Crime
and
Gerontology

Alan A. Malinchak

CRIMINAL JUSTICE PROGRAM
St. Thomas Aquinas College
Sparkill, New York

Prentice-Hall, Inc., Englewood Cliffs, N.J. 07632

Library of Congress Cataloging in Publication Data

Malinchak, Alan A
    Crime and gerontology.

    Bibliography: p.
    Includes index.
        1. Aged—United States—Crimes against. 2. Aged as
criminals—United States. 3. Crime prevention—United States. I. Title.
HV6250.4.A34M34   364   79-22497
ISBN 0-13-192815-5
ISBN 0-13-192807-4 pbk.

©1980 by PRENTICE-HALL, INC.
Englewood Cliffs, New Jersey 07632

Printed in the United States of America.

10 9 8 7 6 5 4 3 2 1

Prentice-Hall International, Inc., *London*
Prentice-Hall of Australia Pty. Limited, *Sydney*
Prentice-Hall of Canada, Ltd., *Toronto*
Prentice-Hall of India Private Limited, *New Delhi*
Prentice-Hall of Japan, Inc., *Tokyo*
Prentice-Hall of Southeast Asia Pte. Ltd., *Singapore*
Whitehall Books Limited, *Wellington, New Zealand*

To Wendy . . .

whose love and encouragement
are an inspiration

Acknowledgments

This author is eternally grateful to Dr. Marc G. Gertz, Assistant Professor of Criminology, Florida State University, whose encouragement, guidance, criticism and faith in this book and author should be a stimulus to other academics; Dr. Vernon B. Fox, Professor of Criminology, Florida State University, whose guidance was a blessing; Mr. Ray Surette, Doctoral Candidate in Criminology, Florida State University, for his critical analysis of statistics; Mr. Stephen E. Cline, Mr. Ken Cashman, and Mr. John Duhring, of Prentice-Hall, Inc., for their guidance; Mr. Bob Walters, President of Walken Graphics, Inc., for his continued support; Ms. Lynn Hengsteler, freelance artist, for her volunteered time and effort; Mr. Thomas Esmond, freelance photographer, for his artistic skills; Mr. Dave Dovel, Criminal Justice Student, University of South Dakota, for his hours of helpful research; Sister Mary A. Heffernan, Ph.D., Professor of Gerontology, Dr. Mary McGann, Associate Professor of English and Speech and Mr. Thomas Spanos, Art/Communications Major, all of St. Thomas Aquinas College, for their photographic portrayals; and Ms. Colleen Huntley, a special thanks for her enduring typing abilities.

Contents

Tables

Foreword

Gerontology has increased in importance in American society since mid-century to the extent that academic programs in this area have been established in universities, retirement settlements and nursing homes have become big business, and occupational specializations have focused on the care of senior citizens. Life expectancy at birth in America in 1920 was 54.1 years. By 1974, life expectancy had risen to 71.9 years—an increase of nearly one third in a half century. This shift in population age has resulted in stresses on almost all social institutions, including the ecomonic and tax structure, the labor market, welfare programs, political leadership, and many other concerns, including the criminal justice system.

This book focuses on the elderly and their involvement in the criminal justice system. The elderly are viewed as victims of crime, and crime prevention programs are discussed to reduce this victimization. The contributions retired senior citizens can make as volunteers working in the criminal justice system are reviewed. The contribution this book makes that has been seriously neglected elsewhere is the discussion of the elderly themselves as criminals.

News stories about retired persons on fixed incomes in predominantly retirement areas being arrested for shoplifting and misuse of welfare programs have been frequent, but most of these charges are misdemeanors. According to the *FBI Uniform Crime Reports* for 1976, there were 75,521 arrests of persons aged sixty-five and over, which is 1.2 percent of all arrests. For Index Crimes (the most serious crimes), there were 13,897 arrests of persons aged sixty-five and over, which is 0.6 percent of the arrests for these crimes. At the same time, a national survey of twenty-six sample states reported in April, 1977, in the *Correctional Compendium*, published in Lincoln, Nebraska, indicated that prisoners aged sixty-five and over average 0.5 percent of the total adult prisoner population, ranging from 0.2 in Colorado, Delaware, and Wisconsin to 1.3 percent in West Virginia. This percentage of the total prisoner population represents an estimated 1,400 prisoners aged sixty-five and over in the United States. Elderly persons arrested for misdemeanors are high in drunkenness and disorderly conduct. The serious offenses for which they serve time in prison include homicide, assault, child molesting, forgery, robbery, and theft.

The long-term response to increased life expectancy has been complex in society, ranging from shifts in housing patterns from extended family units to those with only parents and children, or single individuals, development of the Social Security system that includes Old Age Assistance, and civil actions suits against employment discrimination because of age in violation of the Age Discrimination and Employment Act of 1967. This book addresses the effects of increasing longevity on the criminal justice system. *Crime and Gerontology* should be read by everybody in a social order where a growing segment of the population—the elderly—has introduced new dimensions in American society to the extent that they have become special concerns for the criminal justice system.

Vernon Fox
School of Criminology
Florida State University

Preface

Public opinion polls and surveys have continually earmarked crime as a major concern. Although we are all potential victims of crime, the elderly are more so than other age groups. With the total number of aged persons increasing each year, the study of our oldest and most vulnerable Americans has become a necessity.

Crime is not new. It has been, is, and will continue to play a part in our society. Yet, crime and how it relates to the elderly is a relatively new area of study, one which is just emerging as a national issue. In the past, society focused upon how crime affects youth and the developmental consequences which ensue. The theories of crime and programs of crime prevention which use youth as a guide remain at issue. With the twenty-first century fast approaching, it is time for foresight, particularly with regard to crime and the elderly. It is not the purpose of this book to convince criminologists, criminal justice practitioners, academics or laymen that there is a way to eliminate crime against the elderly. One of the problems of our criminal justice system is its refusal to admit that crime cannot be eliminated, only contained.

Rather, this book will explain and clarify to all interested individuals, organizations, and agencies, what is currently being done for our aged citizens. Once this is understood, consciences of those who possess the responsibility for initiating programs dealing with the aged should receive sufficient stimulation. In addition, if concerned individuals recognize the benefits which accrue from citizen involvement (including the elderly), the liability of crime will be contained. If this book does nothing more than draw attention to the contemporary plight of our elderly, the purpose will be achieved.

A synopsis of the chapters follows:

Chapter One
In this chapter, the reasons why crime and gerontology are of contemporary interest and significance are discussed. A diagram conceptualizing the theme is presented, as well as a brief summary of the following issues: (1) the elderly as victims, (2) crime prevention programs for the elderly (especially those which are environmentally designed), (3) the elderly as volunteers within the criminal justice system, and (4) the elderly as criminals.

Chapter Two

This chapter discusses the reasons why the elderly are more vulnerable to crime than other age groups. Using national and regional data, e.g., LEAA statistics, particular consideration will be given to the following: (1) the special problems of being an elderly victim, (2) violent versus nonviolent victimization, and (3) the fear of victimization causing voluntary self-imprisonment.

Chapter Three

Reasons for the implementation of crime prevention programs for the aged are discussed in relation to the impact of currently existing programs throughout the United States. Highlighted in this chapter, and throughout the book, are personal examples of crimes against the elderly and how the practical value of certain crime prevention programs could eliminate the problems associated with victimization.

Chapter Four

There are numerous reasons why people favor or oppose mandatory retirement of the elderly. Retirement should not be equated with either a lessening of wisdom or a reduction of productivity. The following issues are discussed: (1) why the aged should be volunteers, (2) the advantages and disadvantages to an organization using aged volunteers, and (3) an analysis of some current programs in the criminal justice system utilizing aged volunteers.

Chapter Five

Disengagement theory and activity theory have continually clashed in the field of gerontology. Using concepts such as replacing the old with the efficient (disengagement) and worklike roles (activity), as well as criminological theories, a speculative discussion of how and why the elderly engage in criminal activity/behavior is pursued. Components of this issue include (1) financial dependence vs. financial independence, (2) loss of status, (3) need for companionship/attention, (4) blocked opportunity within the legitimate social structure, and (5) superstructure versus surplus population.

Chapter Six

The reality of the situation is that we are all potential victims of crime as well as victims of the process known as aging. A summary of ideas in the first five chapters will form the basis of preliminary recommendations and reforms in the field of crime and gerontology, such as (1) continuing educational programs for the elderly, and (2) improvement techniques for elderly victimization reporting.

This book offers a synopsis of contemporary information in the area of crime and the aged, both as a text and a source of reference to those whose interest has been aroused.

Alan A. Malinchak
Criminal Justice Program
St. Thomas Aquinas College
Sparkill, New York

Chapter 1

An Introduction

Courtesy of Administration on Aging/HEW

Social research must attempt to be as scientific as possible to the degree that it may direct or determine appropriate, meaningful action in correcting situations that are hurtful to society. Unfortunately, contemporary research involving crime and the aged has been lax in this responsibility. However, for the academic and layman alike, a thorough survey of the existing literature and data surrounding this timely topic does yield an understandable explanation of gerontology and crime—an understanding of which will help alter the present pattern of criminal justice and other bureaucratic policies with respect to the elderly.

Crime and gerontology, topics difficult to study independently, pose complex issues when studied simultaneously. These have not been related studies. Gerontologists have primarily dealt with health-care problems, retirement, housing, and the psychological effects of growing old in society. Criminologists have been trying to unfold the perplexing question, "What are the causes of crime?" For many years both gerontologists and criminologists have concentrated their attention exclusively on their respective fields. Those with doctoral degrees in these fields have focused more and more on less and less—becoming specialists and disregarding other academic disciplines in their own search of knowledge and "the answers." This book relates both fields of study.

Criminologists have devoted much time to the definition and subsequent labelling of the criminal, to theories which desperately try to explain social deviance, and to the treatment or punishment (depending on their moral perspective) of those individuals arrested, tried in court, and sentenced for crime. Only recently has interest, genuine interest, been generated to the other actor in a criminal act—the victim.

Reinterest in the victim began in 1973 with the First International Symposium on Victimology (Jerusalem). Through this symposium and subsequent publications and conferences, the role of the victim within the criminal justice process has widened. Victims are an integral part of the criminal situation. They are not only entitled to compensation, but also the chance to voice their concerns in the hope of preventing further victimization.

There is still a seeming lack of concern for the victim, and an even greater disregard for the elderly victim.

Editor's Note: The author wishes it to be understood that throughout his text he has elected to use the words "he" or "his" rather than "he/she" or "his/her" for brevity's sake alone. The choice is not meant to be exclusionary or chauvinistic.

A steadily rising volume of crime creates an atmosphere of fear haunting all levels of society. It is particularly alarming to those Americans who are most vulnerable—our senior citizens. Unfortunately, scant attention has been focused on this unique and challenging aspect of our crime problem.[1]

Because there has been little attention to the elderly and their battle with crime and the criminal element, this book deals with the following four concerns of crime and gerontology: (1) the elderly as victims, (2) crime prevention programs for the elderly, especially with regard to environmentally designed crime prevention programs, (3) the elderly as volunteers within the various components of the criminal justice system—cops, courts, and corrections, and (4) the elderly as criminals.

WHY STUDY CRIME AND GERONTOLOGY?

Students of crime and gerontology should engulf themselves in this issue not only for gaining knowledge and broadening perspectives, but mainly because of the past avoidance in dealing with it. The issue has not been avoided out of shame, but because of ignorance of the problem and what to do about it. As knowledge of crime and gerontology accumulates, society will be in a better position to make recommendations that will aid the elderly in their battle against crime.

Possibly, the avoidance of this issue is due to the modern, efficient, technological world. This opinion was eloquently expressed by Edward M. Davis, former president of the International Association of Chiefs of Police and chief of police of Los Angeles, California.

Perhaps this lack of concern stems from the fact that we live in a rather plastic and disposable world. We shop at markets and buy convenience items that serve some immediate utility and when we are through with them, we throw them away. Can it be that people are treated in the same manner? Let's look at that possibility: A child is born and develops into a functional human being. As the child advances into adulthood and becomes a productive member of society, a certain utility is attached to that person's functioning and purpose. Once that same human being becomes older and retires and is no longer "a producer," he or she loses utility. When that occurs, no one appears concerned. The elderly are neglected to a position of being isolated from the rest of society. They are discarded, as it were, to a place for "old people." Their wisdom and their judgments are no longer solicited. No one cares for them and no one cares about them. They are lost in a new generation and they are alone.[2]

Perhaps there has not been adequate time to get involved or show concern, but attempts have been made. Six years previous to Chief Davis' statement, the 1971 White House Conference on Aging report, "Towards a New Attitude on Aging," offered suggestions to deal with the problem of crimes against the elderly:

> ...making physical protection and crime prevention an element of the planning of facilities for the elderly; expanding police protection of minority neighborhoods; establishing formal liaison between social service agencies and police departments so that elderly (who are) victims of crime can obtain all necessary assistance; providing better street lighting; making training grants available to police officers and others to acquaint them with the special situation of the elderly and their special susceptibility to particular types of crime; and granting Federal funds to State and local prosecuting officers to expand or establish fraud units which are well acquainted with schemes used to deceive the elderly (p. 78).[3]

Criminologists, gerontologists, and those individuals involved in study closely related to this issue—political scientists, social workers, sociologists, humanists, mental health and allied health professionals—should all concern themselves with the present and future plight of the aged. Rather than brood over the mistake-ridden past, they should learn from past neglect and develop programs which (1) substantially reduce elderly victimization, (2) aid in crime prevention, (3) call for volunteerism, and (4) prevent those senior citizens so inclined from following a criminal career in their later years.

The most poignant and concise rationalizations for concern with the issue of crime and its relation to gerontology are offered by Goldsmith and Goldsmith.[4] Following is a review of some of these rationalizations specifically.

Rationalization One: Many elderly people live below the level of poverty; thus, the impact from any loss of economic resources is greater.

Whether you are a student, professor, housewife or blue-collar worker, consider for a moment: When were you last robbed? Was it financially uncomfortable? Have you never replaced the item? Were you able to manage (for a while at least) without the item? Compare this to the victimized elderly person. Imagine his social security check stolen from him, or his television set—a possession which gives hours of comfort to him and thousands and thousands of lonely elderly people.

As a student, you may do without your television, stereo or other items of entertainment if they are stolen, because you always have your textbooks. Besides, you realize that sooner or later you will be able to purchase whatever was stolen and replace those hours of library reading with electronic sights and sounds. However, the elderly cannot replace stolen items with ease or deferred gratification. They live below the poverty level, often having just enough money to survive. A stolen possession, which might have been purchased years ago, is something they will undoubtedly have to do without, for there is just not enough money for additional expenses.

Rationalization Two: Older people are more likely to be victimized repeatedly, often the same crime by the same victimizer.

Contrary to popular belief, folklore, and the movies, thieves are not an intelligent core of people. Of course there is a rank order of criminals. Those possessing the most knowledge usually escape arrest and conviction, while those with meager intelligence usually spend most of their time in jail or prison. The criminals who fall in the middle of these two groups are of most concern; they realize the potential bullish market of elderly victims.

Picture yourself as a thief. Would you rather rob your professor, a businessman, or the seventy-year old lady who lives in the neighborhood? Which potential victim ensures you the greatest amount of success? No, not the professor; that is revenge. The elderly victim is the most appropriate choice. Success is almost guaranteed. It is a more profitable venture and, of course, there is less risk involved, especially in terms of being identified or physically injured.

Rationalization Three: The aged are more likely to live alone, increasing their vulnerability to crime.

Only 4 percent of those persons aged sixty-five years or older are institutionalized. Ninety-six percent are living among the rest of the potential victims and many are likely to reside alone. The fact that a person lives alone makes him a more likely target of the criminal, for whom it has become safe to assume that an elderly person will offer little resistance—especially a lone elderly person.

Why are the elderly more likely to live alone? Basically, it involves the mobility of their children. The cost and ease of moving from one side of the country to the other makes for a very mobile younger population. Instead of the traditional familial setting, long-distance telephone conversations are keeping family members in touch. The twentieth-century tendency is to relocate—something which the elderly do not particularly cherish at this time of their lives. The elderly are not prone to relocation; therefore, they are prone to living alone.

Rationalization Four: The physical stamina of the elderly is apt to be diminished; therefore, they are less able to defend themselves or escape threatening situations.

It is a fact of nature that as a person grows old, his body loses strength; thus it is comparatively easy for a criminal to knock down an elderly person.

The unsuspecting elderly victim.

Photographed by Tom Esmond

If an elderly person realizes he is about to be victimized, his chances of escape through flight or fight are extremely limited, simply because he can no longer muster up the strength he once possessed.

To avoid being victimized, he may have to use other methods. Here is an example of an elderly person who remained calm in a threatening situation and avoided injury, as told by Mr. R. A. Dorsey of Tallahassee, Florida.

> One Christmas Eve a very presentable man of twenty-five or thirty stopped at my Pine Port motel in Tallahassee, Florida, for a room. Once in the room he drew a pistol about twenty-four inches long, and demanded my money—which I gave him. He wasn't satisfied with the amount, was sure I had more in the office. Playing for time, I told him to come look for himself. He called me "Sir" when he talked, and I tagged him for a service man. I kept talking to him, telling him he looked intelligent, able to make his way honestly, foolish to risk a sure jail sentence sooner or later.
>
> After he searched my desk and found no more money, he asked me if he could use my phone. He referred to a piece of paper and informed me he was calling a taxi and I should wait inside when the taxi came. I continued to talk to him, told him if he'd give me his gun I'd give him the $39.00 he had taken—and I meant it, because he did seem to be a fine young man. He got angry then, snarled that he was wanted all over the country and I should shut up or he'd shoot me.
>
> When the taxi came I followed him out as soon as my office door slammed. I couldn't get the taxi number, but it was a cream and green color. He had yanked out my phone so I flagged down the next car and rode down to a neighboring motel and called the police from there. They were waiting when the taxi man got back to his station, and he told them he had watched the man board a St. Petersburg bus. The policeman arrived at the bus terminal just as the bus was leaving, boarded it, and from the description I had given, nabbed the man—who told Police Chief Montgomery I had kept him off balance by talking to him all the time. He was wanted all over, had retainers in four or five states, had abandoned a wife and two children, and had escaped from a Utah jail. I was glad then I hadn't yielded to an impulse not to call the police.[5]

Rationalization Five: Older people are more likely to suffer physical ailments, such as loss of hearing or sight, therefore increasing their vulnerability.

Criminals usually look for easy marks or victims. If an individual has poor eyesight, the chances of identifying the criminal are narrow. A person with poor hearing would probably not realize that his house was being burglarized. A person confined to a wheelchair has little chance of scaring off criminals. Criminals know this.

Criminals also know that the elderly, apt to suffer such handicaps, provide easy targets and small chance of apprehension. Whenever the risk of being caught is less than the amount of pleasure to be gained from the spoils, a crime will occur. The problem is that crime occurs much too frequently among aged citizens who can no longer count on their physical well-being to combat the criminal.

A related problem is the con artist who takes advantage of the problems of the aged. What better prey than the elderly person suffering from some physical ailment for the sale of defective hearing aids, poor-quality eyewear, dilapidated wheelchairs, and the like. Usually, because of their financial status, the elderly look for bargains—and con artists find suckers.

Rationalization Six: If the aged should opt to defend themselves, they are more likely to sustain injuries, such as broken bones. Recovery is difficult, prolonged, and expensive.

Here the elderly are faced with a decision of whether to maintain pride and self-respect through self-defense or fall victim to the criminal and suffer the consequences without resistance. If the elderly choose self-defense and subsequently break an arm or leg, who is going to provide care? cover medical expenses? give emotional comfort? And if the elderly choose to be victimized, what then? Who will care for them? cover medical expenses? give emotional support? Whether or not the aged opt to defend themselves, they will become another criminal statistic!

In the past there has been little done to aid elderly victims in general. Fortunately, crime victimization programs are being initiated throughout the country. Compensation to victims is, after a long wait, finally a reality. How much of a reality is it? Crime-victim compensation programs currently exist in twenty-four states.

Rationalization Seven: The elderly are more likely to live in high crime neighborhoods than in suburbia. Thus, they live in close proximity to groups most likely to victimize them.

The elderly do not move to high-crime areas, usually the crime comes to them. It does not take too long for their plight to be realized by criminals. They live in the central or inner cities because of low income and family roots. They are dependent upon public transportation. (How many buses have regular schedules in the suburbs?) Also, they must be close to their needs, especially the social security, welfare, and medical offices.

Rationalization Eight: Dates when older persons' monthly pension and benefit checks arrive are widely known to criminals.

Most government checks, whether they are for benefits, pension, or welfare, usually come the first of the month. A potential criminal has two options: (1) steal the check out of the mailbox or, (2) wait until the elderly person cashes the check. With the latter option, criminals usually know when the elderly are most likely to have cash on their persons or in their dwellings.

Picture an inner-city area comprised of a sizable portion of elderly residents. Do you think it would take a thief long to open 100, 200, or even 1,000 mailboxes and fence the stolen checks? No, of course not. And if the thief chose to wait and rob the elderly of their cash, would it not be easy pickings (taking into consideration all the rationalizations discussed so far)?

Yet, there is hope. Prevention of the criminals' two options is already taking place, for example, automatic check depositing, currently in operation for the elderly—a positive way for the elderly to protect themselves from victimization. This and other crime prevention programs will be discussed further in Chapter 3.

Rationalization Nine: Awareness of their own susceptibility to crime causes self-imposed "house arrest" for many elderly persons. Though their fears may be exaggerated, the effects are severe.

Newspaper, radio, television—the media in general—lead people to believe they are the next victims of criminal attack. Although the chance of walking down the street and being victimized is there, the probability of such an occurrence is not likely. The media usually overplays rapes, murders, and muggings because these are the types of sensational events which they consider newsworthy. Whether or not they are, these are the events to which viewers, listeners, and readers are being exposed. The captive audience has little control over the situation, and there is nothing that can instill fear in their hearts like being exposed to "newsworthy" stories of sensational crime.

Unfortunately, the elderly are constantly in fear of being victimized. They sincerely feel that the next criminal attack is earmarked for them, that the next bullet has their name on it. This fear is unwarranted and irrational, but it does exist. It is true that the elderly are victimized proportionately much more than any other age group, but no age group, including the elderly, is victimized 100 percent, 50 percent, or even 15 percent of the time. Before the elderly can learn to fend for themselves, they must first overcome the fear of crime. Fortunately, in the process of learning how to prevent crime, the elderly will realize just how effective a weapon they are to combat criminal behavior.

A focus on the above rationalizations was made to reinforce the picture that there are rational reasons for studying crime and the elderly. Goldsmith and Goldsmith offer many rationalizations. For additional reading on this issue, refer to the Notes at the end of this chapter.

CRIME AND THE AGED

Progress in dealing successfuly with the dramatic problem of crime against the aging has generally been slow and sporadic.[6] Yet, it should be noted that "by the end of this century, approximately 11 percent of our population, or an estimated twenty-eight million people, will be at least sixty-five years old

Table 1–1 Estimates and Projections of the Total Population and of the Population 65 Years Old and Over, by Sex, for 5-Year Intervals: 1975 to 2000
(Numbers in Thousands)

Series and Sex	Estimate 1975	Projecions 1980	1985	1990	1995	2000
Series I[1]						
Total population, all ages	213,540	224,066	238,878	254,715	269,384	282,837
Male	104,202	109,200	116,441	124,232	131,460	138,091
Female	109,338	114,865	122,437	130,483	137,924	144,746
Series III[2]						
Total population, all ages	213,540	220,732	228,879	236,264	241,973	245,876
Male	104,202	107,491	111,315	114,775	117,414	119,162
Female	109,338	113,241	117,564	121,489	124,559	126,714
Both sexes, 65 years and over	22,405	24,927	27,305	29,824	31,401	31,822
65 to 69	8,098	8,700	9,244	10,022	9,791	9,192
70 to 74	5,777	6,793	7,301	7,782	8,433	8,244
75 years and over	8,528	9,434	10,760	12,021	13,176	14,386
Male, 65 years and over	9,176	10,108	11,012	11,999	12,602	12,717
Female, 65 years and over	13,229	14,819	16,293	17,824	18,799	19,105
Both sexes, 65 years and over as percent of total population, all ages:						
Series I	10.5	11.1	11.4	11.7	11.7	11.3
Series III	10.5	11.3	11.9	12.6	13.0	12.9

[1]Assumes 2.7 births per woman
[2]Assumes 1.7 births per woman
Source: U.S. Bureau of the Census, *Current Population Reports,* Series P-25, Nos. 643 and 704.

[Refer to Table 1-1.] Referring to series 3...note that the elderly have the potential to become a larger segment of the total population, but at the very least will not become a smaller portion (series 1) under any circumstances. And if the increasing number of elderly people alone fails to get our attention, continuing public debate on various aspects of Medicare, social security payments, housing for older citizens [and crime against the aged] will certainly increase their social visibility in the years ahead. We can depend on it; the elderly will continue to be visible reminders of human troubles."[7]

The elderly must realize that they are a viable political force. Their numbers alone are a significant statistic. Clark and Anderson note that "in American society today, adult responsibilities are now relinquished relatively so early that there yet remains for most older people a long span of years devoid of social meanings."[8] This need not be the case. There are senior citizen organizations forming all over the United States with such vigor that their future progress and growth is limitless. An organization known as *The Gray Panthers,*

11

whose national headquarters is Philadelphia, Pennsylvania, is becoming so active and prominent throughout the United States that when it musters its forces behind a political force or issue, the chances of victory are greatly increased.

Crime has long been an issue of national importance among Americans. Although the causes of crime are yet to be determined (certain variables present in criminal activity are known), that does not mean crime should be accepted as a normal condition of our society. Crime does exist. It is a problem society is capable of dealing with and reducing in amount. But first must be understood the implications of crime—how it affects each and every person—before crime can be realistically prevented.

It will prove easier to realize the role of the elderly in the prevention of crime if the four major concerns of this book are conceptualized. To bring into focus an understanding of crime and gerontology, consider the components in Diagram 1-1.

Diagram 1—1   Four Major Concerns of Crime and Gerontology

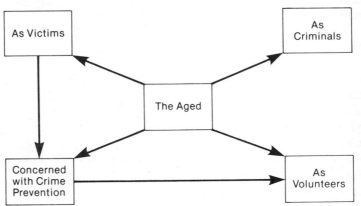

W. M. Beattie Jr. points out the following: "If you are old, you will increasingly need protection and security, not only in your place of residence, but as you attempt to move about the community and are vulnerable to exploitation if not abuse."[9] The police, who have always been our main source of protection, can no longer handle the rapidly increasing crime rate. Whether the fact that crime has become an American way of life is due to a present-day permissiveness, to the economic atmosphere, or to the fact that reporting techniques have improved over the years, is a matter of mere definition. What is of importance is our realization that if we are to protect ourselves from crime, we must fend for ourselves and get involved in all facets of the criminal justice system. As a society we have grown accustomed to having everything done for us. We can no longer depend on others. It is time for us to put our laziness and ignorance of the issue aside—to get involved, not only for ourselves, but for future generations of unsuspecting victims.

THE AGED AS VICTIMS

Goldsmith and Goldsmith[10] question the amount of justice for the victims of crime. They ask, "Is it just for millions of Americans to live each day in fear of criminal activity?" They inquire why the criminal justice system can (and does) equate a twenty-dollar loss to an aging couple striving to survive on social security, to the affluent's loss of the same amount.

> Street crimes such as purse snatchings, muggings, and armed holdups, together with home burglaries and confidence-type frauds, are offenses that most commonly strike the elderly. In the last category, they are victimized out of proportion to their numbers. Typically, of course, older persons are among those least able to afford the depredations of crime. ...Crime leaves a deeper, more lasting mark."[11]

Jaber F. Gubrium has also noted that "the aged are more likely to suffer chronically as an outcome of those crimes of which they are victims. The aged as a group do not possess the physical agility, the financial resources or the social support that allows them to recover as quickly or completely from criminal acts against them as other age groups."[12] A study by the Midwest Research Institute of Kansas City, Missouri, has noted that while it may be of little comfort to victims, it is true that older persons are much less likely to be victims of any kind of crime (with the possible exception of purse snatching) than younger age groups, and that the chances of being murdered or raped are very small. Yet, there is a tendency in some specific neighborhoods for elderly persons to be the more likely victims of burglary, robbery, larceny, or fraud.[13]

Although this may be true in general, students of the criminal justice system must note that "unfortunately, traditional crime statistics do not adequately reflect the extent of the problem of elderly victimization. Many local police and law enforcement agencies do not collect data on the age of victims, and therefore the FBI Uniform Crime Reports also do not include this information."[14]

The problem with statistics is that they can be interpreted in any number of ways, and can be tabulated to present the findings desired simply by asking the right questions. Statistics can aid a theoretical argument or be used to constructively criticize the reliability and validity of the study. Regardless of which side of the fence is straddled concerning statistical analysis, the fact is clear that the elderly are more prone to victimization and suffer greater consequences because of this fact.

Many of the tables and statistics presented in this book are lacking in sample size (mainly because of past inefficiencies in law enforcement data collection); yet all support a contention for more research and data collection in this area. Overall, the tables indicate an increase in the elderly as victims, but there is not enough data to be conclusive. The tables are "indicators" of the issue—reasons to look closely at the problem of crime and the elderly.

Table 1-2 and Table 1-3 reflect why the elderly have a deep-rooted concern for crime.

Table 1-2 Victimization Rates for Selected Crimes Against Persons for the Population 12 Years Old and Over and 65 Years Old and Over, by Sex: First Half of 1973
(Rate per 1,000 population)

Crime	Persons 12 Years & Over			Persons 65 Years & Over		
	Both Sexes	Male	Female	Both Sexes	Male	Female
Total persons	161,502	76,771	84,731	20,149	8,321	11,828
Total selected crimes[1]	64.0	75.2	53.9	15.1	18.4	12.8
Rape	0.5	(B)	1.0	(B)	0	(B)
Robbery:						
with injury	1.2	1.6	0.8	1.0	(B)	1.1
without injury	2.3	3.6	1.2	1.5	2.1	1.1
Assault:						
Aggravated	5.1	7.7	2.8	0.8	(B)	0.9
Simple	8.1	10.3	6.1	1.1	1.6	(B)
Personal larceny	46.7	52.0	42.0	10.6	13.2	8.8

B Base too small for rate to be statistically reliable.

[1]Restricted to crimes shown separately.

Source: U.S. Department of Justice, Law Enforcement Assistance Administration.

According to Table 1-2, the population sixty-five and over suffered about one-fourth as many crimes, relatively, against their person during the first half of 1973 as did the population twelve years old and over—about fifteen crimes per one-thousand population compared with sixty-four per one-thousand. For each of the two age groups, larceny was by far the most frequent crime (approximately 70 percent), followed by assault. In general, Table 1-2 testifies to the fact that the elderly represent a larger proportion of victims than would be expected from their total size in the general population.

In crimes against households, those households headed by a person sixty-five and over were victimized to a lesser extent than all households for each of the three household crimes considered. Motor vehicle theft accounted for a relatively minor portion of household crimes. Burglary and household larceny accounted for the great majority of cases. Of particular significance

Table 1-3 Victimization Rates for Selected Crimes Against Households for Household Heads 12 Years Old and Over and 65 Years Old and Over: First Half of 1973
(Rate per 1,000 Households)

Crime	Head 12 Years and Over	Head 65 Years and Over
Total households (thousands)	68,978	13,397
Total selected crimes[1]	103.9	55.3
Burglary	44.0	28.5
Household larceny	51.4	24.8
Motor vehicle theft	8.5	2.0

[1]Restricted to crimes shown separately.

Source: U.S. Department of Justice, Law Enforcement Assistance Administration.

is the fact that the elderly, as depicted in Table 1-3, represent approximately one-half of all the victims in the crime categories shown.

Crime affects everyone in society, including the elderly, who are not only the victims of violent crimes, but also of nonviolent crimes, especially con games or fraud. As Curt Gentry has noted, "today, ten out of ten adult Americans are the victims of swindles and frauds...age does not automatically confer wisdom."[15] No one is immune to those criminals who feast on the ignorance of others. It is remarkable how many elderly persons fall victim to "get-rich-quick" schemes. Everyone goes through life hearing the comment, "There's no free lunch." Yet many, especially the elderly, do not take the meaning of the phrase to heart.

The following is a story related by Mrs. Alice Brickler about a possible attempt at a con game.

I have a habit of leaving my back door and screen unlocked because it is very convenient for my son who comes by to see me every afternoon and my daughter who lives with me and who comes home from the office in which she works soon after her brother comes. My den is opposite my kitchen and I can sit in the den and keep an eye on the unlocked kitchen door at all times.

This special afternoon I was sitting in the den where I saw a tall well-dressed young man come to the door. Before I could get up from my chair and start to the door he had opened it and crossed the kitchen and greeted me in the den. I was frightened because I didn't know him and I thought he had nerve to enter uninvited. I greeted him and asked what he wanted.

"I've come to help you with your Medicare. Most of you elderly people are being checked by Medicare and I'm going to help you."

"Thanks for your interest" I said, "but my son takes care of all my medical needs. You can't help me" and I began to work him back across the kitchen and toward the door.

"Who is your son?" he asked.

"He is a doctor—Dr. Brickler."

"Oh!" he said, "I know him, he is my doctor. I go to him all the time. He takes good care of me."

I listened to him but said nothing, because by now I had him across the kitchen and through the door. Then I said, "That's wonderful, you must be his most interesting patient because he is a gynecologist" and shut the door and locked it.[16]

Carl L. Cunningham responds to crime and the aged victim with the statement that "behind the cold, numerical descriptions that must be used to describe the criminal victimization of the aged, lies a particularly shocking record of brutalization, deprivation, and intimidation. It is no exaggeration to say that the quality of life of hundreds of thousands of elderly persons is today being drastically degraded by virtue of crime and the threat of it."[17] In addition, Goldsmith and Goldsmith question whether the elderly widow who cowers in her home, imprisoned by fear, is not equally a victim of crime as the person who ventures out and meets it firsthand.[18]

Before leaving this section, it is important to note that the aged victim is no longer as helpless as in the past. There are many crime compensation programs forming throughout the nation. Although these programs are general in scope in that they are aiding all victims of crime regardless of age, the benefit to the elderly is finally outweighing the past costs of criminal victimization. Crime compensation programs for victims will be discussed in more detail in Chapter 2.

THE AGED AND CRIME PREVENTION

In a 1973 *Report on the Criminal Justice System* by the National Advisory Committee on Criminal Justice Standards and Goals, it was remarked that too often, statistical data needed for analyses of the crime problem are inferior, inadequate, or nonexistent (p. 200). Although this is especially so with the aged, there has been some recognition of the problem across the country, which has prompted a few innovative programs to reduce criminal victimization of the aging.[19] Crime prevention programs for the elderly are of an immediate economic and political necessity.

... the ratio of elders to other age groups in the population is growing. This, in turn, is likely to make the influence of the aged in the economics and politics of industrial societies progressively more visible.... And [the elderly] are also a potentially effective group in elections and public referenda.[20]

To be successful in the crime prevention area, it must be noted that "experience can do little to protect the elderly person today."[21] Knowledge and

Objective Three: To involve other Federal agencies and private organizations representing older persons in the creation of a consortium to formulate a national strategy for crime prevention programs for aging persons.

To the end of promoting this objective the Law Enforcement Assistance Administration and the Administration on Aging will: (1) continue discussions with other Federal agencies and private organizations representing the National Elderly Consortium entitled, "National Elderly Victimization Prevention and Assistance Program," which has been submitted to LEAA as a proposal, (2) invite designated representatives of such other Federal and private organizations as considered necessary to attend an exploratory, full-day planning meeting for the purpose of determining appropriate roles and responsibilities for all consortium participants.[23]

Crime prevention for the elderly is taking hold. Seminars and practical techniques for the elderly to combat crime, once scarce, are now in abundance. For example, in the summer of 1977, there was a "Seminar on Crime Prevention for the Elderly" in Tallahassee, Florida. Cosponsored by the Center of Geronotology, Florida State University, and the Senior Society Planning Council of Leon County, Tallahassee, Florida, this seminar was able to instill in its participants (elderly residents of the community) common-sense approaches on how to deal with the possibility of crime as well as to reinforce positive aspects of crime prevention, so that the elderly need not fear crime, but can adequately meet the criminal's challenge. Although the seminar only met on five occasions, it was considered a success. The audience was enthusiastic during all presentations. The loss of participants was practically nil, suggesting that this seminar on crime prevention was of more importance to them than Bingo games, television, or an afternoon of relaxation.

Seminars like the one in Tallahassee are able to educate only an initial number of elderly citizens about crime prevention techniques. The potential lies in having further or continued seminars and spreading the word among the elderly themselves. Crime prevention is the key to combating the aged's fear of crime as well as their actual victimization.

There is no such thing as an invulnerable American (especially an aged American). Vulnerability, however, has its degrees, and the least vulnerable American is one who develops a healthy skepticism—what might be called a consumer's gift sense[24]—which is hoped would evolve from an aged person's meaningful involvement in a crime prevention program. Many such crime prevention programs which combat personal and property crimes of a violent and nonviolent nature will be discussed in Chapter 3.

Utilizing the knowledge gained from crime prevention seminars.

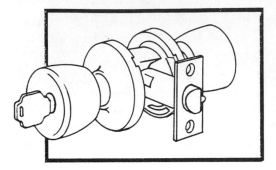

Bored Lock

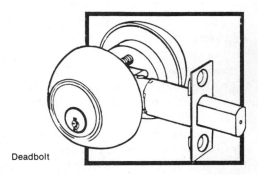

Deadbolt

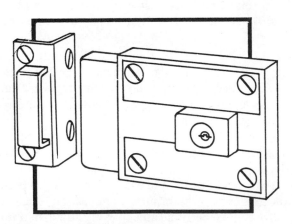

Rim Lock

Courtesy of: Senior Home Security, Inc., a federally funded older workers program through the National Council of Aging, Washington, D.C.

THE AGED AS VOLUNTEERS

Donald O. Cowgill has noted that modern health technology, modern economic technology, and the increase in education and urbanization has tended to diminish the status of the aged.[25] However, this should not mean that the aged are no longer productive. They can volunteer more easily than other age groups, especially in criminal justice activities and programs. By doing so, they can gain a sense of self-satisfaction and meaningful accomplishment—something which retirement seems to take from them. Boyd and Oakes have noted that "the Western tradition includes age-grading throughout the 'expected' life span and even beyond in some traditions. We have not yet discovered what to do with those who do not die. Our constitutional inertia is such that we expel them from the structure rather than modify the structure itself."[26]

In fact, if you believe Cowgill's statement to be true, then you must realize that modern health technology and modern economic technology, although

Sun City posse members assisting injured person located during desert search exercise.

Courtesy of Maricopa County Sheriff's Office

21

diminishing the status of the aged, are increasing the lifespan of the aged. People are living longer, resulting in the desire for fuller and richer lives, not leisurely games and continual boredom.

> In essence, our culture is now producing a new life era—a new phase of considerable duration in the life cycle. With people arbitrarily retired from the responsibilities and economic activities of adult life, sometimes two decades before they experience serious functional impairment, a long hiatus has been created into which we have yet to build new cultural traditions and social institutions.[27]

Volunteering in criminal justice agencies offers the elderly and the criminal justice system a unique solution. Both parties have something which can be gained—for the elderly, a further chance to participate in society, and for the criminal justice system, a reservoir of talent to aid in the reduction or prevention of crime. Tournier writes, "All those who have to do with old people know how difficult it is to break through their passivity when they are turned in upon themselves. One can do something for them only in so far as they themselves react, in so far as one finds in them a desire to collaborate constructively."[28] What more constructive collaboration could there be than between our elderly and a system which is in dire need of support and involvement from the citizenry.

Using volunteers will force modification of the existing system (criminal justice included), as well as give volunteers a chance to remain involved in a system on which they have had so much impact. According to the U.S. Department of Health, Education and Welfare, only about 4 percent of those aged sixty-five and over in the United States are institutionalized (nursing homes, hospitals, community care for the elderly)—about 96 percent are living in the community.[29] Rosamonde R. Boyd affirms the truism that "skills quickly become obsolete and knowledge accumulates too rapidly for many older persons to absorb and acquire new remunerative 'know-how.' But, for the elderly to remain idle a decade or so after retirement scarcely makes sense in a society where longevity is constantly increasing and where needed talent is scarce. This is an abuse and waste of human resources."[30]

What is shocking is the general feeling among other age groups that when a person reaches sixty-five, the so-called "legal limit" for middle age, he automatically becomes an "old person"—no longer productive and mostly a burden to family and society. What no one seems to realize is that once a person is born, he begins to age and continues this aging process until death. There is no set age at which abilities, desires, or egos begin to diminish. True, the process known as aging does affect certain biological characteristics—physically and mentally. But take a look around—there are probably more competent and intelligent elderly persons (proportionately) than middle-aged or young adults. All the aged need is a chance to remain active, to be given the opportunity to fight the overriding generalization that old people are inept.

Take a good look at your parents and grandparents. Before you know it, you will be among the ranks of the elderly. Hopefully, you will not have to face the problems which are common to the elderly today, including early retirement.

Retirement should not mean nonresponsibility. Through volunteering, an elderly person's years of accumulated knowledge could prove productive. Harriet H. Naylor has remarked:

> ...often the older volunteer has rich knowledge of what has happened in the community...information all very helpful to professional staffs. In addition volunteers have time to listen carefully, time to encourage people—services which are hard to cover in budgets. Yet, volunteers alone are not the answer, responsible administration is the key to a good volunteer program by senior citizens. Strong administrative support is required to persuade staffs of agencies to allow senior citizens opportunities to share their wisdom and skill.[31]

Commitment to goals in criminal justice and the commitment of the elderly to the criminal justice system through volunteering is the practical answer. Beattie remarks, "In a society which is future and change for the better oriented, the basic orientation concept of 'urban renewal' is to tear down and replace the old for the new. We have failed, to date, to define as a people those goals of social existence and purpose for the adult beyond the occupational-work role and the parent-spouse role. The concept of leisure, if it is relevant at all, only has meaning if there is the alternative option of productivity and work."[32] Volunteering is just such an alternative.

THE AGED AS CRIMINALS

Over the years the study of gerontology has produced two countertheories: disengagement theory, which was originally introduced by Cumming, Dean, and Newell in 1960, and activity theory.[33] Disengagement theory is "a functional approach to the place of the aged. Its concept is that it is functional for a social system to disengage its elders, since a system, especially an urban-industrial one, is only as sound as its members. They assumed that the quality and quantity of a person's work diminished as he/she aged. Thus, it was 'best-for-all' that the elderly voluntarily withdraw from a number of social roles, so that the roles could be filled by younger, more efficient occupants."[34] If you consider disengagement theory as the thesis, then its antithesis is found in activity theory. "The proponents of activity theory feel that life satisfaction (adjustment) results from the maintenance of active involvement in any number of worklike roles in old age."[35] The needed synthesis will be found by combining concepts from each theory in the formation of a positive approach to life for the elderly.

Criminologists can see that each of these gerontological theories could make a contribution to an aged person's involvement in a criminal behavior. For example, an aged person who has difficulty adjusting to retirement and the loss of socially acceptable roles, might pattern his life style around criminal activity. In the face of being replaced by the young and efficient, it could be argued that the elderly escalate to a deviant identity as a consequence of their reaction to the dominant social audience (those under sixty-five years of age). It might be further argued that the elderly no longer possess a shared symbolic universe: that is, they have fallen from the graces of those in society who assign influential societal roles. Consequently, disengagement from society could cause deviance.

With respect to activity theory, the plight of the elderly might be equated to the sociological concept of blocked opportunity. Activity theorists feel involvement in worklike roles is a necessary ingredient for successful transition to old age. If so, when normal pathways to legitimate involvement in the system are blocked—for example, by mandatory retirement at seventy— elderly persons could follow illegitimate paths such as criminal behavior to fulfill needed worklike roles.

If you think that the possibility of the elderly turning to crime is bizarre or unwarranted, that picturing your grandmother engaged in burglary, larceny, or carrying a weapon is outrageous, you had better take a breath. In Rochelle Jones' book entitled, *The Other Generation: The New Power of Older People,* she identifies an increase in crime by the elderly. Because her statistics were compiled in the 1960s from the FBI Uniform Crime Reports and statistics separating data on arrests of people over sixty-five are no longer compiled by that agency, it is difficult to generalize her results. However, she does give sufficient food for thought in Table 1-4.[36]

As Jones states, "Since many crimes are not reported, the actual increase is undoubtedly higher. If criminal activity can be linked to lack of social status and ambiguous social expectations, we can expect an upswing in crime among retirees."[37]

Table 1-4   Criminal Offenses Compared[38]

Offense	Increase in the Population at Large	Increase among People Over 65
Homicide	57	144
Burglary	36	38
Larceny	48	67
Carrying and possessing firearms	92	101
Driving under the influence of alcohol	−46	60
Total property crimes	41	62
Total crime index	42	54

In addition to the components of these two gerontological theories contributing to an elderly person's involvement in crime, there are two other aspects which need to be looked at. First, not only the aged's loss of status and occupational roles in society, but their financial status may cause them to consider crime as a means of support (Table 1-5).

Elderly persons living on a fixed income may find shoplifting, petty theft, larceny, etc., a supplement to their meager incomes. Jones revealed several interesting facts with regard to Table 1-5, as follows:

Table 1-5 Resources of the Aged[39]

Source of Income	Percentage of Couples with This Source	Percentage of Total Income from This Source
Social Security	100	37
Interests, dividends, and rental income	64	17
Earnings	53	25
Private pensions	22	6
Veteran's benefits	20	5
Public retirement benefits other than Social Security (military, civil service, etc.)	9	55
Public assistance	5	1
Private group annuities	4	Unknown
Contributions (relatives)	1	Unknown
Others	Unknown	3

(1) Older adults derive income from a variety of sources, but most sources contribute relatively little to their total income. No source of income is sufficient by itself to provide an adequate income in retirement. Older adults must rely on makeshift arrangements, some money here and some money there, to get by.

(2) Although over half of the older adults earned some income, this represented only a fourth of their total income. Older adults are penalized by reductions in their Social Security benefits if they earn more than the so-called retirement test allows each year. The retirement test was $3,000 a year in January 1977. After they have earned $3,000, one dollar is subtracted from their Social Security check for every dollar that is earned. The number who already receive some income from their earnings means that employment could be a substantial source of retirement income if jobs were available and older adults were permitted to work.

(3) Private pension plans are relatively unimportant sources of retirement income. Although many workers are covered by pension plans at some point during their working years, very few have actually collected in retirement. Arcane rules and regulations have added Catch 22's to most pension plans. Many who thought they were covered by a pension plan have found, to their surprise, that they could not collect after retiring because of a loop-

hole or obscure requirement. Although Congress passed a pension reform act in 1974 to safeguard retirement benefits, this legislation does not help those who are already retired. Those who do collect often find benefits to be less than expected.

(4) Older adults now rely on public rather than private sources of income. Only one percent receive financial help from relatives. Five times that many receive public assistance. Although the majority have some savings or investments, less than one-fifth of their total income is derived from that source.[40]

The facts are startling. The revelation is horrifying. If elderly citizens are forced to turn to a life of crime to provide themselves with the necessities for survival, drastic measures of reevaluation are needed.

The other aspect which could lead an elderly person to crime is loneliness. The elderly are in such a state of flux in adjusting to old age that criminal behavior may be a way of attaining the companionship and attention which they gradually lose, but suddenly realize is missing from their lives.

Gubrium says that for an aged person "three important factors may enhance or limit activity: (1) health, (2) financial solvency, and (3) state of social support."[14] Depending on an elder's potential, activity resources determine the flexibility to decide upon a course of action that persons have at their disposal.[42] If an elderly person is healthy, yet he is financially poor, he lacks social support, and he finds volunteer programs unavailable, criminal activity might pose the logical, although somewhat irrational, solution to his predicament. Delinquency, contrary to popular belief, is not reserved for juveniles only.

The lack of social structures that provide opportunities for aged people to perform meaningful social roles offers a distinct challenge to older persons in the United States[43]—a challenge which might be responded to by criminal behavior, a probable way of drawing attention to the aged's contemporary plight.

A thorough study of the aged as criminals will appear in Chapter 5, which will prove noteworthy to the beginning student who is unfamiliar with theoretical issues in criminology or gerontology. The chapter will include a review of related theories, both criminological and gerontological, and a speculative discussion of the aged as criminals—an entertaining idea, and one which should stimulate research in this area.

SUMMARY

Before concluding this introduction to crime and gerontology and proceeding to further discussions of the areas/issues outlined, a few remarks may prove significant.

Statistically, the elderly rank "fear of crime" as the most serious problem they experience.[44] Once the fear of crime can be overcome, society will be able to actually prevent its occurrence. "All Americans share a concern about the crime problem because we all share the status of potential victims. We also share the fact of life known as aging: It is to our advantage to seek justice for aging victims of crime."[45]

Rationalizations for looking at crime and the elderly have been discussed. Statistics to stimulate interest have been examined. It is now up to the student to go further in this book and truly understand the issue—the inherent problems that elderly people face regarding crime. There must be understanding before there can be help; otherwise aid might be misdirected and involvement useless.

Boyd and Oakes have put it all together, stating:

> Several authors emphasize that only a minority of the aged, perhaps not more than 5 percent, are institutionalized and thus excluded from the mainstream of life. If and when they exist, then, the problems of the majority seemingly result from inevitable factors presently associated with becoming old. The solutions to these problems may be simple if the talents of all citizens are mobilized and this is the challenge which confronts us today. As the challenge is adequately met, we will discover that what may today be defined as a social problem, or what may presently be considered inevitable consequences of becoming old may tomorrow be merely the easily circumvented contingencies of a normal phase in the life cycle.[46]

Before leaving this chapter, please read the following essay by Florida Scott-Maxwell. First heard on the Third Programme of the British Broadcasting Corporation and printed in *The Listener* and later in *Harper'sBazaar* during the 1950s, the stream of thought is truly classic in nature and will echo its message even after the pages of this book have yellowed with age.

WE ARE THE SUM OF OUR DAYS (ABRIDGED)
Florida Scott-Maxwell

...[A]ge cannot spend all its long days, and often wakeful nights, in seeing itself in the light of eternity. Old people may, at a deep level, be facing their inner judges and doing it valiantly. At a more ordinary level they spend much of their time being astonished at their own unimportance. They feel so minute and ephemeral, that they doubt that their identity will last as long as it decently should. They are tired of themselves, and ready to relinquish the rags and tatters of themselves that still cling together.

They are also constantly bedevilled by a question that they cannot get rid of, and this is 'How long must we make ourselves last?' For the haunting thought is always in our heads that perhaps we know nothing of age. It may all lie ahead, and can only be faced day by day to its unseeable end. Each hour nibbles at our solidity, and we relinquish something in every little humiliation. Trying twice before one's knees get one upright. One's own knees! Not seeing what others see, not hearing what they hear, missing the point, and so—pretending one was not interested. Often it was true: one was not interested. The emphasis, noise, and clamor of life seem out of proportion to sense. Something else is true and must be admitted: dullness becomes very attractive. Sitting in a decent silence, enjoying the presence of the you that does not talk, and liking even better the absence of the one that does. One's mind open, in case there is any peace about; but turning away from the too personal, in search of the impersonal—we need a good deal of blankness for that.

Yet it is cold to be left out, and who wants to be treated like an effigy that no longer functions? So we demand with energy, 'Who should be interested if not we? Who else started these lives and events?' We have a great need to know certain things. We long to follow the logic on which we were a link, and—if we can—to catch a glimpse of the new thing that lies beyond us. We watch, all the time, to see where life fructifies, and where it lies dormant. If suffering comes to those we know well, we care above all that the suffering should be used to further life. Perhaps we have come to care more for the quality of life than we do for those who carry it; the old want to learn who, among the young, has the gift of learning. For the old can feel justified, or condemned, by all that they engendered.

But all that is what we long for, fruitlessly, very often. What we get is an odd experience of anonymity, as though we moved along the cracks between the lives of other people. I know one woman who was once so lovely that, as she walked, all eyes were on her and, if she turned round, others turned to look at her. As she aged she noticed that everyone looked right through her, as though she were not there at all. It gave her a funny sense of freedom, but also a sense that she had become invisible. She felt she could go anywhere, into houses and out again. No one would stop her for no one would see her. She even wondered if she dared dance instead of just walking, but thought it more prudent not to try.

It may be this experience of being invisible that makes so many old people give up wearing their social masks. No longer greatly impressed by humanity, no longer sure that they themselves exist, feeling it hardly matters if they do, they gain a new ease in remaining as uncovered and limpid as children. If to be tempered in the fires of insight is the task of age, perhaps this childlike naturalness is its reward. Old people tend to enjoy indulging in mild eccentricity. This could be one aspect of our anonymity, combined with the fact that the old have so much life in them that cannot be lived; we dare to be natural at last, and really care little for the opinion of others. I have heard it said that the vigour and richness of character in a country is proved by the number of great eccentrics that it produces. So, let old people make their contribution here.

There is another aspect to age somewhat akin to this, that is almost embarrassing to speak of because of its extreme improbability. One wants to shield it from younger ears. Yet it is innocent, and may be forgiven us. It is this—the old feel very young. At moments, that is. Though we are aching, inadequate wrecks, there are times when, in our hearts, we are incurably, deliciously young. I have no idea whether we should be or we should not be. Who is to say? Undoubtedly the quality of this strange youthfulness matters greatly. And observation tells us that it varies greatly. All that I am sure of is that an unexpected freshness comes to one when old. I have seen it rise in the lined face of a woman in her nineties, and it suffused her with virginal lightness. And who has not been struck by the guileless purity in the eyes of many old men?

This puzzling newness is so buoyant a thing it is a problem how to deal with it discreetly. Explain it as you will, it feels like happiness: but also like release and exemption. If taken in too literal a manner it may make you want to start again, and how can this be done? For the absurd fact is that an irrational and very high spirited you is convinced that it now knows how to live. And could: there is the danger. For two pins it would try. In fancy, and very nearly in fact, it is ready to start out at once and see the world. It knows clearly that the necessary physical strength is lacking, as well as the robust purse, and that the perfect companion, who would like exactly what you like has not been met in a lifetime of looking. Yet this unconquerable you, who might easily make a fool of you, must be honoured. It must be honoured greatly, for the leap of expectancy that rises in its heart is authentic, and I beg you to believe me when I say it is pristine in its freshness.

This gaiety in age is accompanied by, perhaps even partly caused by, the realization that though our drama has been played, and that nothing much will now happen to us in the outside world, our battle too is over. And that fills us with a surge of triumph. It is like a great thrust of cognition, for we have lived our lives. We have been through that mystifying travail. We have worked and suffered, and sinned and loved, and known happiness. We have done harm and done good. We have seen ugliness and beauty. We have been broken, and we have come through. So that some part of us is free: free of trying, free of any need of hope. And somewhere we are clear. A little clear: as though at the core there was an infinitesimal diamond, and there the conflict of living is stilled.

If age is at all as I see it, then age is undeniably stormy. Stormy, but quiet; contradictory, in fact. Very well, that is what age can be. And how could it be anything less? If our true occupation is accounting for our lives, and relinquishing ourselves, no one can say that such a great matter could be accomplished easily. It is only after the combat that rest comes to the wrestler.

Facing our own truth, giving ourselves up—think of these a moment longer. Even a hint of truth feels like a spear in the heart. And so relinquish yourself? Who else have you? This question could be answered in two ways. Caution seemed to ask it, and caution could answer it. But so could abandon, and I feel that here abandon is the better guide. Let us say again: 'If you relinquish yourself what have you?' The answer comes with a rush of relief: 'Everything that isn't me!' And so we fall heir to a new richness, and marvel and meaning are clearer; and sometimes the candle of sentience which we each carry may burn with a new brightness.

It hardly needs saying that the old keep an eye on death, even trying to peer beyond death. We feel that we may indeed end there, as we have already diminished so much. But with equal strength we feel there is that within which cannot be put out. Those who have experienced, in the recesses of the soul, that which feels immortal, rest content. And since even the poorest of us receive so much, is it not natural, at the end, to bid adieu to life in the words that Jacob spoke to the Angel: 'I will not let thee go, except thou bless me'?[47]

Personal communication with Mrs. Florida Scott-Maxwell indicated she wrote this essay at age seventy-three and now, at age ninety-four, says, "I back now, what I said then, and realized that it pointed to me what I still had to learn, and that was the greatness of life."

QUESTIONS

1. Why should we study how crime affects the elderly?
2. Shouldn't the Criminal Justice System concentrate on the youth? After all, isn't this where our deviance begins? And, if we eliminate the deviance caused by the youth, aren't we eliminating the problems for the aged?
3. Why should we concern ourselves with the plight of the elderly—they won't be with us much longer anyway?
4. Is there statistical evidence to warrant research in this area?
5. Why is crime prevention a positive approach to crime?
6. How will volunteering in the Criminal Justice System help the elderly?
7. Why are the aged turning to crime?
8. What can we do to aid the elderly in their fight against victimization?
9. What crimes seem to haunt the elderly the most?
10. Is the fear of crime an issue to consider?

SUGGESTED READINGS

Richard Cloward and Lloyd Ohlin, *Delinquency and Opportunity* (New York, N.Y.: The Free Press, 1960).

E. Cumming., L. R. Dean, D. S. Newell, and I. McCaffrey, "Disengagement—A Tentative Theory of Aging," *Sociometry,* Vol. 23, No. 1, 1960, pp. 23–5.

B. W. Lemon, V. L. Bengtson, and J. A. Peterson, "An Exploration of the Activity Theory of Aging: Activity Types and Life Expectation Among Inmovers to a Retirement Community," *Journal of Gerontology,* Vol. 27, No. 4, pp. 511–23.

John Lofland, *Deviance and Identity* (Englewood Cliffs, N.J.: Prentice-Hall, Inc., 1969).

NOTES

1. Clarence M. Kelley, "Message From the Director...," *FBI Law Enforcement Bulletin,* Vol. 45, No. 1, January 1976.

2. Edward M. Davis, "Crime and the Elderly," *The Police Chief,* February 1977, p. 3.

3. Barbara Puls McClure, "Crimes Against the Elderly," Library of Congress Congressional Research Service: Education and Public Welfare Division, HV 6251-A, 75-23OED, October 21, 1975, p. CRS-3.

4. S. S. Goldsmith and J. Goldsmith, "Crime, The Aging and Public Policy," *Perspective on Aging,* Vol. 4, No. 3, May/June 1975.

5. R. A. Dorsey, participant, "Seminar in Crime Prevention for the Elderly," Center for Gerontology, Florida State University and Senior Society Planning Council, Tallahassee, Florida, sponsors, June 21–July 5, 1977.

6. S. S. Goldsmith and J. Goldsmith, "Crime, The Aging and Public Policy," p. 16.

7. George L. Maddox, "Growing Old: Getting Beyond the Stereotypes," *Foundations of Practical Gerontology,* eds. Rosamonde Ramsay Boyd and Charles G. Oakes (University of South Carolina Press, 1973), p. 5.

8. M. Clark and G. Anderson, *Culture and Aging: An Anthropological Study of Older Americans* (Springfield, Illinois: Charles C. Thomas Publisher, 1967), p. 10.

9. W. M. Beattie, Jr., "Plight of Older People in Urban Areas," *Aging,* January 1968, Vol. 159, p. 10.

10. Goldsmith and Goldsmith, op cit., p. 17.

11. Kelley, loc. cit.

12. Jaber F. Gubrium, *The Myths of the Golden Years: A Socio-Environmental Theory of Aging* (Springfield, Illinois: Charles C. Thomas Publisher, 1973), p. 141.

13. *Crime Prevention Handbook for Senior Citizens* (Kansas City, Missouri: Midwest Research Institute, 1977), p. 2.

14. McClure, op cit., p. CRS-1.

15. Curt Gentry, *The Vulnerable Americans* (Garden City, N.Y.: Doubleday and Company, Inc., 1966); pp. 11–12.

16. Mrs. Alice Brickler, participant, "Seminar in Crime Prevention for the Elderly," Center for Gerontology, Florida State University and Senior Society Planning Council, Tallahassee, Florida, sponsors, June 21–July 5, 1977.

17. Carl L. Cunningham, "Crime Against the Aging Victim," *Midwest Research Institute Quarterly,* Spring 1973, p. 8.

18. Goldsmith and Goldsmith, op cit., p. 18.

19. Goldsmith and Goldsmith, op cit., p. 16.

20. Jaber F. Gubrium, *Time, Roles and Self in Old Age* (New York, N.Y.: Human Sciences Press, Behavioral Publications, Inc., 1976), p. vi.

21. R. N. Butler and M. I. Lewis, *Aging and Mental Health: Positive Psychosocial Approaches* (St. Louis, Missouri: The C. V. Mosby Company, 1977), p. 105.

22. "Statement of Understanding Between the Law Enforcement Assistance Administration and the Administration on Aging," Information Memorandum AOA-IM-76-66 (Washington, D.C.: Department of Health, Education and Welfare, Office of the Secretary, May 10, 1976).

23. Ibid.

24. Gentry, op cit., p. 324.

25. Donald O. Cowgill, "Aging and Modernization: A Revision of the Theory," *Late Life: Communities and Environmental Policy,* ed. Jaber F. Gubrium (Springfield, Illinois: Charles C. Thomas, Publisher, 1974), p. 144.

26. *Foundations of Practical Gerontology,* R. R. Boyd and C. G. Oakes (University of South Carolina Press, 1973), p. ix.

27. Clark and Anderson, op cit., pp. 8–9.

28. Paul Tournier, *Learn to Grow Old,* trans. Edwin Hudson (New York, N.Y.: Harper and Row, Publishers, 1972), p. 37.

29. E. Grant Youmans, "Some Views on Human Aging," *Foundations of Practical Gerontology,* eds. R. R. Boyd and C. G. Oakes (University of South Carolina Press, 1973), p. 17.

30. Rosamonde R. Boyd, "Preliterate Prologues to Modern Aging Roles," *Foundations of Practical Gerontoloty,* eds. R. R. Boyd and C. G. Oakes (University of South Carolina Press, 1973), p. 42.

31. Harriet H. Naylor, "Volunteerism with and by the Elderly," *Foundations of Practical Gerontology,* eds., R. R. Boyd and C. G. Oakes (University of South Carolina Press, 1973), p. 201.

32. Beattie, op cit., p. 10.

33. Gubrium, op cit., p. 52.

34. Ibid.

35. Ibid.

36. Rochelle Jones, *The Other Generation: The New Power in Older People* (Englewood Cliffs, N.J.: Prentice-Hall, Inc., 1977), pp. 50–51.

37. Jones, op cit., p. 51.

38. Ibid.

39. Jones, op cit., p. 123.

40. Jones, op cit., pp. 123–24.

41. Gubrium, op cit., p. 38.

42. Gubrium, op cit., p. 39.

43. Youmans, op cit., p. 23.

44. Goldsmith and Goldsmith, loc cit.

45. Goldsmith and Goldsmith, op cit., p. 18.

46. Eds. Boyd and Oakes, op cit., p. xvii.

47. Florida Scott-Maxwell, "We Are the Sum of Our Days (Abridged)," in *Culture and Aging: An Anthropological Study of Older Americans,* by Margaret Clark and Barbara G. Anderson (Springfield, Illinois: Charles C. Thomas, Publisher, 1967), pp. 434–38.

Chapter 2

The Aged as Victims

Each day the probability of victimization is increased. Crime just does not happen to the "other person."

Those of you who have never been victims of crime might wonder what your reaction would be if you were suddenly victimized. Would you experience a horrid feeling of helplessness? Would your financial world come tumbling down upon you? Would the psychological impact of such an event provoke a prejudiced attitude? Would the emotional disturbance of being victimized be unbearable? What punishment would you want doled out to the criminal? These questions and others like them need to be asked, for no one really considers such questions until victimized. Remember, the probability of victimization cannot be escaped, but the reduction of victimization can be attempted through preparation.

The aged are the most vulnerable to crime. A sense of understanding the issues involved in the victimization of the elderly can be gained from reading the following excerpt of Mr. John M. Gallo in a statement to the House of Representatives, Ninety-Fourth Congress, Second Session.

STATEMENT OF JOHN M. GALLO, PRIVATE CITIZEN

MR. GALLO: I was victimized about four times, as you say, but one instance was the worst one I ever had. One man got me into the elevator, and I had plenty of money with me because it was Friday. I had to pay my people to work. I had $140.

MR. BIAGGI: Are you still in business, Mr. Gallo?

MR. GALLO: Yes; I keep going yet and I keep going until 100. I have plenty of power to go yet. I am not afraid to go out and I keep going without any fear in the streets.

Now, when this man come in, he says, "Where is the money?" because I had one bag with some seeds in them. My wife wanted me to take it home. But being that I come out from the bank, he thought that I had a lot of money in the bag. So he says, "Where is the money?" and he tried to knife me right then and there, and I was perspiring because I knew this was the end of me.

The knife was about six inches long, a very strong knife that would go into anything. He says, "Where is the money?" I says, "Here's the money." I says, "Calm down, calm down. Maybe you need money better than I do." I says, "Don't get all excited," and I touched him, see, and I smiled although I was really in bad shape.

I says, "There's the money. That is all I got." I says, "Take this but watch out, somebody is coming." I says, "Go away, go away, somebody is coming." That was the end of it. He ran and left me there. I didn't know if I was going to go out, if I stay there, I didn't know what to do.

I just went out and looked for an officer, but what could the officer do, the whole thing was over. So I didn't even report the case. What could I do? What could they do to me? That was all over and I had forgotten.

MR. BIAGGI: Why didn't you report the case, Mr. Gallo?

MR. GALLO: Well, I feel like a fool to go there and tell them what happened. So what do you want us to do now? That is what I say.

MR. BIAGGI: Don't you know you could be helpful? Perhaps this fellow has committed a crime in other areas. You could describe him perhaps a lot better than some other victims.

MR. GALLO: Now I know better. See, one time—this is a good time to tell you what happened to me in the Bronx because I didn't see anybody mention this. I was in the Bronx and I was lost, looking for the address and I was turning around. It was about four o'clock in the afternoon in the winter.

I knew I was lost, so I got scared because the neighborhood was kind of funny, and I didn't know where to go. So I look around and I saw two boys, no more than thirteen or fourteen. So they come out from nowhere, I don't know, and they were looking at me in a funny way.

I says, "Oh, oh, here I am now." I didn't just go away and run. I says, "I am going to fight with them, they are small anyhow." As small as I am, I push one. The other one with the knife, he turned around and slashed me right on my shoulder, but I didn't feel any pain.

So the other one ran and whistled. He had a whistle in his hands. So that whistle, two big men came out from the bar. I figure now that those two punks, they tried to get money from me, or from anybody else for that matter, and those two big people get from me, may give them so much percent, because they know these little punks, they don't get hurt by the law.

The cop has no power in the street. My business is on 39th Street and 8th Avenue, and believe me that is the worst district for everybody. I don't say—this year the men in there, they don't fear the cop, and one man cannot be arrested. Three cops fought with him very, very fiercely. We tried to help them out but he ran away. What happened, three policemen couldn't arrest a man because the cop has no power, and people know that the cop has no power. That is why they do so much.

Other times I won't even mention because that is ridiculous, but I am not afraid, and I would advise anybody not to stay home and bury yourself for no reason at all. Go out and don't have the bags—once a woman has a bag, say, "Come on, take it, here it is." Don't show no bags, no nothing, and if you can go out, try and pick up a friend, a friend that is on the same floor and say, "You want to go to the store, to the A. & P., let's get together." Three or four together is not so bad as one. One is very bad.

That is my advice. Those little punks, they have got to be punished, and the law now, they give them to the father and mother. That is a terrible thing to do because the father and mother, they are not good to take care of that little boy. What happens, the boy goes home, finds nobody. The man is in the bar and the woman is walking the streets because she is making a lot of money.

What can you do? He goes again to do something wrong and goes again in the custody of the father and mother.

MR. BIAGGI: Mr. Gallo, do you think the law should be changed so that these young people should be treated in the same fashion as adults in the serious crimes?

MR. GALLO: Not exactly the same fashion, but at least take them out of the street. Put them in some place where they can learn a trade. They have to learn a trade because if you give them back to the father and mother, but they are no good, it won't do him any good. It won't do the father any good.

MR. BIAGGI: Some fathers and mothers are very good and they have boys that go bad.

MR. GALLO: If they are very good, let them pay for the damages that their children do, so this way the father will take care because I have children myself, that they are perfect. I have wonderful children and I am proud to have those children because I was a very strict father.

MR. BIAGGI: You were victimized four times, weren't you?

MR. GALLO: Yes.

MR. BIAGGI: When was the first time?

MR. GALLO: The first time was about four or five years ago. They come into my office.

MR. BIAGGI: Why haven't you gone out of business or left the city? Aren't you afraid?

MR. GALLO: I don't want to do that. I love my New York. I have faith in my New York. I know New York is going to go back, and it is going to go back like in 1920s although things were not so good, you know, in money matters and things like that. But still I leave my office about twelve, one o'clock in the night because that was the time I tried to make good in my business, and I succeed now, and nobody bothered me in the street, nobody, nobody bothered me in the street. I used to take the subway, go over to my home.

Now, my first wife died. Now I live in New York because I love New York. I won't leave New York for anything. I live in Lincoln Center but I am lucky that I can pay the rent but the poor people that live in places where they are in bad shape, I am sorry for them.

The only thing to do is not to go out with bags for the women and not to go out alone. That is the only thing. The law has got to do something, but I don't know what can probably be done.

MR. BIAGGI: I want to thank you, Mr. Gallo.

MR. GALLO: That is all I can tell you—my poor English. I didn't go to school. I came to America, it was about 1918, and here I am working yet.

MR. BIAGGI: I appreciate your spirit.

MR. GALLO: Well, it's all right. I wish everybody would listen. Thank you. It was a pleasure being here.[1]

Mr. Gallo's statement focuses on the following issues regarding victimization of the elderly:

(1) Nonreporting of victimization
(2) Feeling of helplessness when victimized
(3) Lack of faith in the police
(4) Suggestion of safety in numbers (don't go out alone)
(5) Fear of crime
(6) Compensation to victims

All of the issues to which Mr. Gallo points can be generalized to the aged as a whole. Victimization or the fear of victimization may force the elderly to an existence of hibernation. Must the aged incarcerate themselves because of the seemingly hopeless situation outside the security of their residence? Self-imprisonment is not necessary if the elderly learn how to protect themselves from criminals. The first positive step the aged must take is the reduction or elimination of the "fear of victimization."

THE FEAR OF CRIME

In discussing fear of crime among the aged, Pope and Feyerherm[2] summarized recent trends of the effects of crime on the elderly. These trends are as follows:

(1) In early 1974, the National Council on Aging commissioned Louis Harris and Associates to conduct a study concerning problems of the elderly. Over 4,000 household interviews were conducted, resulting in the following:

(a) Among the elderly interviewed, 31 percent of those with incomes under $3,000 a year responded that fear of crime was a major social problem. This is in contrast to the elderly with incomes of $15,000 or more per year, of whom only 17 percent felt fear of crime to be a major social problem. Thus, those elderly with lower incomes perceive social problems to be more serious than those who are financially advantaged.[3]

(b) Quite obviously, variables such as income, race, sex, and education differentially affect the attitudes of the elderly toward social problems, or, more specifically, toward fear of crime. Of particular concern to the elderly is that their perceptions of crime have a direct impact upon their ability to feel safe and secure when leaving their residences.[4]

(2) The Law Enforcement Assistance Administration (LEAA), in cooperation with the U.S. Census Bureau, completed a survey of crime victims in eight separate impact cities (Atlanta, Baltimore, Cleveland, Dallas, Denver, Newark, Portland, and St. Louis).[5]

(a) Overall, the data substantiates the fact that many elderly citizens are not reporting personal victimizations to the proper officials.

(b) It is not surprising, for example, that the rape rate for the elderly is substantially less than that of the general population. Yet, it must be remembered that the crime of rape is as heinous for an elderly woman as it is for a woman in any other age group. Of more interest, however, is the comparatively high victimization rate among the elderly for crimes of personal larceny involving contact between victim and offender. The victimization rate for larceny among the general population is 317 per 100,000; the rate for those aged fifty to sixty-four is 342; the rate for those aged sixty-five and over increases to a rate of 362.[6]

Goldsmith and Tomas referred to the aged's concern over victimization quite succinctly, stating that "in certain respects a crime against an older person may be considered simply as if it were a crime against a person of any age, and indeed, traditionally, this has been the case within the criminal justice system ... [however], these crimes against the aged warrant treatment as a special category. Older people receive no special consideration from potential victimizers; in fact, their special vulnerability serves as a green light to criminals."[7]

It is time the agents of the criminal justice system implement a green-light policy to prevent further victimization of the aged, so that incidents like the following, which occurred to Mrs. Gayhe E. Curtis, cease to exist.

I went to the corner grocery store to get some fresh peaches. I was going to lay down my purse in order to put the peaches in a bag. Hovering around me were two tall young fellows. Intuition told me to keep hold of my purse, so I did.

When returning home I had to walk up a hill. I noticed the two fellows walking a distance behind me but paid no attention. I was waiting in the entrance lobby of my apartment building when I looked out the glass door and saw the boys frantically rummaging all the apartments (the bills were by the mail boxes). Suddenly one ran through the door, up the nearby stairs, and the other boy walked behind. As I turned to watch the latter boy, the first fellow sneaked up behind me. He fastly hooked his foot around one of my ankles and gave me a big shove on my shoulders with his hands. I fell straight down. While I was falling, he tried to rip the purse strap from my arm. The purse handle got stuck on my arm and he was unsuccessful. Then, with his foot (he wore sneakers) he kicked me in the head and said "Stay down!" Then both ran out the door. I hollered after them that God would punish them. I never have forgot the experience.[8]

THE AGED: ARE THEY PRONE TO VICTIMIZATION?

A review of related literature shows most authors to be in agreement that the aged are more prone to victimization than other age groups. However, there are some authors who feel as Rifai does, that "there is a strong connection between age, visibility, and the type of crime of which one might become a victim. The so-called 'young-old' [sixty to sixty-four years of age], who are more mobile in the community and the highly visible active older person [Mr. Gallo], were more likely to become victims of burglary and street robbery. The increased incidence of street robbery...probably coincides with increased amounts of exposure. This may lend some credence to the hypothesis that older persons are not victimized more than other age groups because they are not, as a group, as visible as other age groups."[9]

The issue of whether or not the aged are more victimized has proponents of both sides, but, regardless of the viewpoint, there is a substantial amount of concern among scholars over the question of elderly victimization. The following discussion should help the student clarify a position on this issue.

Ottie Adkins states, "Many of our senior citizens are prime targets for criminals who take advantage of the seemingly careless and sometimes naive older person. Crime in the street...is often directed at the elderly because they are relatively defenseless and are most often alone. [And] there is no possibility of changing the attitude of a thief, trickster, or swindler to the point where he might give consideration to a victim merely because he is older."[10]

The latter portion of Adkins' statement reflects the business aspect of crime. Soft-core sentiment and emotions play no part in the hard-core dealings of criminal activity. A criminal cannot afford to be generous. Crime involves the element of risk. It is only natural for the criminal to prey upon the elderly, for there is less risk in being apprehended and suffering the consequences of a prison term.

Although crimes of violence are more identifiable, crimes involving fraud are more numerous. Since there is little risk attached to nonviolent crimes (e.g., the elderly are less likely to report fraud) and since there is usually no physical harm involved, the criminal, if apprehended, will undoubtedly receive a lighter sentence. (This is a fault in the criminal justice system, which is blind to the harm caused by confidence games, crimes of fraud, and white-collar criminals.) An excerpt of an actual account taken from *On Guard,* a publication of the State of California's Attorney General's Office, may best illustrate the business attitude of criminals.

> Jim Norris of our Los Angeles Crime Prevention Unit staff discovered the following scheme during an appointment with an Orange County Police Department. The scheme went like this, in one instance: Two men in plain clothes approached an elderly woman who was in her front yard and presented badges explaining that they were detectives. They said they had just arrested a young boy in the neighborhood who claimed he had robbed her of some money. They asked her to check in her home to see if her money was missing, and followed her into the house. While they were in the house they followed her around to see where she hid her money. She of course did not suspect. The "detectives" then told her that there must have been some mistake and that perhaps the boy was lying—while one suspect had the woman's attention the other was stealing the money from her hiding places. The two detectives then left. About twenty minutes later, they called her back telling her they had arrested another boy. They asked her to check her hiding places again and this time, her money was missing. They assured her everything was okay. They told her that they had her money but that it would be needed for evidence for a few days and would then be returned. The money was never returned, of course. The phone call they made to her had put her mind at rest. She believed that there was no need to call the cops since they were already handling the case.[11]

For anyone who experiences the same situation as the elderly woman mentioned above, the possibility of "taking the bait hook, line, and sinker" would be just as great, regardless of age. There are many gullible and naive people waiting to be victimized, yet criminals seem to zero in on the elderly.

One reason for the elderly woman being sought by the criminals is that the elderly are more likely to keep sums of cash hidden in their household. Crime prevention techniques to foil such schemes will be discussed in Chapter 3; but, as an example, what the elderly woman could have done to prevent her victimization should be obvious: (1) she could have checked the detectives' credentials more thoroughly, possibly calling police headquarters to see if they were cops or (2) refused to let the detectives follow her about the house and checked her hidden money alone. Regardless, the elderly woman was victimized mainly because she put too much faith in authoritative strangers and paid too little attention to her common sense and good judgment.

Pope and Feyerherm noted that "compared to crimes of a personal nature, the victimization experiences of the elderly (as with the population in general) are far more substantial with respect to property offenses."[12] They further remarked that "while expressed fear of violent crime is understandable considering the increase in the number of rapes and muggings reported in most major cities throughout the country, the fact remains that chances are much greater of becoming the victim of a property as opposed to a violent offense... [and] certain offenses (whether violent or property related) may wreak more havoc with the lives of elderly victims."[13] (See Charts 2-1 and 2-2.) With regard to property crime, Mr. R. A. Dorsey recalled the following incident:

Chart 2—1: Victimization Rates, 1974*

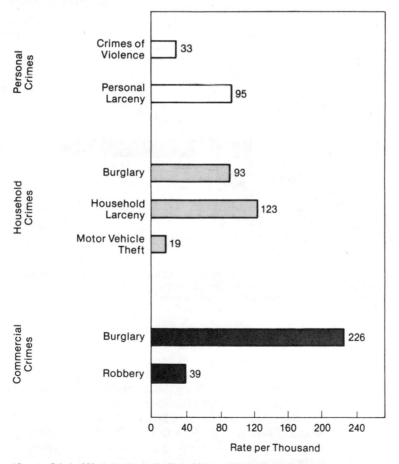

*Source: *Criminal Victimization in the United States, 1974: A National Crime Survey Report,* U.S. Department of Justice, Law Enforcement Assistance Administration, National Criminal Justice Information and Statistics Service, December 1977, p. 13.

Chart 2—2: Victimization Rates, 1975*

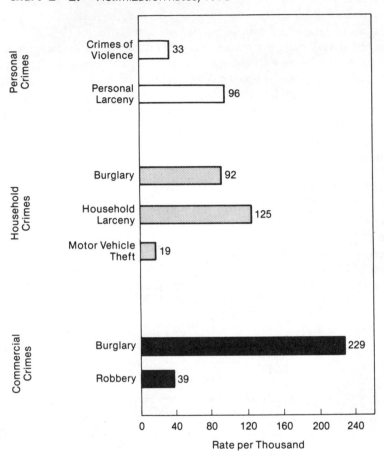

*Source: *Criminal Victimization in the United States, 1975: A National Crime Survey Report,* U.S. Department of Justice, Law Enforcement Assistance Administration, National Criminal Justice Information and Statistics Service, December 1977, p. 13.

My wife and I came back to our Pine Port Motel (we lived in a home attached to the motel) from a grocery shopping trip. Nothing seemed amiss until I opened our refrigerator to store some of our purchases. I noticed half a dozen bottles of Pepsi, a wedge of cheese and some cold cuts missing.

My wife, about then, called to tell me the change we used in the motel was gone. I laughed at her at the same time holding a finger to my mouth to tell her to be quiet—I thought I had heard a noise in our bedroom.

I called the sheriff first, then armed with a baseball bat, I foolishly pushed open the bedroom door. The room was empty, but an open window told me someone had been there.

And the not too unpleasant ending—in about ten minutes Deputy Sheriff
Monk rang our bell. In his car were two frightened and bewildered boys.
Monk had seen them as he was answering our call, munching cheese and
drinking Pepsis as they walked along. It developed that they were running
away from home and had stopped to ask for a handout. When no one answered
the bell they had tried the back windows and found one open.

I told Deputy Monk that if they would go back home I would not press
charges. He took them to jail, gave them a good scare and contacted their
parents. The grateful letter I got from one of the parents more than repaid me
for the few items I had lost.[14]

Gubrium states that "according to popular belief, aged persons as a
group are greater victims of crime than those in any other age group," yet
he also feels that there are sufficient data from a variety of surveys which
indicate that "the aged, in fact, are among the least victimized."[15] Not
accounting for elderly victims like Mr. Dorsey, Gubrium reiterates that
these statistics do not reflect the relative impact of crime on the lives of
persons and that there is much underreporting involved.[16] In other words,
the underreporting of crimes, by all age groups and the elderly in particular,
may be the rationale some researchers use in suggesting the elderly are not
being victimized any more than other age groups. Not only are the elderly
less likely to report crimes against them, whether from feelings of incompe-
tence or lack of faith in the criminal justice system, but an elderly person
who does not exercise caution is bound to suffer greater physical and mental
stress from victimization than the college student, young professional, or
the middle-aged suburbanite.

Gubrium perceives surveys as a false indication of the actual amount of
elderly victimization and offers three hypotheses as food for thought.

(1) The extent of victimization of the elderly is greater in nonprotective
than in protective housing environments.

(2) Concern about the extent of crime is greater among persons residing
in protective, age-concentrated housing, than among those residing in nonprotective age-heterogenous housing.

(3) Among the aged, fear of crime is likely to be greater in nonprotective,
age-heterogenous housing than in protective, age-concentrated housing.[17]

Perhaps a definitive explanation of Gubrium's hypotheses will aid in
determining the extent of elderly victimization. Please keep in mind that
these are only hypotheses and not quantified research findings.

Concerning the first hypothesis, *protective housing* refers to a housing
environment which is properly secured, such as a private home (correct
locks, lighting, etc.), a senior citizen apartment complex having proper

security measures (guards, camera equipment, voice boxes to identify callers), and a senior citizen community, built and protected with the elderly in mind. *Nonprotective housing* refers to inadequately secured homes, apartments, or rooming houses, where the possibility of breaking and entering is greatly enhanced.

The second hypothesis, regarding protectiveness and concern about crime, draws the distinction between the aged who live in age-heterogenous housing, for example, an aged couple living in a neighborhood comprised of many couples of varying ages, as compared to the aged who live in protected age-homogenous housing, such as an elderly resident living in a multiunit senior citizen apartment complex. In other words, the protected age-homogenous elderly are likely to have more concern about crime because the issue is constantly being reinforced through social interaction.[18]

Lastly, the hypothesis concerning protectiveness and fear of crime essentially suggests that fear of crime is greater among nonprotected age-heterogenous elderly because these elderly have few supportive relationships to help them cope with anxiety.[19] Fear runs rampant because they do not have the means to talk out their concern about crime. It seems that social interaction is the elderly's release mechanism for their greatest fear—crime. Significant to note is Furstenburg's indication that a person's response to crime may vary depending upon whether one is focusing on concern about crime or fear of victimization.[20]

To determine whether or not the elderly are actually victimized more often than other age groups, some recent statistics will be reviewed.

STATISTICS

Goldsmith and Tomas refer to the study of criminal victimization as highly complex. They feel the major roadblock to obtaining accurate data is underreporting. The most commonly cited reasons for failure to report a personal or household crime to the police are (1) a belief that, because of a lack of proof, nothing could be accomplished by reporting the incident, and (2) a belief that the incident was not important enough to warrant police attention.[21] These, along with the other reasons described concerning the underreporting of crimes, should not lead to the conclusion that the elderly are not being victimized. There is an enormous amount of elderly victimization, especially against elderly females. Goldsmith and Goldsmith reported a study of robbery in Oakland, California, conducted by the Center on Administration of Criminal Justice at the University of California at Davis. This study concluded that older persons, especially women, were among the most vulnerable segments of the city's population.[22]

The St. Petersburg, Florida Police Department, using St. Petersburg statistics, reported the following in their publication, *Crime and the Elderly:*

(1) St. Petersburg, Florida, has long been known as a haven for elderly citizens.

(2) Florida ranks fourth among states in the total number of elderly residents, representing a 37 percent population increase since 1970.

(3) Of the St. Petersburg, Florida population, approximately 37 percent or slightly over 88,000 persons are sixty years of age or older.

(4) Of this over-sixty population, slightly over half (53%) are female and a majority (84%) are white.

(5) Most residents reside in the central city.

(6) Fifty-one percent of the residents subsist on less than $5,000 a year.

(7) Thirty-one percent of the residents live in the $5,000-to-$10,000-a-year-bracket, while only 3 percent have an average income of more than $20,000.[23]

(8) Within certain categories, elderly persons are overvictimized in relation to their representation in the city's population.[24] (See Table 2-1.)

Table 2-1   Crime and the Elderly—1974 and 1975, St. Petersburg, Florida

Crime	1974 Total Crime	Victims 60 & Over	Total	1975 Total Crime	Victims 60 & Over	Total	% Change Number of Victims 1974–1975
Homicide	33	5	15%	16	3	19%	− 40%
Rape	81	3	4%	90	5	5%	+ 67%
Robbery	844	238	28%	805	319	40%	+ 34%
Aggravated assault	968	34	3%	1298	45	3%	+ 32%
Simple assault	2265	104	5%	2348	97	4%	− 7%
Residential B & E	5124	1364	27%	6627	1445	22%	+ 6%
Auto B & E	1449	130	9%	1299	131	10%	+ 1%
Pickpocket	54	17	31%	32	17	53%	0
Purse snatch	278	184	66%	240	174	73%	− 5%
Commercial B & E	1950	—	—	1306	—	—	—
Shoplifting	1602	—	—	1798	—	—	—
Larceny							
Auto parts	1914	303	16%	2029	296	15%	− 2%
Bike theft	2284	52	2%	1662	45	3%	− 13%
From buildings	1159	120	10%	825	92	11%	− 23%
Miscellaneous	2144	394	18%	2614	556	21%	+ 41%
Auto theft	783	56	7%	597	59	10%	+ 5%
TOTAL	20982	3004	14%	20187	3284	16%	+ 9%

Source: St. Petersburg Police Department, St. Petersburg, Florida.

Consider the following statistics concerning elderly victimization, from Tables 2-2, 2-3, 2-4, 2-5, and 2-6, gathered from various cities in the United States.

Table 2-2 reflects a study by North Texas State University in Denton, Texas. After compiling data for one year, this study revealed that "the elderly (people sixty-five and over) experienced 29.8 crimes per 100 people,

Table 2–2   Victimization by Age

Crime	Under 65 (Per Hundred People)	65 and Over (Per Hundred People)
All crimes	41.7	29.8
Robbery	4.7	5.6
Burglary	13.8	7.9
Auto theft	4.7	3.0
Theft	10.0	4.9
Swindling	2.2	3.8
Purse snatching	1.3	3.2
Assault	3.5	1.3
Rape	2.5	0.0
Murder	0.03	0.08

Source: Raymon Forston and James Kitchens, North Texas State University, "Criminal Victimization of the Aged: The Houston Model Neighborhood Area," Community Service Report #1, Center for Community Services, School of Community Service, North Texas State University, Denton, Texas, 1974, p. 10.

Table 2–3   Senior Citizens as Victims of Crime in Comparison with the Total Number of Victims

Crime	1971	1972[1]	1973
Total robbery	6,766	3,802	4,895
Senior citizens	2,296	1,147	1,352
Percent of total	33.9	30	27.6
Total breaking and entering	30,798	20,156	21,154
Senior citizens	3,442	4,552	5,899
Percent of total	24	22.5	27.9
Total robbery (armed)	12,227	7,908	9,934
Senior citizens	2,082	1,201	1,701
Percent of total	17	15	17.1
Total homicides	690	500	751
Senior citizens	65	51	98
Percent of total	9.4	10.7	13
Total rapes	472	359	692
Senior citizens	21	21	35
Percent of total	9.4	5.9	5.1

[1] 9 months

Source: *In Search of Security: A National Perspective on Elderly Crime Victimization,* Report by the Subcommittee on Housing and Consumer Interest of the Select Committee on Aging, 95th Congress, First Session, April 1977, p. 13.

while those under sixty-five experienced 41.7 per 100 people of all crimes included in the study. Considering all crimes combined, the elderly are not overvictimized. However, for certain crimes, namely, robbery, swindling, purse snatching and homicide, those sixty-five and over are more highly victimized than the under-sixty-five group."[25]

The Detroit Police Department prepared the data shown in Table 2-3 in a report entitled, "Senior Citizens as Victims of Major Crimes." The elderly, comprising 22 percent of the population, nevertheless, experienced 27.6 percent of the unarmed robberies in 1973, a 5.4 percent increase in burglaries from 1972 to 1973 and a 3.6 percent increase in homicides from 1971 to 1973.[26]

In New York, the elderly experienced a 46 percent increase in homicides from 1971 to 1975.

Only a few statistics regarding elderly victimization have been reviewed since space does not allow numerous statistical data, but students should reserve forming an opinion on this issue until the following is discussed.

Table 2–4 City of New York—Total Homicides per Month (1971–1975)

	1971	1972	1973	1974	1975	Total	Percent of Annual Total
January	128	149	153	143	140	713	8.4%
February	112	128	128	103	136	607	7.1%
March	151	135	146	140	138	710	8.4%
April	110	138	153	137	118	656	7.7%
May	104	128	169	126	134	661	7.8%
June	124	138	152	143	130	687	8.1%
July	145	176	157	140	136	754	8.9%
August	158	196	156	139	138	787	9.3%
September	145	165	137	136	154	737	8.7%
October	134	164	138	118	136	690	8.1%
November	129	143	143	132	150	697	8.2%
December	182	155	146	160	156	799	9.4%
TOTAL	1622	1815	1778	1617	1666	8498	

Source: *Crime Against the Elderly,* Hearing before the Subcommittee on Federal, State and Comm Services of the Select Committee on Aging, House of Representatives, 94th Congress, Second Session, New York, N.Y., December 13, 1976, USGPO, Washington, D.C., 1977, p. 54.

Table 2–5 City of New York—Homicides of Persons Older than 65 Ye (1971–1975)

1971	1972	1973	1974	1975	Total
74	72	88	88	108	430

Source: *Crime Against the Elderly,* Hearing before the Subcommittee on Federal, State and C Services of the Select Committee on Aging, House of Representatives, 94th Congress, Second Se in New York, N.Y., December 13, 1976, USGPO, Washington, D.C., 1977, p. 54.

Table 2–6 Miami Beach, Florida[a]
Part One Crimes Against the Elderly—60 Years or Older
(January–June 1976)

Crime	Crimes Against People Younger than 60	Against Elderly
Robbery	81	129
Aggravated assaults[b]	51	28
Larceny (pickpocket)	116	168
Larceny (purse snatch)	87	146

[a] Some 59% of the city of Miami Beach's permanent residents are over 60.

[b] Simple assaults not counted, only aggravated assaults or better.

Source: Adapted from John H. Tighe, "A Survey of Crime Against the Elderly," *The Police Chief*, February 1977, p. 19.

WHAT DOES IT MEAN TO BE A VICTIM (STATISTIC)?

Whether the crime against an aged person is of a violent or property nature, or involves a confidence scheme, the consequences of the actual victimization are not only damaging financially and physically, but also psychologically, forming a more permanent scar.

Clark and Anderson make reference to seven problems elderly people face as they grow older. They are as follows:

(1) A change in physical appearance
(2) Partial or total retirement from active duties
(3) Lower energy level
(4) Greater possibility of ill health
(5) Greater possibility of need for help
(6) Changes in cognitive and intellectual functioning
(7) Greater uncertainty about the duration of life[27]

When all of these problems are combined with the trauma of victimization, the psychological effects can be devastating. Goldsmith and Tomas remark that "there are two dimensions to the threat of criminal victimization: the actual and perceived threat. Both have a negative impact on the individual, e.g., self-imposed incarceration. Elaine M. Brody of the Philadelphia Geriatric Center notes the psychological consequences of actual victimization... the landlord who raises the rent excessively, the salesman who exploits, etc. ...inflict wounds to pride and dignity as well as to purse and person. Violent crime injures not only the physical self, but reinforces feelings of helplessness. Even a small loss may be the most recent in a series of 'insults,' though superficially trivial, it may represent the proverbial last straw, or restimulate previous experiences of losses with their attendant painful emotions."[28]

The easy targets.

Courtesty of Administration on Aging

In fact, an elderly's reaction to a crime might stem from the continuous feeling of helplessness. Maybe the next crime will cause the elderly victim to crack from nervous strain and tension or push the elderly to personal combat with the criminal. Mrs. Hanna Burdick relates just such an incident.

One never knows how one is going to react in a crime situation. Common sense dictates one behavior—submission—yet anger may cause one to react quite differently and perhaps rashly. I have in mind a couple of incidents which occurred to a friend when I lived in Chicago, Illinois.

In leaving work one day while it was still light, in transferring from the 35th St. bus to the nearby Rapid Transit Station, my friend felt her handbag being seized by the strap held in her hand. Instead of letting go of the handbag, fury seized her and she thought, "Who in the world is this punk to do this to me?" She held on, keeping up with the running young black lad until he suddenly let go, running away, and she dropped to the ground. A few days later she saw the boy, wrist bandaged, on the bus. They eyed each other wordlessly, he with fear in his eyes, and she watching him closely. She never saw him again.

In another incident, my friend was standing on the "el" platform waiting for her train, when through an open window of a waiting train, an arm reached out and grabbed her handbag strap. Again, she held on tightly, thinking to herself, "What does he think he's doing anyway?" The train started to move, and he released his hold and drew his arm back into the moving car. Had he held on, he might have dragged my friend off the platform to certain death.

My friend knew the hazards of resisting, but her immediate reaction in each case was anger, not caution.[29]

Just as Mrs. Burdick's friend, many elderly reach their boiling point and all too frequently their breaking point. Restating Goldsmith and Tomas's theme, the St. Petersburg, Florida Police Department reports that "to most, the loss of money in a wallet or purse would prove more an inconvenience than a devastating loss, as one could rely on savings or other sources. However, to an elderly person, the loss of money would prove disastrous, since it may be all the money they have. Also, the experience of being 'accosted' and the loss of personal mementos may be damaging psychologically —many personal items are priceless and their value is in memory, emotions, and pleasant thoughts. Although an antique vase may be worth $1,000, the monetary loss is insignificant when compared to the psychological damage caused by the theft of such a possession. All things considered, the aged face an entirely different set of problems when they become victims of a crime."[30]

Although violent crimes are a personal affront to an individual, nonviolent crimes, such as fraud and confidence games, can be just as financially and psychologically damaging. Goldsmith and Goldsmith point out, "Street crime and residential crime are not the only types of crime victimizing the aged; they are especially vulnerable to frauds, con games, and swindles, robbing them daily of previous financial resources or even subsistence. Health frauds, and sale frauds, phony investments, home-repair schemes, pigeon drops, fraudulent retirement plans...these and many other deceptive business practices are directed against the elderly."[31] Adkins also notes that being educated and intelligent is no guarantee that people will not be swindled when they are targets of con artists.[32] The following should illustrate the psychological damage and loss of faith and trust in the system which the elderly encounter.

The con artist watches for a potential victim, usually an elderly lady walking home from the grocery store, on the presumption that she has already cashed her government check. The con artist appears at the door claiming to represent the Social Security Administration. He tells her that under a new provision of social security, she is entitled to $15 additional benefits per month. This is an excuse to get in her front door. The con artist then gives her a fake form to complete. Sometime during his stay in her house, he requests a drink of water, or makes some excuse to get the victim to leave the room. While the victim was filling out the form, the con artist had time to "case" her house, or look around for items of value. When she left the room to get the con artist a drink, he took the goods and left. The con artist does this by gaining the trust of the victim. To make sure the victim won't call the police, the con artist memorizes the victim's phone number before leaving the house. Once away, the victim gets a telephone call from the con artist, who is impersonating a cop with a disguised voice. She is told by this "police officer" that someone reported a man leaving her home with valuables and that he is calling her to confirm or deny it. He then assures her that the police are aware of her plight and will do everything they can to apprehend the suspect. Confident in this knowledge, she probably will not call the police since she believes they are already investigating.[33]

Even though the general population may not consider con games criminal activity, the fact remains that they are very profitable. Farace and Camera note, "The monetary loss in confidence games goes well beyond that of bank robberies when one realizes that many successful schemes go unreported for reasons of embarrassment, fear, age of victim, etc. Many confidence operators are well aware of this fact, a situation which gives added impetus to their activities."[34]

What does it mean to be a victim? Much more than being a statistic! Aged persons are not just numbers, they are a reflection of the future. If the general population shows no concern for the plight of the aged victim now, the chances are no one will show compassion for those currently in young adulthood when they reach the full potential of victimization—old age.

In an article entitled, "Youth Gives Way to Graying of America," Robert Reinhold disseminates reasons to consider policy implications involving the elderly.

> ...low fertility and mortality rates have combined to produce a population that, while increasing for many decades, will probably have a larger proportion of elderly people and a smaller proportion of the young. Although it is hazardous to forecast the consequences of this trend, it seems unlikely that any aspect of American life will be untouched....the fertility rate of American women continues to slide dramatically. For the first eleven months of 1976, the rate was 65.7 births for each 1,000 women in the childbearing ages (15-44), down from 66.7 in 1975. At the crest of the postwar "baby boom" in 1957, the figure was 122.7; the previous low was 75.8, set in 1936 during the Depression. Even the absolute number of babies born remains extremely low, in comparative terms. About 3,159 babies were born during the twelve months that

ended November 1976, the same as during the comparable period of 1975. During the baby-boom years, with a far smaller population, over 4,000,000 babies a year were born.[35]

Considering the modern phenomenon of the birth-control pill, vasectomies, and zero-population cries, and assuming human fertility will remain low (not as many new babies and the "baby-boom" babies growing old), society can expect an enormous population of elderly Americans by the twenty-first century. With crime reduction nonexistent at present and the elderly population steadfastly growing, can elderly victimization be dismissed so lightly?

WHAT IS THE KEY TO ELDERLY VICTIMIZATION?

Crime prevention and crime compensation are the answers to victimization of the aged. Until the knowledge is produced to eradicate crime and criminals effectively, realistic attempts to help the aged should be implemented through crime prevention programs as well as compensation to elderly victims in the form of monetary reimbursement, free medical care, replacement of personal belongings and emotional support from significant others, in particular the various actors of the criminal justice system. Goldsmith and Tomas state that "in large disasters, the aged victim can at least take some comfort in the fact that he is not alone in his troubles, and that there is a national spotlight on the problem, and, hence, sympathy and emergency relief on the way."[36] It seems only humane to offer the same service for the most natural disaster a human can experience—crime.

Goldsmith and Tomas further state that evidence is mounting that the elderly constitute a unique class of crime victims and that crimes against the aged can be dealt with most effectively when considered as a distinct category of criminal activity.[37] Some categories of persons—namely, children, women, political leaders—are already recipients of special security measures "derived from a public policy which recognizes that, for some groups, equal protection of the laws can best be realized through specialized or differential treatment."[38] If there exists any age group in need of special security/protection and compensation, it is the aged.

VICTIM COMPENSATION

The fact that victim compensation has resurfaced as a national issue is due to the increased awareness of its importance among scholars and practitioners alike. In 1973 the First International Symposium on Victimology took place in Jerusalem. This conference dealt extensively with the question of compensating victims of crime, especially through schemes employing state systems and national support.[39]

In addition, the American Society of Criminology devoted an annual meeting to victim compensation, with Robert Childres suggesting the question be viewed with regard to personal injury; James Starrs viewing victim compensation as a part of the general problem of insurance law; Marvin Wolfgang suggesting that the principle of crime compensation was neither new nor radical, yet legislation providing it by a state would be innovative in contemporary criminal law; Schafer supporting the idea that compensation should be the personal responsibility of the criminal as a portion of the correction process;[40] and many others taking differing views with how to implement victim compensation since then, yet all agreeing it is a much needed component of the criminal justice system.

Helping aged victims should be mandatory. Yet Brooks mentions that as of 1971 there were only six crime compensation programs in the United States (California, New York, Maryland, Hawaii, Massachusetts and New Jersey).[41] Of these, California was the first, providing monetary compensation to victims of violent crime. A point to note is that crime compensation or victim compensation (different nomenclature for the same issue) develops with the needs of each particular state; thus, like our criminal code, existing crime compensation programs are also unilateral. State crime compensation programs may yet blossom into an issue of considerable political consequence[42] —recall the potential number of elderly citizens (voters) in the years ahead. As of 1977 there were twenty-four crime-victim compensation programs in the United States.

The Crime Control Act of 1976, enacted October 15, 1976, by the Ninety-fourth Congress, Second Session, United States of America, requires that each state establish a planning agency which is charged with developing a comprehensive plan for the improvement of law enforcement and criminal justice, coordinating state activities, and establishing priorities. The plan developed by this agency must meet certain criteria for the state to be eligible for Federal anticrime funding.

One of those requirements is that the plan *must* provide for the development of programs and projects to prevent crimes against the elderly. Advocacy groups representing older citizens should be able to use this office's resources to assure that the crime-related problems of the elderly are adequately addressed within their communities. They should also be aware that the state planning agency is required by this act to assure that citizen and community organizations participate at all levels of the planning process.[43]

To avoid confusion over the term compensation, Schafer distinguishes compensation from restitution. Believing that the two terms are used interchangeably, but in fact represent different viewpoints, Schafer offers the following distinction: "Compensation means making amends to the victim, it is an indication of society's responsibility being civil in character, thus representing a noncriminal goal in a criminal case. Whereas restitution concerns restoring the victim's position and rights that were damaged or destroyed by and during the criminal attack. It is the responsibility of the offender, being penal in character and thus represents a correctional goal in a criminal case."[44] Compensation requires the victim to make application, and payment is issued by society; whereas restitution comes in the form of a court decision, and payment is made by the criminal to the victim.[45]

Regarding elderly victimization, the term compensation is most appropriate and efficient. Compensation would enable the elderly victim to readjust to his victimization in a reasonable period of time—letting time heal all physical and psychological wounds. Restitution, on the other hand, could possibly take "forever." Once a case enters the court system, the opportunities for stalling on the part of the defendant (alleged criminal) are limitless, causing the aged victim additional pain and suffering through procedural delay. For a more comprehensive study on victimology and crime compensation, the interested can further read Schafer. (See reference at end of Chapter 2.)

Another issue which merits special attention with regard to victim compensation is the amount of support given the victim from actors within the criminal justice system, especially the first line of contact victims have with the system—the police. Goldsmith remarks, "One area currently undergoing profound and very rapid change in law enforcement is the area of police-victim relations. Within that broad category, the problems of crime and older victims has recently emerged as a topic of serious concern for law enforcement."[46] Clarence M. Kelley, former FBI director, stated:

> In dealing with the victims of crime, particularly in those instances where violence has occurred, the police officer should be prepared to exhibit, among other professional attributes, a high degree of sensitivity, compassion, and interviewing skills. The welfare of the victim is, of course, a foremost consideration and, in this regard, care should be taken by the contacting officer to avoid needlessly adding to the traumatic effects of the crime experience. The often crucial role of the victim in the solution of cases also clearly warrants a a special concern by the contacting officer. Indeed, a recent study involving a number of serious offenses indicated that in more than half of those cases solved, the police learned of the identity of the suspects through victim reports. In many such instances, a cooperative attitude on the part of the victim and a willingness to provide needed information may largely hinge on the manner in which the officer has handled the contact.[47]

Furthermore, Goldsmith offers the following checklist for police-older-victim programs:

(1) Do the police have a sound knowledge of any state victim compensation programs? Do they distribute information and material on such programs in order to facilitiate filing claims?

(2)   Where victim services are available through nonpolice agencies, do police have information or directories to give to elderly victims to assist them in getting such assistance?

(3)   Do patrol officers provide the victims information, short-run or emergency assistance, or referral to available medical care, mental health, public assistance, and legal aid services?

(4)   Does the officer provide an explanation to the older victim of how the case will be processed through the criminal justice system? Are there materials which can be distributed? Is there an officer for the older victim to call for further information?

(5)   Have feedback mechanisms been established in order to provide older victims with information regarding developments in their cases?

(6)   Are there special police training programs dealing with the nature and needs of older persons, the special problems they face, and sensitivity training for better police-older victim relations?

(7)   Is there a departmental victim services liaison officer when victim services are housed in another agency?

(8)   What kind of crime control public information program does the department have? Are local older persons, local senior centers, clubs, and other organizations actively involved in target-hardening training?

(9)   Are there departmental programs or means to provide technical assistance for establishing older people's programs for team shopping, neighborhood watches, escort services, and so forth?

(10) Have special police units concerned with crimes such as bunco and purse snatching or offenders such as juveniles who are particularly associated with the criminal victimization of older people been given training specifically designed to improve communication with and providing assistance to older persons?

(11) Does the department pursue outreach to involve social workers, area aging-agency personnel, social security personnel, and others working with older people in crime prevention and personal security programs for older persons?

(12) Has the communications dispatch room staff been trained in crisis intervention and counseling techniques?

(13) Finally, is there a firm commitment rather than lip service at all levels of the department from chief to patrol officer to improve and expand victim services to older persons?[48]

The aged should receive special consideration from local police agencies. As Pope and Feyerherm note, the elderly constitute (1) a group which is favorable to crime prevention programs, (2) their victimization is ever present, and (3) the respect the elderly have for law enforcement is high.[49]

The following article, partially reproduced from *Aging,* emphasizes the contemporary relationship between law enforcement and the elderly, as discussed by the executive director of the International Association of Chiefs of Police, Mr. Glen D. King:

AGING: ...Because police departments are usually a first line of help for older people...do police departments around the country really care about the elderly?

MR. KING: ...The unique nature of the group makes them dependent to a greater degree on the police agency. It creates a greater need, and I think most police agencies respond to this very positively. In my view, law enforcement agencies, rather than feeling that the aged are a burden, feel that they have the first claim.

AGING: ...We have discrimination of all kinds, but we also have age discrimination, and it's rather typical of a tendency in our country to push them off and forget about them. How do police departments escape that tendency?

MR. KING: Well, you don't totally escape it, I guess, because police agencies themselves, insofar as their own employees are concerned, have to be concerned with the younger person more than in most jobs. The policeman's job is one that requires physical stamina. And we have earlier retirement for police than for most people. ...We get more telephone calls, I would suspect, per capita, from older people, because their needs are greater. And I think the departments respond to this relatively well.

AGING: ...Are you satisfied, or are police departments generally satisfied, with the cooperation that they get from other community agencies or groups, or is there something to be desired in the matter of cooperation from other groups in the country?

MR. KING: My experience doesn't indicate this. I think there is an interest on the part of the agencies. There may not be agencies set up with adequate resources to give the kind of assistance that's honestly needed. But I didn't find, in the city in which I worked and in the department of which I was a member, any lack of interest. I didn't find any unwillingness to become involved. I frequently found people who didn't have the answers, who weren't able to provide a totally satisfactory response. But I think this was not generally caused by a lack of interest or a lack of willingness to do what needed to be done.

AGING: What about those younger police officers on the beat that you mentioned? Are police departments able to provide them with training in the specific problems of older people and in dealing with older people, and do they?

MR. KING: Yes, it's covered by most departments in recruit training. Of course it's only been within very recent years that a large number of departments in the country were able to provide training for their officers. The advent of the minimum standards commissions in the state, mandating training for law enforcement agencies, has created the ability of agencies to train their officers before they are put on the street. So, in recent years I think the level of training has improved because the availability of training has improved. It's still going to be addressed in relatively minor detail when you take into consideration the total instruction that comes in a department, but I think most departments and most law enforcement officers now have some understanding of the unique problems of the older person.

AGING: Well, what can police departments do to protect older people that they're not doing for the population as a whole?

MR. KING: Well, you have a number of programs that are in operation across the country. Most major departments have a specialized program they've developed.... They vary a little bit but more in detail than they do in the overall, basic concept.... I really believe that effectiveness in this area, though, lies not in specialized programs. I think you need these because there are unique needs that have to be met.... But I think the overall benefit has to come from normal, routine, operational police activities.... But if you rely on specialized programs, you have access to such a limited number of specialized programs that you really don't get the kind of benefit that you need.

AGING: Alright, let's assume that there are some special needs. What would your advice be to professionals who are working for and with older people in a community? What can they do to help reduce the susceptibility of older people to crime?

MR. KING: I think they can inform older people about the nature of crime that occurs most frequently with the older person—thefts from persons, purse snatching...they can inform the older person about the nature of the offenses to which they are most susceptible, and they can talk to them about procedures and things they themselves can do to reduce their vulnerability. Now, this calls for a direct relationship with them. This calls for representatives of a police agency meeting with groups of the elderly, the older citizen, and instruction programs. I think you can also involve them in law enforcement activities. There's a wealth of talent there. There's a wealth of experience. There's a wealth of knowledge that's looking for an outlet.

AGING: We've now got crime-victim compensation in twenty-four states. Do you find that older people are taking advantage of these programs, and should we have such a program in all states, or should we federalize it?

MR. KING: This is something that we have addressed over several years. We have urged that there be victim compensation... with crimes against property there is a growing belief, I think that you ought not to be simply because you happened to be the immediate target of the thief, or of the burglar, called upon to bear that total load. There ought to be a sharing of it, and this is a point of view that we have officially adopted, in resolution by our members, and we have urged it in Federal legislation. We have urged it in state legislation, and I think it's a completely valid approach.

AGING: What are police departments learning from the demonstration projects which the Administration on Aging has funded with several of them through the IACP?

MR. KING: I think they really are looking for programs that have been effective. They're looking for ways they can supplement their own activities. They're looking for approaches that they can take. I think that there are characteristics of cities that require you to adapt something, sometimes, before you can move it from one to the other. But I think the projects that you have funded have a much wider impact than the narrow jurisdiction that receives the original funding. I think the benefits can be transferred, and I think that they are. We have, for the last two years, one full issue of our professional publication here, our in-house publication, devoted solely to crimes against the elderly. And a very major part of that has been a description of programs that have worked. Very few people want to write about the programs that haven't worked and sometimes they do like to exaggerate the degree to which they have worked. But most of the time, if they are willing to write about it, it has some elements that can be used by other departments. And I think this is good.

AGING: Maybe older people can function in some ways as assistants to police departments. Do you think that's feasible?

MR. KING: I think they can function in a great many ways as assistants to the police departments, and I think the police departments ought to utilize them more. But there's a lot of difference between the citizen working in direct concert with his police agency and the citizen operating as the vigilante. I think he creates more danger than he eliminates when he does that.[50]

Before concluding this section on elderly victimization, it should be noted that the aged need the cooperation of all facets of the criminal justice system. Yet, until such cooperation exists, eliciting help from the private sector will remain a viable alternative. One such source is an organization known as Aid to Victims of Crime, Inc., St. Louis, Missouri, which provides emergency supportive services to victims of rape, robbery, burglary, assault and homicide. Even though the organization does not concentrate on the aged, its efforts are beneficial to the elderly, especially through such services as:

(1) Helping the victim or family contact a public or private agency, such as welfare department, social security office, or hospital.

(2) Contacting employers to ask that a victim's position be held in case recuperation is needed from the victimization; also trying to persuade employers to give victims time off to go to court once the criminal is apprehended and slated for trial.

(3) Arranging for transportation to court, hospital, police station, etc.

(4) Arranging for home care, child care, grocery shopping, etc.

(5) Providing emergency food and clothing.

(6) Arranging funerals.

(7) Replacing items stolen or broken that are essential, e.g., eyeglasses, walking canes, and locks on doors.[51]

In short, organizations such as Aid to Victims of Crime, Inc., are assuming the responsibility which actually belongs to society, in particular the state or locality where the victim resides. When the elderly victim receives emotional and financial support from private organizations instead of governmental agencies, law enforcement can lose "the elderly's generalized support for the agency involved, cooperation with law enforcement investigators, e.g., swearing out of complaints and showing up in court as witnesses, and most importantly, the elderly might not be receptive to future reporting of criminal activity and crime prevention suggestions"[52]—which is one of the keys to eliminating elderly victimization.

SUMMARY

In this chapter elderly victimization has been discussed, noting the nonreporting of crime by the elderly, their concern over victimization, their fear of crime, and the reasons they are more prone to victimization.

The criminal justice system must assume a more active role in elderly victimization and, in particular, in compensation to aged victims. What everyone has in common with this most venerable segment of our race, the aged, is sharing the same problems. All are susceptible to violent crime, property crime, and confidence schemes, yet younger people are better able to cope with the consequences than the elderly. If people refuse to get involved in eliminating the hardships elderly victims suffer, they have only the same to look forward to in years to come.

QUESTIONS

1. How can we improve the elderly's reporting of crimes to the police?

2. What can be done to quell the aged's fear of crime?

3. Must the fear of crime be controlled before realistic attempts at reducing victimization begin?

4. What do you think is the reason for the slow start in victim compensation among the states?

5. If the criminal justice system has properly identified the elderly victimization problem, why isn't more being done?

6. Why are the aged prone to victimization? Or is this a misnomer?

7. Are the elderly more naive than other age groups, or are they more trusting and less cynical, thus leaving themselves open to criminals?

8. What is the impact of crime upon an elderly victim?

9. Does it matter where an elderly resides with regard to his concern or fear over crime?

10. Do the statistics reflect elderly victimization as a growing problem?

11. Are the psychological wounds of victimization more devastating to the elderly than other age groups?

12. Although violent and property crimes against the elderly are feared the most, which crime against the elderly is the source of the loss of millions of dollars a year?

13. Why should the young concern themselves with the plight of the elderly?

14. Is there a victim compensation program being operated in your state? If so, how does it operate with regard to the elderly; if not, why not?

15. Does your local law enforcement agency have a program specifically designed for the elderly victim?

SUGGESTED READINGS

T. W. Condit and S. Greenbaum and G. Nicholson, *Forgotten Victims—An Advocate's Anthology* (Sacramento, California: California Office of Criminal Justice Planning, Alameda Regional Criminal Justice Planning Board, 1977).

P. H. Hahn, *Crimes Against the Elderly—A Study in Victimology* (Santa Cruz, California: Davis Publications, 1976).

NOTES

1. John M. Gallo, statement, "Crimes Against the Elderly," Hearing Before the Subcommittee on Federal, State and Community Services of the Select Committee on Aging, House of Representatives, Ninety-fourth Congress, Second Session, Held in New York, New York, December 13, 1976 (Washington, D.C.: U.S. Government Printing Office, 1977), pp. 60–62.

2. Carl E. Pope and William Feyerherm, "A Review of Recent Trends: The Effects of Crime on the Elderly," *The Police Chief,* February, 1976.

3. Pope and Feyerherm, op cit., p. 29.

4. Ibid., p. 30.

5. Michael J. Hindeland, *Criminal Victimization in Eight American Cities,* Final Report, L.E.A.A., 1975, p. 377.

6. Pope and Feyerherm, loc cit.

7. Jack Goldsmith and Noel E. Tomas, "Crimes Against the Elderly: A Continuing National Crisis," *Aging,* June/July 1974, p. 10.

8. Mrs. Gayhe E. Curtis, participant, "Seminar in Crime Prevention for the Elderly," sponsors, Center for Gerontology, Florida State University and Senior Society Planning Council, Tallahassee, Florida, June 21–July 5, 1977.

9. Marlene A. Young Rifai, "The Response of the Older Adult to Criminal Victimization," *The Police Chief,* February 1977, p. 32.

10. Ottie Adkins, "Crimes Against the Elderly," *The Police Chief,* January 1975, p. 40.

11. Evelle Younger, Attorney General, State of California, *On Guard,* Vol. 4, No. 4, October 1976, p. 5.

12. Pope and Feyerherm, op cit., p. 31.

13. Ibid.

14. R. A. Dorsey, participant, "Seminar in Crime Prevention for the Elderly," sponsors, Center for Gerontology, Florida State University and Senior Society Planning Council, Tallahassee, Florida, June 21–July 5, 1977.

15. Jaber F. Gubrium, "Victimization in Old Age: Available Evidence and Three Hypotheses," *Crime and Delinquency,* July 1974, p. 245.

16. Gubrium, op cit., p. 245.

17. Ibid., p. 248.

18. Ibid., p. 249.

19. Ibid., p. 250.

20. Frank F. Furstenberg, "Public Reaction to Crime in the Streets," reprinted from *The American Scholar,* Vol. 39, No. 4, Autumn, 1970. Copyright © 1970 by the United Chapters of Phi Beta Kappa.

21. Goldsmith and Tomas, op cit., p. 11.

22. Sharon S. Goldsmith and Jack Goldsmith, "Crime, The Aging and Public Policy," excerpted from *Perspective on Aging,* Washington, D.C.: National Council on the Aging, Inc., Vol. 4, No. 3, May/June, 1975, p. 18.

23. St. Petersburg Police Department, *Crime and the Elderly,* St. Petersburg, Florida, 1974–75, p. 1.

24. Ibid., p. 2.

25. Raymon Forston and James Kitchens, "Criminal Victimization of the Aged: The Houston Model Neighborhood Area," Community Service Report No. 1, Center for Community Services, School of Community Service, North Texas State University, Denton, Texas, 1974, pp. 3–4.

26. "In Search of Security: A National Perspective on Elderly Crime Victimization," Report by the Subcommittee on Housing and Consumer Interests of the Select Committee on Aging, Ninety-fifth Congress, First Session (Washington, D.C.: U.S. Government Printing Office, April, 1977), p. 13.

27. Margaret Clark and Barbara G. Anderson, *Culture and Aging: An Anthropological Study of Older Americans* (Springfield, Illinois: Charles C. Thomas, Publisher, 1967), p. 60.

28. Goldsmith and Tomas, loc cit., p. 11.

29. Mrs. Hannah Burdick, participant, "Seminar in Crime Prevention for the Elderly," sponsors, Center for Gerontology, Florida State University and Senior Society Planning Council, Tallahassee, Florida, June 21–July 5, 1977.

30. St. Petersburg Police Department, op cit., p. 2.

31. Goldsmith and Goldsmith, loc cit.

32. Adkins, loc cit.

33. Evelle Younger, "Welfare, Social Security, Pension Check and Food Stamp Frauds," *On Guard,* October 1976, p. 1.

34. Theodore Farace and Andrew Camera, "Confidence Games," *The Police Chief,* January 1975, p. 37.

35. Robert Reinhold, "Youth Gives Way to Graying of America," *Tallahassee Democrat,* February 13, 1977, pp. 1E–2E.

36. Goldsmith and Tomas, op cit., p. 11.

37. Ibid, p. 12.

38. Goldsmith and Tomas, op cit., p. 13.

39. Stephen Schafer, *Victimology: The Victim and His Criminal* (Reston, Virginia: Reston Publishing Company, Inc., 1977), p. 125.

40. Schafer, op cit., pp.128–9.

41. James Brooks, "Compensating Victims of Crime: The Recommendations of Program Administrators," *Law and Society Review,* Vol. 7, Spring 1973, p. 445.

42. Ibid.

43. *Action on Aging Legislation in Ninety-fourth Congress,* Special Committee on Aging, U.S. Senate, November 1976, pp. 15–16.

44. Schafer, op cit., pp. 112–13.

45. Ibid., p. 113.

46. Jack Goldsmith, "Police and the Older Victim: Keys to a Changing Perspective," *The Police Chief,* February 1976, p. 21.

47. Clarence M. Kelley, "Message From the Director...," *F.B.I. Law Enforcement Bulletin,* Vol. 46, No. 1, January 1977.

48. Goldsmith, op cit., p. 23.

49. Pope and William, loc cit.

50. "IACP Executive Director Talks About Crime and the Elderly," *Aging,* No. 281–82, March/April, 1978, pp. 18–22.

51. Aid to Victims of Crime, Inc., University Club Building, Suite 705, 601 N. Grand, St. Louis, Missouri, 63101.

52. Goldsmith, op cit., p. 20.

Chapter **3**

The Aged and Crime Prevention

Sun City posse members conducting monthly meeting at Sun City Office.

Courtesy of Maricopa County Sheriff's Office

Criminologists are not alone in trying to answer such vague questons as: "What is being done to prevent elderly victimization?" As criminologists attempt to determine what is being done about the crime problem, gerontologists are inquiring about what is being done for the aged population and demanding that crime prevention programs for the elderly be established. Literally thousands of questions are continually asked of social scientists actively involved in criminological and gerontological research and development. Although their answers to crime prevention questions may be vague at times, their achievements in the area of crime prevention for the elderly are readily visible.

Criminological and gerontological theorists and researchers are constantly criticized and evaluated by their colleagues as well as the general public. Yet, such constructive criticism has fostered ideas and academic pursuits which have enabled the implementation of various crime prevention programs. Although the term *prevention* has been used for years, e.g., insurance prevention, dental disease prevention, medical disease prevention, the term has only recently resurfaced and been connected with crime.

Even though crime prevention has become popularized in recent years, its spectrum has not been broad enough. Though most law enforcement agencies see their role as crime prevention, in actuality they have barely slowed the crime rate, not prevented it. In addition, most police departments are generalists in crime prevention because of limited manpower and financial resources; therefore, particular attention to specialized forms of crime prevention (such as for the aged) is taking time to develop. Unfortunately, the aged cannot wait forever, "law enforcement must thrust into the area of crime prevention. We've relied on the traditional police approach too long, with nothing to show—no satisfactory results. Even if we were able to rehabilitate, deter and cure, the devastating impact on the victims remains."[1]

This chapter focuses on the following:

(1) Crime prevention in general

(2) Crime prevention through environmental design

(3) Examples of specific crime prevention programs, with regard to both personal and property crime

(4) Crime prevention against confidence games and frauds, specifically those to which the elderly fall victim

CRIME PREVENTION FOR THE ELDERLY

Evelle Younger, Attorney General for the State of California, noted as recently as 1971 that the study of elderly victimization had largely been ignored. Since studies have only recently attempted to struggle with this particular area of victimization, it follows that crime prevention programs for the aged have also been lacking. One reason for this lack of concern of involvement in crime prevention programs for the elderly is the conflicting data from victimization studies.[2]

Brown and Rifai state that "there has been conflicting information concerning the actual incidence of victimization among older persons; the second report of *Criminal Victimization in the U.S. (1975)*[3] indicated that in terms of personal crimes, persons sixty-five and over had the lowest rates of victimization of all persons studied. While there is still an urgent need for clarification of data, a study prepared by Louis Harris and Associates, Inc., for The National Council on the Aging, Inc., Washington, D.C. © 1975,[4] showed that on a nationwide level, the highest concern among older Americans was the problem of crime."[5]

Home burglary prevention inspection.

Courtesty of:
Senior Citizens Crime Prevention Program
Cottage Grove Police Department
Ron Willis, Chief
400 Main Street
Cottage Grove, Oregon 97424

This disparity in elderly victimization—are they or are they not being victimized and to what extent—is reasonably explained by Ernst, Jodry, and Friedsam (1976) in four points:

(1) Different research projects may have used differing age categories. One project may have classified everyone fifty-five and above as an older adult while another project used sixty-five years of age and over.

(2) Two projects may also have been completed in vastly different geographic and socioeconomic sectors of the city, for example, one project in the central city (ghetto or slums), another in the suburbs.

(3) Differing results also could have been obtained by grouping all crimes together without considering the vulnerability of the population to specific types of crime. For example, the elderly are more prone to fraud and purse-snatching victimization than to rape and auto theft.

(4) Divergent statistical results leave the relationship of victimization and age subject to debate, especially since most law enforcement agencies do not record the age of the victim.[6]

If the criminal justice system and sociologists in general are to quarrel over whether elderly victimization even exists, they are wasting valuable time. Whatever else remains, older Americans, as all Americans, are concerned with crime and how to prevent it. A reasonable approach for the aged can be found in crime prevention programs specifically designed for them.

Traditional law enforcement has devastated funds which might have been spent more wisely or economically, such as for crime prevention. Although the overall picture of crime prevention seems weak (Table 3-1), it is a start in the right direction.

Table 3–1 Crime Prevention Programs Implemented for Senior Citizens

Type of Program	Police Departments Involved	Percent of All Departments
Operation identification	125	69
Self-defense program	63	35
Residential security	120	67
Business security	77	43
Anti-purse snatching, pocketpicking	96	53
Anti-fraud program	91	51
Mailbox security	42	23
Check-cashing program	46	26
Other	15	8
None	19	11

Source: Philip J. Gross, "Law Enforcement and the Senior Citizen," *The Police Chief,* February, 1976, pp. 9–12.

Gross, interested in how many crime prevention programs have been implemented for the aged during the last five years, sent surveys to 500 police agencies, in association with the International Association of Chiefs of Police (IACP). Of the 500 departments surveyed, only 180 or 36 percent returned the requested information.[7] Why did the other 320 police departments not comply? Is it to be assumed that they were too embarrassed to send data? Are the 64 percent nonrespondents unconcerned over the issue of elderly victimization and appropriate prevention programs to deal with the problem? Although underlying reasons for the low response rate are not known, an upsurge of crime prevention programs can be anticipated, so data will be available for any future IACP-sanctioned surveys—a bureaucratic guarantee.

CRIME PREVENTION IN GENERAL

Crime prevention is not merely the responsibility of law enforcement offices or the criminal justice system. Rather, crime prevention is the responsibility of all components of the criminal justice system and most importantly the responsibility of a component indirectly related to the criminal justice system—the public. If the growing crime problem is to be solved, a commitment on the part of the community is a must. In the ten-year period from 1964 to 1974, crime increased 125 percent, while the population only grew 6 percent.[8] Yet, if the community sincerely gets involved in crime prevention and makes the criminal's job a tough one, a reduction in the number of criminal victimizations, i.e., the crime rate, can realistically be expected.

> We shall see no abatement in the spiraling crime rate until responsible persons in every community act promptly to support law enforcement. Citizens must be the eyes and ears of the police....The terrifying rise of criminality has created a genuine state of national emergency...we must win the war against crime.[9]

So, exactly what is crime prevention? Basically, crime prevention is protecting oneself from criminal attack or criminal behavior by using techniques which place oneself out of the reach of the criminal. Criminals are essentially lazy people—why work when they can steal? Most criminals are amateurs; therefore, by investing a small amount of time (for instance, by making sure the locks at home are sturdy), a person can force the criminal to search elsewhere for spoils.

Is crime prevention effective? Yes, but to what extent it is effective is impossible to determine. Remember, exactly how much crime exists will never be known because of nonreporting of victimizations. And how much crime has been prevented through crime prevention efforts will never be known because the statistics will never be available. It is unlikely that an apprehended criminal would inform police of the various neighborhood burglaries that he attempted but failed because of a Neighborhood Watch program or Operation Identification. Criminals will never admit to the number of crimes they have attempted unsuccessfully. Because of this fact, it will never be known if the crime prevention programs that have been implemented are effective. The only possible satisfaction may come from one of two statistics: (1) the crime rate remains the same; therefore, we know that additional crime has been prevented, (2) the crime rate decreases; therefore, we know that efforts at crime prevention have been successful. This, of course, assumes that crime rates reflect crime and not demographic fluctuations, such as changes in the mean age of the population.

If crime prevention is believed to be effective, the next logical question is "Is crime prevention costly?" The cost of crime prevention can be seen as a necessary expense. Considering the amount of time, energy, money, and increased insurance premiums invested after being burglarized, the cost of crime prevention is minimal. However, there are some law enforcement offices and agencies which consider crime prevention programs as very expensive ventures. They desire tangible results—criminals in hand to justify their existence as law enforcement officers. Unfortunately, catching criminals is a very tedious and often fruitless quest. There are more criminals "out there" than there are police officers. The only realistic response to the cost of crime prevention programs and the cost of utilizing police officers in the task is, Why risk a crime when prevention techniques are readily available? Crime prevention is a safe and sound investment in reducing victimization.

What part or function does crime prevention play in the criminal justice system? In other words, why do we need it and if we do, how much do we need? Is there such a thing as "too much crime prevention?"

Beerbower and Sheppard stated:

> In our opinion, serious consideration should be given to the establishment of an additional component to the criminal justice system. The traditional concept has included three major divisions in the system: police, courts, and corrections. A comprehensive examination of the system reveals that crime prevention permeates the entire system without coordination and has resulted in considerable fragmentation.[10]

They feel that a separate crime prevention component would develop a "unity of purpose" toward the prevention of crime.[11] We cannot afford to disagree with these men. Our criminal justice system is growing with each crime reported, therapy encountered, diversion program instituted, etc. We must face reality—the criminal justice system is a bureaucracy, unfortunately with departments which do not "share" vital information. Although the LEAA and the National Criminal Justice Reference Service have attempted to spread the word, there still remains a separateness between criminal justice components. This idea of a crime prevention component, one which would be the center of all crime prevention efforts, is an innovative approach to finally uniting cops, courts, and corrections. Undoubtedly, the greatest advantage this "Fourth Dimension" would have would be its accessibility to the public, especially elderly groups.

What function does crime prevention play in the criminal justice system? It is the key to reducing crime. Recall its effectiveness. Now the opportunity exists for it to become efficient as well. Crime prevention is definitely needed —all other efforts to combat crime have failed. Crime prevention is today's response and the future's answer to eradicating criminal behavior. Can there be too much crime prevention? Well, can there be too much crime? The tolerance level for the amount of crime prevention used will reflect the amount of crime we, as a society, are willing to accept. Since we prefer not to be victimized, then we must accept enough crime prevention to do the job effectively and efficiently.

CRIME PREVENTION THROUGH ENVIRONMENTAL DESIGN

Crime prevention through environmental design is not new to the twentieth century. Kings and noblemen of the Middle Ages built moats around their castles, the U.S. Army built walls around their forts, and Englishmen put up street lamps to lighten the criminal darkness which swallowed English towns in the nineteenth century. The 1950s and 1960s brought chainlink fences to the suburbs, barriers of shrubbery between residential neighbors, and garages for the protection of modern-day necessities—bicycles, automobiles, and garden tools. Yet, even with all the effort to prevent loss, crimes still occurred and losses of personal property rose. What was the reason? All the money that individuals, groups, and communities were spending to protect themselves from crime was only fostering more criminal behavior. Among scholars, only a handful proposed a workable solution.

Contemporary interest in environmental design as a crime prevention approach was stimulated by ideas presented by such people as Jacob, Wood, Angel, and Jeffrey in the 1960s. Jacob's contention was that *street surveillance* is the key to crime prevention. She argued for diversifying land use to create more activity on the street, thereby creating more surveillance possibilities and stimulating informal social controls. Wood suggested that paid surveillance, project police and guards could never exert the control provided by an involved and interested community. She indicated that the design must provide, at the very least, the opportunity for *communities to exercise social control.* Angel developed the critical intensity zone hypothesis: Public areas become unsafe not when there are either a few or many potential victims present but when there are just enough people on the scene to attract the attention of potential offenders, but not enough people for surveillance of the areas. He suggested *alteration of physical configurations to concentrated pedestrian circulation* and thereby eliminate critical intensity zones. Jeffrey noted the "failure" of prevention and the inadequacy of post prevention and rehabilitation models. He suggested that *urban planning* and *design* be employed to control crime.[12]

The National Institute of Law Enforcement and Criminal Justice has been studying environmental influences on the problems of crime and the subsequent fear of crime since 1969. In 1974, the Institute established CPTED (Crime Prevention Through Environmental Design program) based on the positive aspects of Newman's work,[13] which suggests that the "physical design features of public housing affect both the rates of resident victimization and the public's perception of security."[14] Design features include (1) height of building, (2) number of apartments per floor, (3) number of entrances and where they are located, and (4) the site of the building. All these concepts have become known as Newman's "defensible space."[15] Although Newman's research almost entirely concentrated on public housing projects, especially high-rise apartments, his principles have been studied when considering housing designs of the 1970s, such as town houses.[16] Though early studies have not earmarked "defensible zones" as "the" answer to crime prevention, research will continue until a solution is eventually reached.

Because the environment within a populated area is partially the cause of crime, e.g., a deteriorated Central Business District (CBD), a solution to preventing crime can be readily seen—clean up the CBD. This task, although easy to say, is quite difficult to perform. Yet, the principle involved holds the key to preventing or possibly reducing criminal behavior. When we shape our environment, we are in control. If we don't shape our environment, it will dictate our lifestyle, e.g., fear of crime, less use of CBD, and eventual deterioration of an area.

The environment is our lifeblood. We have shaped our existence around our cities—its pollution, unemployment, schedules, crime rate, etc. If we sit idly by, our environment will slowly choke us or fatally victimize us through crime. It is time we learned a lesson from the antipollution advocates. If polluted air can kill us, it is worth an investment of our time to eradicate its potential threat. Crime is such a killer that it is time we get serious about its increasing rate and start preventing it. Crime prevention through environmental design is just the white knight we have been looking for. As an example of its effectiveness, look at Diagram 3-1, page 73, and try to visualize ways to improve the surroundings.

Diagram 3-2, page 74, has the home improvements—environmentally designed improvements—to prevent criminal victimization.

Diagram 3—1

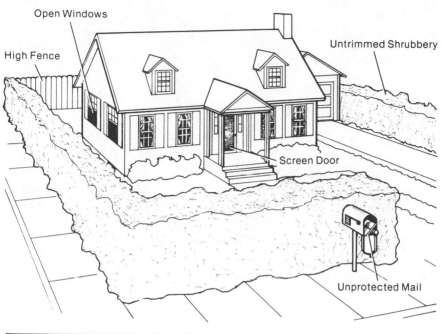

Open Windows

High Fence

Untrimmed Shrubbery

Screen Door

Unprotected Mail

Sliding Glass Doors

Diagram 3—2

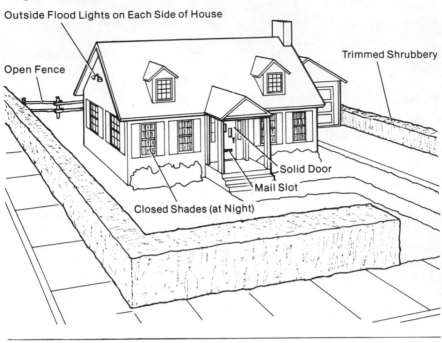

Outside Flood Lights on Each Side of House

Trimmed Shrubbery

Open Fence

Solid Door

Mail Slot

Closed Shades (at Night)

Solid Back Door

Although the diagram examples are illustrations of residential areas, think of how many places within a city which you've visited that are potential crime targets. For example, how many times have you driven by the local mini-market and noticed movement within the store? Not many times. Many such stores have their windows covered with signs as sales enticements. Well, criminals are enticed because of the low risk of being seen from the outside. It is nearly impossible to visualize whether a customer is buying or taking. An environmentally designed store would leave enough open space in the windows for the store clerks' movements to be easily seen by an outsider, and thus a transaction could be easily distinguished from a robbery. What about that dead-end street near the park, the shortcut you've been using, the street with no streetlights, the dark narrow alleys along Main Street, the basement laundry room in your high-rise apartment, the subway? The list is endless, and something can now be done about it.

City planners have tried for decades to bring growth and population back to the city, concentrating on transportation, housing, and education. All these variables are important; however, if the transportation is terrific, the housing beautiful, the educational settings superb, yet the crime rate remains, their efforts have been fruitless. A major political push by the voters should be to inform city, county, and state governments that they want city planning with an eye on crime prevention. Once criminologists and city architects, designers and planners team up to battle the crime problem through environmentally designed programs such as CPTED, we will all prosper. At present, "our cities are unsafe because they present opportunities for the commission of crimes," yet, "crime can be controlled through urban design wherein safety and security are designed into streets, buildings, and parks."[17]

Daryl F. Gates offers the following Do's and Don'ts for avoiding the construction of architectural crime problems.

Do ensure that:

(1)   Address numbers are easily visible on the front, and when necessary, on the back of the building.

(2)   Building address numbers are lighted or otherwise visible at night.

(3)   A map is placed at the main entrance of large complexes.

(4)   Illumination of exterior areas is designed with vandalism-resistant light fixtures.

(5)   Apartment numbering systems follow a logical order.

(6)   Sufficient tenant and guest parking is provided to reduce on-street parking.

(7)   Good quality deadbolt locks are installed on apartment front doors.

(8)   Apartment windows are placed to allow surveillance of entrances and public areas.

(9)   Apartment front doors are provided with door viewers (minimum 170° view) or similar devices.

(10) Building designs do not provide unnecessary concealment (such as doorways and recesses) for possible assailants.

(11) Apartments are situated to facilitate patrol observation.

(12) Entrances are visible to patrol observation or neighbors.

(13) As much as possible, stairwells are open and visible from the public areas.

(14) Elevators are visible from nearby public areas.

Don't allow:

(1) Vulnerable windows or sliding glass doors to be placed in isolated areas.

(2) Blind corners in public highways. Require good visibility along paths and hallways.

(3) Walkways to be placed next to areas of possible concealment.

(4) Stones or other landscaping material that may be used as weapons or missiles.

(5) Exterior lighting systems to be operated by easily accessible switches.

(6) Elevator stopbuttons that may be activated without an alarm sounding.

(7) Laundry rooms and similar facilities to be located in areas not visible to passing foot traffic.

(8) Shrubbery and trees to offer concealment. Specify landscaping that provides a clear field of vision between two and five feet above the ground.

(9) Walls or partitions to provide concealment for would-be burglars and attackers. Consider the use of chainlink fences or similar barriers instead of solid walls.[18]

Crime prevention through environmental design is a challenge which can be met by concerned individuals. Once we accept the fact that environment can be controlled, we will know crime can be modified.

PERSONAL AND PROPERTY CRIME PREVENTION PROGRAMS FOR THE ELDERLY

It is important to note that there are at least four government agencies which the elderly may inquire of for crime prevention assistance. The Department of Health, Education, and Welfare and the Administration on Aging lists these agencies as follows:

(1) *Agency on Aging*. In every state and in 550 communities throughout the United States, an agency on aging has been formed under Title III of the

Poor environmental crime protection.

Improved environmental crime protection.

Photographed by Tom Esmond

Older Americans Act. These agencies (1) serve as an advocate for older persons, (2) coordinate activities in the elderly's behalf, and (3) provide information about services and opportunities for them, e.g., local information on prevention of crime against the elderly or possible sources of funding for such efforts.

(2) *Criminal Justice Planning Agency.* These agencies operate in all states and territories of the United States. Each agency receives financial assistance from the LEAA, U.S. Department of Justice, pursuant to the Crime Control Act. These funds are used in designing and developing improved methods for dealing with the nation's problems of crime and delinquency, including crimes against older persons, which is a specific priority area included in the 1976 revisions of the Crime Control Act.

(3) *Department of Housing and Urban Development.* Funds made available through Community Development Block Grants provide a wide range of activities, such as home security against crime for the elderly, and home improvements or neighborhood facilities for the elderly. Also, funds for housing repair assistance are made under the Home Improvement Loan Insurance Program, Title I of the Housing and Community Development Act of 1974.

(4) *Farmers Home Administration.* An agency of the Department of Agriculture, the FHA makes loans available to senior citizens for a variety of purposes under its rural housing programs. Although security against crime is not the primary purpose of these loans, it can be a benefit of the program.[19]

Either the aforementioned agencies or footwork on your part will put you in touch with currently existing crime prevention programs for the elderly. In this section, you will be looking at specific programs in various parts of the United States. With an introduction to some of the various crime prevention programs and a discussion of a few in depth, you will gain a sense of where crime prevention for the elderly is at present.

There are many law enforcement agencies and communities actively involved in crime prevention programs for the elderly. The keys to these progressive and effective programs are community concern and involvement between the police and the elderly. As an example, let us look at Cottage Grove, Oregon. The city of Cottage Grove faced an increasing crime rate and a diminishing budget. With community support, the police department established a Senior Citizen Crime Prevention Program. Willis and Miller note that Cottage Grove, a community of 7,000 people, had a 1975 crime rate which doubled the crime rate of 1974. With 22 percent of the city's population aged sixty-five and over, most of whom are on fixed incomes, the local police urged and gained support from the public, especially from the elderly. Community awareness and pride in the activities of the senior volunteers has raised the public consciousness about crime prevention.[20]

Cottage Grove, Oregon, and the west coast in particular, especially the state of California, have led this country in innovative crime prevention programs. California's Attorney General, Evelle J. Younger stated:

> Giving emphasis to the positive aspect of prevention efforts minimizes the pervasive climate of fear among seniors, who often fear crimes of personal violence considerably out of proportion to the actual likelihood of incidence.[21]

With the cooperation of local, state, federal, and private organizations, and the elderly themselves, crime prevention programs will soon exist within each and every community plagued with victimization of the elderly.

The source of each crime prevention program for the elderly will be given directly beneath the title. This enables easy reference if the student wishes to contact a particular program or agency for further details. Although there are many crime prevention programs available to the elderly, the limitation of space allows only a few to be discussed. Please bear in mind that the programs mentioned here are successful programs. Those programs which failed did so not because of lack of need, but because of lack of community and police support.

PERSONAL CRIME PREVENTION

California Attorney General's Crime Prevention Unit

Through Evelle J. Younger's dedication to crime prevention programs for the aged, the Attorney General's Crime Prevention Unit (CPU) has developed methods of prevention to minimize the likelihood of elderly victimization. In general, CPU offers the following:

(1) Detailed information on residential methods of improving resistance to forceful entry through windows and doors.

(2) Lectures noting the importance of thinning and lowering shrubbery for visual survey [crime prevention through environmental design].

(3) Encourage self-help projects, e.g., Neighborhood Watch, Operation Identification, and Organized Security Checks.[22]

Because of Younger's belief that there is a credibility problem for the government and for a society when it is not actively concerned about enabling its seniors to live their old age in peace and dignity, as well as his alarm over the fact that the number of older citizens is growing at a rate of 900 daily or 330,000 a year, he incorporated the following objectives in *all* CPU crime prevention programs (even going so far as listing the steps for a committee to accomplish these objectives).

(1) To alert and inform senior citizens in your community about consumer fraud, street crime, bunco, and burglary as it could affect their age group, and to present methods of avoiding incidents.

(2) To inform older citizens of their rights and entitlements under laws governing health, welfare, consumerism, and crime.

(3) To inform seniors where and how to complain if victimized.

(4) To alert and orient local law enforcement and regulatory agencies regarding crime and consumer fraud problems of the elderly.

(5) To train and organize senior volunteers throughout the state to act as crime prevention chairpersons in local senior centers, neighborhoods, and organizations.[23]

The following are examples of crime prevention programs for the elderly implemented by the California Attorney General's Crime Prevention Unit.

Becoming a Good Witness

Through one-day seminars, CPU trains the aged to become better witnesses. They stage a crime during the seminar, thereby forcing the aged audience to witness a criminal act. CPU has employed the use of memory training exercises, thus enabling the aged to learn to recognize and recall important facts concerning the crime. The following acronym is used as an aid for the elderly's recall:

C —Color of car?
Y —Year of car?
M—Make of car?
B —Body shape of car?
O —Occupants of car; how many? race? sex?, etc.
L —License; remember the number like a sentence and a price tag, e.g., ABC-127: *All Boys Color* for $1.27[24]

Purse Snatch

Elderly women are the most vulnerable group to purse snatchers because they are basically poor and dependent upon public transportation—the most likely area for a purse snatch to occur. The following tips will be useful in thwarting a purse snatcher.

(1) Although it may seem nontraditional or nonfemale, do not carry a purse.

(2) Only carry essential items in your purse. Do not consider your purse a vault to store your valuables.

(3) Use checks or credit cards. If cash must be used, carry only the amount of money you will need for the purchase.

Suspect identity chart

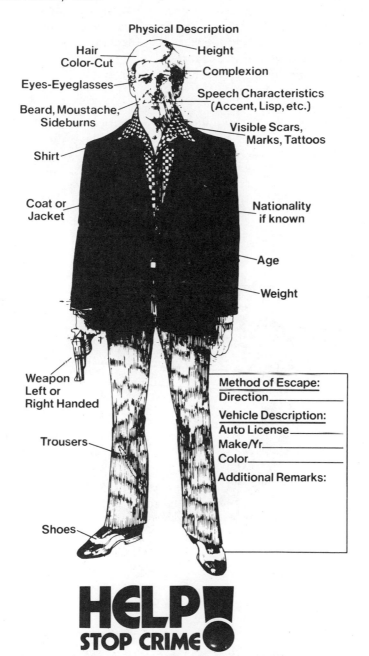

Physical Description

Hair Color-Cut

Height

Complexion

Eyes-Eyeglasses

Speech Characteristics (Accent, Lisp, etc.)

Beard, Moustache, Sideburns

Visible Scars, Marks, Tattoos

Shirt

Coat or Jacket

Nationality if known

Age

Weight

Weapon Left or Right Handed

Method of Escape:
Direction_____

Vehicle Description:
Auto License_____
Make/Yr_____
Color_____

Additional Remarks:

Trousers

Shoes

HELP! STOP CRIME

Courtesy of:
Help Stop Crime! Office of the Attorney General, State of Florida, Governor's Council on Criminal Justice

(4) Do not dangle your purse or carry it loosely by its strap.

(5) Do not wrap the strap around your shoulder, neck, or waist. Since most purse snatchers are hit-and-run criminals, they might pull you down to the pavement, possibly injuring you when they tug on your purse.

(6) Put your wallet in an inside coat pocket, not in your purse.

(7) If attacked, do not fight; surrender your purse.

(8) Call the police immediately.[25]

Recently elderly women—in fact, quite a few women—have been purchasing tear-gas sprays, mace, and plastic lemon squeezers filled with ammonia to

CRIME PREVENTION UNIT
MIAMI BEACH POLICE DEPARTMENT

Courtesy of Miami Beach Police Department

use against an assailant. These items may or may not be legal, depending on the laws in a particular state. Catherine V. Nelson tells of a related incident.

> While going to work in Miami about five years ago [1973, at the age of seventy], I was waiting for a bus when three teenage boys came up to me. One got behind me, one stood beside me and the third one asked me for a smoke. I knew what was about to happen so I opened my bag and quickly pulled out my tear gas and gave the boy a shot of it which scared them all off.[26]

Mrs. Nelson was fortunate not to have the tear-gas gun taken away and turned against her. A more reasonable defensive tactic in the situation would have been to turn her purse upside down, empty all the belongings and simultaneously scream for help. Although the boys had not made a criminal gesture, her suspicions were enough to cause fear and immediately react with the tear-gas gun. How awful this event would have been if the boys were merely there to take the bus and were trying to be friendly. It will never be known for sure what would have happened; but it can be assumed that a series of events led Mrs. Nelson to be fearful, and her instinct for self-protection caused her to react aggressively to the situation instead of cautiously.

Safety on Public Transportation

As previously mentioned, public transportation is the basic mode of transport for the elderly. Bus companies, subways, and even some cab companies have offered discounts to the elderly. Criminals know this and use the areas earmarked for public transportation to prey on senior citizens. The following safety tips for using public transportation are offered by the Attorney General's Office of the State of California:

(1) Know where you are going and how to get there. Many criminals will take advantage of a person who looks lost.

(2) Notify your family or a friend of your destination and approximately when you will return, especially if you are going out in the evening.

(3) Avoid going alone. Travel with another person; most of the time you will find a friend who needs to run an errand also.

(4) On your way to the public transportation, use streets; avoid taking shortcuts through parks or vacant lots.

(5) When waiting for the bus, stand near other people who are waiting.

(6) When on the bus, avoid sections where a group of juveniles may be involved in loud and boisterous conduct. Also, be aware of persons around you.

(7) If the bus is near empty or empty, sit as close to the driver as possible.

(8) While seated, keep your purse on your lap, not on the floor or the seat next to you.

Tips for Holiday Dangers

During the holidays there are greater crowds in stores, using public transportation, and wandering the streets. Pickpockets, thieves and con artists roam the streets and shopping centers in droves. The aged, as well as the general population, should take note of the following suggestions when shopping or traveling, especially during the holidays.

(1) Use a check or credit card to pay for a purchase.
(2) If you do carry cash, keep money in an inside pocket of your coat or jacket.
    (a) Keep varying amounts of money in different pockets.
    (b) Avoid showing large sums of money in public.
(3) Check your wallet· or purse immediately if jostled or brushed in a crowd.
(4) Avoid shopping alone. A woman alone is a prime target.
(5) Do your shopping during daylight hours.
(6) Put your purchases in the trunk of your car.
(7) When you leave home, keep a light on. If possible, use timers for different lights.
(8) Lock all doors and windows of your residence.
(9) During the holidays there are many parties. While at a party do not leave your coat, purse, or other valuables in a vacant room which has access to it via a window.[27]

The above guidelines should not be practiced during holidays only. Your New Year's resolution should be to implement what you practice during the holidays all year long. Crime is not seasonal; therefore, crime prevention should not be seasonal either. For further information concerning other crime prevention programs from the state of California, contact:

State of California, Office of the Attorney General
Crime Prevention Unit
3580 Wilshire Boulevard, Suite 938
Los Angeles, California 90010

**Cass Corridor Safety for Seniors Project—
Detroit, Michigan**

Wayne Bradley, project director and Detroit city policeman, is directly responsible for the Cass Corridor Safety for Seniors Project, an inner-city attempt at crime prevention in Detroit. Initially, there were four general concerns for establishing this project: (1) median age of a street-crime victim was approximately 67.8 years, (2) in many cases, it was difficult to get a senior citizen to testify about crime [faint powers of recall, intimidation, fear, and the "swiftness" of the criminal justice system in bringing an alleged criminal to trial being the causes of this discouraging phenomenon], (3) a great majority of crime-prone youth are located in the same area as the aged, and (4) senior citizens are in close, unavoidable contact with precisely the element of society most likely to attack or steal from them.[28]

The Cass Corridor of Detroit was selected as the site of the project because of its high concentration of aged citizens and its high incidence of street crimes. Its goals are outlined below.

(1) To coordinate existing resources and mobilize potential voluntary resources in a complementary manner, in order to increase the safety of senior citizens in the target area.

(a) To involve and coordinate at least twelve existing agencies, institutions, and organizations.

(b) To mobilize the same over the course of the project.

(c) To fund five community project grants which will be implemented by community organizations or agencies and involve from ten to one hundred volunteers each.

(d) To mobilize at least four additional volunteers per month to work with existing agencies or services.

(e) To generate at least one new project per month involving at least five volunteers each.

(2) To document the impact of the project, e.g., is the safety of senior citizens in the target area increasing?

(a) To assess the existing level of crime against the elderly in the target area utilizing a composite estimate of unreported crime.

(b) To document the level of crime against the elderly during the course of the project.

(3) To develop mechanisms for continuation of the project and application to other communities.

(a) To develop and implement mechanisms capable of sustaining the resources mobilized after the term of the project.

(b) To develop a model and methods of implementation for application of the project concept to other communities.[29]

Although the Detroit area which encompasses the Cass Corridor had been deteriorating for many years, it is refreshing to know there is an ongoing program consisting of police, government, and community cooperation that is attempting to prevent further elderly victimization. For further information contact:

Detroit Police Department
Cass Corridor Safety for Seniors Project
3165 Second Avenue
Detroit, Michigan

Crimes Against the Elderly Program—Sarasota, Florida

The Sarasota Police Department, working with Senior Friendship Centers and Sarasota's Council on Aging, sponsors the Crime Against the Elderly Program, involving radio presentations and seminars for those organizations which request their service. The seminar presentations include (1) an introduction to the goals of the program, (2) distribution of printed material, (3) a movie entitled "Senior Power," and (4) a question and answer session. It is usually during the question and answer period that tips are presented on:

(1) Prevention of purse snatching
(2) Prevention of physical assault
(3) Telephone harrassment
(4) How to use a whistle as a defensive weapon
(5) How to protect your home

For further information contact:

Sarasota Police Department
Post Office Box 3528
Sarasota, Florida 33578

Operation Lifeline—Huntington, West Virginia

Operation Lifeline, a telephone service for the elderly, is offered by the Huntington Police Department's Crime Prevention Unit. It offers the aged a sense of security, protection, and reassurance. The procedure operates as follows: (1) the elderly recipient must call the police department between 9:00 A.M. and 10:00 A.M. each morning, (2) if the police department does not receive a call, the police department calls the elderly person, (3) if there is no answer, a patrol car is dispatched to the elderly's person's residence to see if there is a need for assistance.

Through this program, the police department is able to monitor the aged's physical, emotional and psychological problems. At the same time, the elderly can inform the police of suspects, con artists, or strangers in the neighborhood. Since the program's inception in August of 1974, the number of elderly persons involved in Operation Lifeline has increased immensely (from twenty to two-hundred). Not only has the response been excellent, but the program has become an integral part of Huntington's law enforcement operation. For further information contact:

Huntington Police Department
Crime Prevention Unit
City Hall
Post Office Box 1659
Huntington, West Virginia 25717

Operation Good Morning—Charleston, West Virginia

Operation Good Morning, a program offered by the Charleston Police Department, is quite similar to Operation Lifeline. However, one unique, additional component is a check-cashing program for the eldery. Once a month, the police escort a bank teller to and from senior citizen housing projects. This enables the elderly to cash their social security and pension checks in the privacy of their own homes and without the risk of being robbed enroute to or from the bank. For further information contact:

Charleston Police Department
Post Office Box 2749
Charleston, West Virginia 25330

Operation Good Neighbor—Evansville, Indiana

In order to establish better rapport with the Evansville citizenry and in particular the elderly citizens, the Evansville Police Department established the following programs as part of Operation Good Neighbor:

(1) *Ride-Along.* Elderly persons are able to ride along with a patrolman during an eight-hour shift, thus enabling citizen observation of the patrolman's actual working conditions.

(2) *Scanner Club.* Confined elderly citizens listen in on police calls and become additional eyes and ears for the police.

(3) *Block Meetings.* During these meetings the local residents are able to express their concerns and discuss solutions about crime in their area. This affords a rather direct line of communication with the police.

(4) *Police Cooperation.* The police offer movies, lectures, free tours of police headquarters and jail to all interested citizens. In addition, the police department will send a patrolman to a residence for a safety inspection in order to ensure that the residence is not vulnerable to criminals; if the pa-

trolman discovers an improper lock or an easily accessible place of entry, he will suggest appropriate measures to eliminate the problem.

Whereas the Evansville Police Department has been successful in its crime prevention efforts, it should be noted that:

> It is not an easy task to sell the public on crime prevention, and some of our more experienced [law enforcement] officers are even more hesitant in accepting the idea. Some officers are having difficulty realizing that arrest is not the only method of fighting crime. They have a difficult time realizing that policing today is different than it was twenty years ago when they were given a club, gun, and badge and told to go to work....the objective...is getting to the problem and solving it before it becomes serious enough to make an arrest.[30]

For further information contact:

Evansville Police Department
15 Northwest Seventh Street
Evansville, Indiana 47708

Crime Prevention and Senior Citizens—Jacksonville, Florida

The Crime Prevention Unit of the Office of Criminal Justice Planning initially began its efforts for senior citizens by surveying 660 elderly residents to determine (1) the elderly's level of awareness regarding prevention, (2) their patterns of victimization, and (3) their fears. This survey was compared to a similar study which concerned itself with Jacksonville residents in general. Some of the most significant findings are listed below.

(1) Senior citizens exhibit a much higher fear of walking alone in their neighborhoods at night (72 percent as opposed to 34.2 percent in the general survey).
(2) Of the elderly surveyed, approximately 10 percent had been victims of crime within the past two years.
(3) Twenty-two percent of the elderly stated they do nothing special to prevent crime from happening to them.
(4) Those elderly who take precaution against victimization tend to stay home or keep doors and windows locked as preventive measures.
(5) Senior citizens over seventy years of age reported being victimized more than any other age group of senior citizens.
(6) The elderly saw the need for more police officers and severe punishment for criminals as priorities for preventing crime.[31]

The information obtained from the surveys indicated the elderly are victimized by a narrow group of crimes. The CPU is currently developing a program which involves the elderly in the crime prevention effort. For further information contact:

Office of the Mayor
Criminal-Justice Planning
1245 East Adams Street
Jacksonville, Florida 32202

Crime Cautions for Seniors—Minneapolis, Minnesota

The Crime Cautions for Seniors program was developed cooperatively by public and private agencies because the city found seniors not making use of facilities the community had to offer. This program, an educational one, was established to increase the elderly's enjoyment of their retirement years and to aid in city development.

Concentrating on the fear of crime among the elderly, the program instructs the aged in prevention of victimization and the procedures to follow if they witness or suspect a crime is occurring. The program's format is as follows:

(1) Notices are posted in senior citizen high-rise apartments several days prior to the program.

(2) A local policeman is in charge of the program the day of the presentation.

(3) On occasion, a prearranged crime is enacted and audience participation is solicited.

(4) The film, "Senior Power" by William Rose is shown.

(5) A question and answer period follows.

For those elderly actively involved in the presentation (the prearranged crime), a Junior Police Badge is presented. All the elderly residents receive brochures and a plastic phone ring with the Crime Cautions emblem and an emergency number for the police department. For further information contact:

Minneapolis Police Department
Community Relations Division
Room 118, City Hall
Minneapolis, Minnesota 55415

PROPERTY CRIME PREVENTION

Senior Citizens Crime Prevention Program—
Cottage Grove, Oregon

In July 1975, the senior citizen volunteers of Cottage Grove, Oregon, attired in emblem-adorned blue blazers provided by the police department, launched Operation Identification. Soon, both volunteers and training officers of the program realized that they were offering a feasible and economical approach to reduction of criminal opportunity. Through a door-to-door campaign, the volunteers (1) discussed household needs, such as locks, (2) marked personal belongings with engraving pencils, (3) developed inventories of property, (4) placed stickers on windows which read "Inventory Guarded Home."[32] For further information contact:

Cottage Grove Police Department
Crime Prevention Unit
400 Main Street
Cottage Grove, Oregon 97424

Lock Program—South Bend, Indiana

In South Bend, Indiana, the Bureau of Police Crime Prevention Unit surveyed evaluated applicants for a federally funded lock program for the aged using the following qualifications for recipients: (1) over sixty years of age, (2) own their own home, (3) the home must not be a multifamily dwelling, and (4) income must be less than $5,000 with limited savings. Those who qualified were then asked to sign a statement approving the installation of the lock on their home. The crime prevention unit then sent letters to local locksmiths for competitive bids.

The chosen locksmith then installed one-inch double-cylinder deadbolt locks in the homes. Once installed, a sample questionnaire was sent to the recipients asking their reaction to the program. Overall, the response was positive. Currently, of all the homes which had a lock installed, none have had an incident of burglary or even an attempt reported. The South Bend Bureau of Police feels this program has been a successful deterrent to residential burglary. For further information contact:

South Bend Police Department
701 West Sample Street
South Bend, Indiana

Senior Citizens Robbery Unit—Bronx, New York

Since October 1974, the Bronx Senior Citizens Robbery Unit in New York, comprised of eighteen officers, investigated all robberies occurring inside a building when the victim is sixty years and over. Of the eighteen officers mentioned, nine are investigators with the following responsibilities: (1) identifying and lifting forensic evidence, (2) identifying crime patterns, (3) disseminating information on crime-prone locations, and (4) offering crime prevention seminars. Listed below are examples of just some of the assistance given the elderly complainants by the BSCRU.

(1) Transportation to and from court if the aged person's presence is required.

(2) Visit hospitalized victims to see if needs are being met.

(3) Notify other social agencies if they feel there is a need.

(4) Advise members of complainant's family if the victims are unable to cope with the trauma of the situation.

(5) Assist victims with the crime compensation board.

(6) Maintain a portable suspect file which is brought to the complainant's home, thus causing little hardship and a minimum amount of inconvenience to the victims.

(7) Crime prevention lectures and seminars to organizations which request them.

For further information contact:

Senior Citizens Robbery Unit
450 Cross Bronx Expressway
Bronx, New York 10457

Operation Identification—St. Paul, Minnesota

Crawford noted in 1974 that over 150 police and sheriff departments in Minnesota are involved in Operation Identification. This program is successful because marked property is dangerous. Criminals realize that marked property can be traced rapidly and easily. In addition, Crawford states that "according to the St. Paul Police Department, since March 1972, there have been 9,200 homes, businesses, schools, and churches enrolled in this program in that city. Out of these 9,200 enrollees, only forty-one have been the victims of burglary. During the same period of time, there was a total of 12,000 burglaries in St. Paul."[33]

Security for the Elderly—St. Petersburg, Florida

The St. Petersburg Florida Office of Crime Prevention, funded by LEAA, state, and local contributions, concluded a home security program for the elderly in March, 1978.

The project provided some 600 homes with needed security devices—free of charge. For an elderly person to have been eligible, he had to have four qualifications: (1) own his home, (2) be at least sixty-two years of age, (3) have an income of $5,600 or less, and (4) have been victimized by a burglar since January 1974. Once an application was approved, a home security inspection was done of the premises. Needed security devices were installed, for example, deadbolt locks, window and sliding glass door locks, door viewers, metal mesh screens, etc. The objective of this program was to provide house security to an elderly population which otherwise would have been unable to afford it.[34] Although they no longer provide free security services, they are still actively involved in surveying the security needs of the elderly. For further information contact:

Office of Crime Prevention
Security for the Elderly
1510 First Avenue, North
St. Petersburg, Florida 33705

Home security is important for the elderly. Statistics in Tables 3-2, 3-3 reveal why all people should involve themselves in crime prevention in order to protect their property and should insist that local law enforcement agencies provide necessary inspection of their homes. The elderly, being less able to protect themselves, should be even more involved than other age groups.

Table 3-2 Percentages of Burglaries by Point of Entry (State of California)

Point of Entry	Residential	Industrial	Other Facilities*
Door	59.6	57.7	50.9
Window	36.6	30.0	40.9
Not specified/unknown	3.1	2.7	4.2
Roof (existing opening)	0.2	4.2	1.6
Roof (makes opening)	0.0	0.4	0.0
Wall (existing opening)	0.1	0.6	0.0
Wall (makes opening)	0.1	3.0	0.0
Floor	0.1	0.1	0.0
Other	0.2	1.3	2.4
TOTAL BURGLARIES	5,506	1,876	381

*Other facilities include schools, churches, and public facilities.

Source: Crime Prevention Training Manual, Senior Home Security, Inc., 1200 South Grand Avenue, St. Louis, Missouri, 63104, p. C-1.

Table 3–3 Percentages of Burglaries by Point of Entry (Dallas, Texas)

Daytime Residential Burglaries		Nighttime Residential Burglaries	
Front door	40.9 percent	Front door	43.5 percent
Rear door	20.3 percent	Rear door	19.1 percent
Side door	2.8 percent	Side door	4.3 percent
Front window	5.6 percent	Front window	8.6 percent
Rear window	15.0 percent	Rear window	10.0 percent
Side window	14.8 percent	Side window	14.4 percent
Roof/floor	.3 percent	Roof/floor	0.0 percent
DOORS—TOTAL	64.0 percent	DOORS—TOTAL	67.0 percent
WINDOWS—TOTAL	36.0 percent	WINDOWS—TOTAL	33.0 percent

DAY/NIGHT TOTALS:
Doors—64.8 percent
Windows—35.2 percent

Source: Crime Prevention Training Manual, Senior Home Security, Inc., 1200 South Grand Avenue, St. Louis, Missouri, 63104, p. C-2.

Blockwatchers—Jamaica, New York

The Senior Citizens Advisory Committee of Jamaica, New York, encouraged its elderly residents to participate in the Blockwatchers program, as well as in Operation Identification. The Blockwatchers are elderly volunteers who are on the lookout for suspicious occurrences or actual crimes in their neighborhood. All volunteers attend a one-day seminar for training in (1) what to look for and (2) how to describe alleged criminals and events accurately. The volunteers remain anonymous, only giving their Blockwatcher number when reporting to the police. For further information contact:

New York City Police Department
Deputy Commissioner
Public Information
1 Police Plaza
New York, New York 10030

CRIME PREVENTION AGAINST CONFIDENCE GAMES

Confidence games, swindles, and consumer fraud all have one fact in common—rarely, if ever, is physical force used by a criminal to victimize the elderly. All that is usually needed to rob an elderly person of money, valuables, or even their life savings, is a glib tongue and trusting eyes—in short, an experienced and effective liar. Again, an examination of programs will give insight on how to prevent losses to nonviolent criminals.

California Attorney General's Crime Prevention Unit

The Door-to-Door Salesman

Almost everyone has been approached by the door-to-door salesman at some point in his life. Similar in technique, the door-to-door charity worker offers a sentimental sigh or touches one's heart in quest of a donation. Although it is difficult to doubt the work of someone asking for a donation for cancer research or muscular dystrophy, it is wise and appropriate to donate with the following in mind:

(1) Ask for identification and a phone number to call. If they want the donation, they'll return.

(2) Do not make a commitment over the phone. Ask them to mail information before making a decision.

(3) Be aware of a charitable organization's principles and check on its legitimacy.

(4) Realize that legitimate charities have no need for high pressure tactics.

(5) Never donate cash. Write a check to the organization.

(6) If a solicitor cannot wait for a donation and continually presses for an immediate contribution, that solicitor is probably a phony.

(7) Get proof that the donation is tax deductible.

(8) After donating, check with the organization to make sure they have received it.[35]

Investment Schemes

The elderly are eager to invest. One of the major reasons for this is their status of "fixed income" citizens. Many investment schemes "seem" to be the answer to their financial dilemma. The elderly should pay particular attention to any scheme or investment which offers them a quick way to make money. Generally, investments always involve some degree of risk, but particular attention should be given to the following guidelines for investing:

(1) Know the investment promoter. A legitimate investment promoter can be verified by contacting a state Corporation Commission regarding the promoter's license or regulation.

(2) Learn all about the investment. If possible, obtain a list of other investees and personally contact them or a reputable brokerage firm for information.

(3) Review the investment with a third party, preferably an attorney.

(4) If the investment yields an immediate loss, report the experience to a regulatory or enforcement agency at once.[36]

Medical Quackery

Elderly persons are victims of medical quackery in seven out of ten cases involving medical fraud. The following are ways to identify the medical quack:

(1) Suspect any person who "guarantees" to cure a disease.
(2) Suspect any person who has a "secret formula" or "special treatment" known only to him.
(3) Suspect any medical advice via direct mailing.

> Because of the convenience, many elderly persons transact business and handle their personal affairs by mail . . . in fiscal year 1975, 34,900 complaints were handled by the U.S. Post Office under an unsatisfactory mail-order program, with 27,000 or 78 percent resolved to the satisfaction of the consumers. In fiscal year 1976, 32,845 or 90 percent of the 36,315 complaints which received attention under the Consumer Protection Program were resolved.[37]

(4) Suspect any person who endorses or markets some food fadism and false nutritional therapy.

For further information concerning guidelines to confidence games prevention contact:

State of California
Office of Attorney General
Crime Prevention Unit
3580 Wilshire Boulevard
Suite 938
Los Angeles, California 90010

Mail Fraud

The U.S. Post Office experience has been that senior citizens are particularly susceptible to certain schemes. The following statistics and schemes to which all age groups fall victim are disclosed by the Post Office.

The Business Scheme: Business opportunities which offer high profits and guarantee success induce many elderly people. Whether the investment is in worthless distributorships, franchises, or vending machine operations, the objective remains the same—to entice the victim to believe this "opportunity" is a way of expanding his meager fixed income.

The Home Improvement/Land Fraud: Elderly persons wanting to purchase retirement homes or property are easily victimized by the pleasant and polite salesman whose "property" may be of poor quality or nonexistent. Concerning home-improvement frauds, the elderly are an easy target primarily because of their physical limitations, which prevent them from accomplishing home repairs themselves. Such frauds as these resulted in an estimated public loss from 1973 to 1975 in excess of $25 million.

Table 3-4   Mail Fraud Investigation

	Fiscal Year 1975	Fiscal Year 1976
Customer complaints	127,044	135,717
Investigations completed	6,332	5,793
Arrests	1,618	1,674
Convictions	1,260	1,458
Questionable promotions	4,133	2,761
Discontinued	—	—
Current investigation	—	3,771

Source: C. Neil Benson, Chief Inspector, U.S. Post Office, Washington, D.C., 20260, Personal communication 1/26/77.

The Medical Fraud: Due to the rising cost of medical attention and, possibly, insufficient insurance coverage, the elderly are often victimized by promoters of "cure-alls" for whichever geriatric problem they possess.[38]

The medicine man who conned the western towns of the 1800s with his famous "elixir" is not dead. The contemporary con artist can be of either sex. The female usually plays the beautiful, sympathetic, and helpful role. The role is still defined as a thief—a thief with female charm.

To be discussed now is the crux of the elderly's concern—the Bank Examiner, the Home Repairman, and the Pocketbook Drop. Though there are many confidence games, these pose the most serious potential financial loss to the elderly. The names of these con games may be different in various parts of the country, but the games themselves are all variations on a theme —swindle the elderly. Again, the purpose behind explaining these con games is to educate the elderly, as well as ourselves. Swindles occur repeatedly during the year in any given location. Why? Because no one has taken the time to explain the swindle. Educating the public to these con games is the most effective measure of preventing victimization.

The Bank Examiner

There are many ways in which the bank-examiner con game can be pulled off; however, the following highlights must be included in the scheme:

(1) A person telephones a home and identifies himself as an official from

the bank, police department, or federal law enforcement agency. This person uses an official title and arranges to meet with the victim at home.

(2) Acting very serious, the "examiner" will inform the victim that an employee at the bank where the victim does business is suspected of embezzling funds from customers' accounts.

(3) The phony examiner will often bring official receipts and documents used by the bank. He will ask to see the victim's savings account and quickly tell him that the records at the bank reflect a much smaller amount than what is posted in his deposit book.

(4) He will ask the victim's help in catching this employee by asking him to withdraw funds from his account and give them to him for examination. The victim is informed that the entire process should take only a few days to investigate, the money will be returned, and he will have done a great service for the community.

(5) When he gives his money away, he will never see it or the "examiner" again.

Common sense dictates that when a person is solicited by a bank or law enforcement agency, he should take a moment and investigate the investigation. If the investigation of a dishonest employee is legitimate, not only will the dishonest employee be working the next day, but the investigation will be ongoing. If potential bank-examiner victims would only take the time to call the law enforcement agency or the bank and ask to speak to an official, they might find the phony examiner making tracks.

Remember, neither banks nor law enforcement officers will ever ask a person to cooperate in an investigation by using large sums of money from his personal savings account. One particular preventive measure to schemes which call for large withdrawals from a bank account is having more than the bank teller approve the withdrawal. If bank tellers were trained in what to look for in these bunco operations, there would be fewer elderly victims. The phony examiners victimize the elderly in this scheme because elderly people are naturally more trustworthy and, unfortunately, easier marks.

The Home Repairman

Elderly people usually live in homes in which they have resided all their lives and which they have finally paid off. There is no appliance, tool or home which lasts forever without repair. Yet, has a car mechanic ever come to your house to fix your car, a small-engine mechanic ever shown up to inspect your washer and dryer? Of course not. When your property—whether it be your car, washer, dryer, or house—needs repair, you call someone for the necessary assistance. The first rule of thumb is to be wary of people who offer to inspect your house. The following highlights usually occur during the home repairman scheme:

(1) A person wearing work clothes and carrying a tool box or ladder appears at a victim's front door.

(2) He says that he is a repairman, engineer, or inspector of some kind. He asks to inspect the premises—e.g., chimney, furnace, electrical wiring, plumbing or septic tank—usually using the excuse that this is an old house and there might be some serious damage present which could cause a fire.

(3) After the inspection, he reports there is serious damage which needs to be taken care of immediately, and he'll have to notify the city building inspector.

(4) Now he makes the victim pay. He will offer to repair the damage—and at a substantial saving. He may quote a low price, asking for a cash deposit; or he may have the victim sign an order which is much more expensive than what was quoted, but, because of certain words in the order, legally bound to be paid.

Do you check references or identification of strangers, officials or salespersons?

Photographed by Tom Esmond

99

There are numerous rules to follow when a person is approached by a home repairman:

(1) *Caveat emptor*—let the buyer beware.

(2) Let the repairman explain the work he can do and its cost, but not inspect alone.

(3) Ask the person for credentials and the phone number of his company (which should be called immediately).

(4) Call the better business bureau.

(5) Check with neighbors.

(6) See if he or his company is listed in the phone book.

(7) Never pay for repair work until the job is satisfactorily completed.

If these simple preventive rules are followed, the buyer will never find dark oil on his driveway instead of tar, or painted plumbing instead of new pipes.

The Pocketbook Drop

The best way of explaining the pocketbook-drop scheme is by drawing on the statement of Mr. John Murphy, of the Pickpocket and Confidence Squad, New York City Police Department.

> The pocketbook drop is the best con game in the country, the one that makes the most money. It is primarily done by two con girls. As far as what they look like, it could be anything, black and white, two whites, two blacks. Black and white is a very popular team in New York because of the mixed neighborhoods. What the con girls do is usually go in a car and start driving up and down a neighborhood. They are looking for a woman alone. They prefer an older woman. They work during the early part of the day, banker's hours—they have to work during the time the banks are open. They are looking for a woman alone, not one with a child by the hand because she is in a hurry.
>
> When they spot her, one gets out of the car and approaches. She will start a conversation, the number one girl, as we call her. She will start a conversation with the possible victim, ask directions in the neighborhood: "Excuse me, I am looking for an address, 4922 Fifth Avenue." There will be no such address. They will start gabbing about this address and the young girl will probably say, "I was looking to get an apartment in their neighborhood and it looks like such a lovely neighborhood. I was looking to move in."
>
> They start gabbing for a few minutes and the victim finds this is a lovely young woman she is talking to. Very friendly. The victim might say, "I have been living in the neighborhood for thirty years." In the conversation the girl brings out the fact that she has to move because where she is living now there are too many bad memories because she lost her husband only a couple of months ago; he died in a car accident. A couple of years ago it was Vietnam.
>
> She would say, "Yes. I was hoping to move in today and I was going to get

an apartment in this block and I was going to put my money in the bank,'' and she pulls out a load of money and it is a fake roll of money, what we call a "mich." She shows that she has a lot of money and she puts it back in the purse and forgets about it. She keeps talking.

If the victim is friendly enough and the con girl figures she is a possible sucker she gives a sign to her partner who comes out of a car. The partner walks down, usually carrying a plain white envelope or brown envelope, and as she is going by and she sees the two women and says, "Can you help me. I was just on my lunch hour and I found this envelope and I wonder if there is a lost-and-found in the neighborhood.''

Her partner says, "I don't live here but this lady does.'' Now the conversation starts. Eventually the girl will open the envelope to see what is in it. She opens it up and it is loaded with money, $40,000 or $50,000. Again a "mich." When the con girl opens it she doesn't take it out of the envelope; she goes part way and closes it again.

Inside that envelope there is always a note and the note will say, "Dear Brother: I did it again, I hit the OTB (off-track betting) for $50,000. I have to take off because the Internal Revenue are on my back, send me the money... usually next month to Switzerland or Cuba. If it is a Jewish neighborhood it says, "Send me the money next month to Egypt." A cute little twist to it.

The one girl who found the money will almost always work for a lawyer. It is almost a guarantee. She says, "Let me ask my boss what to do.'' She "goes to the boss'' and she comes back and says, "This money will never be claimed by the people who lost it. So my boss says we have to agree to put the money in the bank three months because that is how long it takes him to legally make it ours. So we have to put it in for three months.'' So with $50,000, the lawyer gets $5,000 for his share and they get $15,000 each. So they have to agree to only one thing, put it in the bank and not spend it. Because he is a lawyer he wants a little guarantee that the money will not be spent, it will be saved for three months. How do you do that? You show them that you have money of your own in the bank to live on for three months. One girl says, "I don't have to show him because he pays me a salary every week so you two have to show.''

The little widow says, "I have my husband's insurance money, will that be enough?'' The one who works for the lawyer says, "I will take it up and show it to my lawyer,'' she comes back and says, "there is your $5,000 back and here is your $15,000.''

Now they look at the victim. That woman's heart is going. I do not think it is greed to want to share in $15,000 legitimate money. We are all out there trying to make money and this is a way to make it legitimately. The woman's heart is pounding, she is all excited and she doesn't have anybody around here. These girls keep talking with her. They will take her home and get her bank book. They have a cup of tea with her while she is getting dressed, so they can go to the bank.

She will have about $10,000. They tell her to take out about $7,000. Then give the banker a story; tell him you are going to buy property or real estate or jewelry. Sometimes the banks insist on giving a check so they take it to another bank and cash it. So she takes the money out and gives it to the woman who is to go up and give it to the lawyer.[39]

Educating the elderly about these confidence games is the first and most important step in preventing elderly victimization. Along with preventive education, Major Orlando P. Ragazzi, Chief Organized Crime Task Force, Connecticut State Police, offers the following:

(1) Of course, the best way to deal with crime is to prevent it from ever happening, in the case of the elderly, we in Connecticut would like to see a national intelligence clearinghouse, to alert the various states to the types of fraud prevalent nationwide. This is essential for us, to protect our elderly from the traveling "scams" that begin in one state and move on to others.

(2) A national intelligence clearinghouse, using modern computer technology, would also benefit prosecution. Most times, local prosecutors have no idea how many persons have been victimized by the accused. With information on past ripoffs, state prosecutors could pattern the sentence to fit the magnitude of the crime.

(3) And, while prevention and quick arrest are essential, there is another consideration that is even more important—especially to the victims. Convicted frauds must be made to repay their victims in full. The cost of crime should be borne by the convicted—not by the law-abiding members of society.[40]

All the aforementioned crime prevention programs and examples of confidence games are illustrations of what is going on throughout the United States. The cry for crime prevention programs has been heard since 1931 because, as has been stated:

> It is better for the individual, better for society, and cheaper for the taxpayer, to prevent crime rather than to wait until the crime had been committed, and then apprehend the criminal and correct him.[41]

It is only logical to address the issue of crime prevention. Crime prevention is the answer to the elderly's victimization rate and fear of crime. If an elderly person is victimized by personal attack, property loss, or financial ruin from a con artist, he should not sit back and be ashamed. There are several agencies which can be of assistance to the elderly victim. At the least, these agencies will be able to prevent other senior citizens from being victimized merely by the information they provide.

AGENCIES

(1) Local
  (a) Police Department
  (b) Newspapers, television, and radio stations
  (c) Better Business Bureau

(2) State
   (a) Attorney General's Office
   (b) Licensing Offices
   (c) Department of Insurance
   (d) Securities Division
(3) Federal
   (a) Office of Consumer Affairs
      Executive Office Building
      Seventeeth and Pennsylvania Avenue, N.W.
      Washington, D.C. 20201
   (b) Federal Trade Commission and Bureau of Consumer Protection
      Pennsylvania Avenue at Sixth Street, N.W.
      Washington, D.C. 20580
   (c) Postal Inspection Service
      475 L'Enfant Plaza West, S.W.
      Washington, D.C. 20260
   (d) U.S. Department of Justice
      Constitution Avenue and Tenth Street, N.W.
      Washington, D.C. 20530

If the above agencies are unable to provide assistance, they will eventually put a person in touch with an agency that can help.

> Helping citizens to resist crime is not another community relations program. It is, indeed, a distinct law enforcement function. Educating and alerting people to how they can reduce their vulnerability to the crimes about them is a continuing responsibility of law enforcement, and it is as necessary as a patrol force...crime resistance is resistance not only to the reality of crime but to the fear of crime that has narrowed the lives of so many people [especially the aged].[42]

SUMMARY

Crime prevention for the elderly is on the rise in America. Various components of the criminal justice system, especially local law enforcement agencies, are implementing programs specifically designed to eliminate the elderly's fear of crime and ensure that the elderly are sufficiently learned in prevention techniques, thus avoiding the traumatic experience of victimization.

In gathering data through victimization studies, the LEAA estimated twenty million people over the age of sixty-five in the United States. Although these twenty million elderly only represent 8 percent of all the victims of crimes surveyed by the LEAA studies, the problems the elderly face with victimization haunt them more than any other age group, e.g., hospitalization, financial ruin, emotional stress, and even psychological collapse. LEAA holds the key to successful crime prevention programs.

> An important step in devising more effective crime prevention and peace-of-mind programs for older people is the development of more meaningful victimization data. As part of our continuing National Crime Panel, LEAA will conduct victimization surveys to monitor the risk of victimization associated with the elderly and to firmly establish the relationship between age, fear of crime, and avoidance behavior.[43]

As long as we realize that crime prevention is everyone's concern, we are headed in the right direction. Every known source, organization, and criminal justice agency must be employed in the prevention of elderly victimization. We have heard of the expression, "Two heads are better than one"; in this case, helping hands is the solution. Remember, the elderly themselves must be involved in the process of crime prevention if they are to benefit. As Goldsmith's notion of segmental community crime prevention states, "Potential victims are specifically concerned with preventing crimes against its own members and is a reason for the elderly to unite."[44]

> In solidarity lies power. Without a sense of group consciousness among older adults, a senior power movement can neither be strong nor lasting. Older adults must first recognize that their problems are not individual concerns but group problems, shared by millions of others like themselves.[45]

The two most important benefits to be gained from the concept of segmental crime prevention are that (1) participants have a greater state and commitment to the program, and (2) more emphasis is placed on the specific crimes committed against the group,[46] such as hearing-aid fraud—a crime which is not of particular concern to the general population.

What has been learned from this chapter? At the very least, it should be realized that there is an effective, though not universally known, technique to prevent victimization. The years slip by quickly and what is learned and practiced during youth will remain as habit when the status known as elderly is reached. A person is never too old to learn. There is no better time than the present for both young and old to actively participate in crime prevention. Diagram 3-3, page 105 is provided here for your convenience and in the hope that it inspires you to begin preventing crime immediately.

QUESTIONS

1. How does emphasizing the positive aspects of crime prevention minimize the fear generated by crime?
2. Why should special crime prevention programs be established for the elderly?

Diagram 3—3

OPERATION IDENTIFICATION RECORD

Valuable property should be marked with an electric engraver or any sharp etching tool with your Florida Drivers License number (FL DL _____). If you are not a driver, you can obtain an I.D. card and number from any Division of Drivers Licenses Issuing Station. Avoid marking on removable parts such as lids, doors, plates, etc.

Items which cannot be marked, antiques, china, coins, etc., should be photographed in color with the owner's identification. A complete description of the article should be written on the back of the photograph.

SUGGESTED ITEMS FOR MARKING: Bicycles, T.V.'s, stereos, tape recorders, cameras, appliances, sporting goods, guns, typewriters, sewing machines, clocks and watches, power tools, lawnmowers, outboard motors, golf clubs, etc. Credit card numbers should also be recorded.

Property marked with your Drivers License Number FL DL _____

ARTICLE	MANUFACTURER AND MODEL	SERIAL NUMBER	LOCATION MARKED

Keep this list in a secure place. DO NOT SEND A COPY OF THIS LIST TO THE POLICE.

HELP
STOP CRIME

OFFICE OF THE ATTORNEY GENERAL
Governor's Council on Criminal Justice

3. Why have studies concerning elderly victims surfaced in the late 1970s?

4. Why is there conflicting data over elderly victimization?

5. Explain crime prevention through environmental design.

6. Can positive results be tabulated from crime prevention programs?

7. Is crime prevention costly?

8. Is crime prevention effective?

9. Is the "Fourth Dimension"—a crime prevention component of the criminal justice system—a realistic idea?

10. What are the general ideas behind the con games which victimize the elderly?

SUGGESTED READINGS

Dennis J. Dingemans and Robert H. Schinzel, "Defensible Space Design of Housing for Crime Prevention," *The Police Chief,* November 1977.

Oscar Newman, *Defensible Space: Crime Prevention Through Urban Design,* (New York, New York: MacMillan, 1972).

Your Retirement Anti-Crime Guide, pamphlet, American Association of Retired Persons and National Retired Teachers Association, Washington, D.C., 1973.

NOTES

1. Evelle J. Younger, "The California Experience: Prevention of Criminal Victimization of the Elderly," *The Police Chief,* February 1976, p. 13.

2. Younger, op cit., pp. 13–16.

3. *Criminal Victimization in the U.S. (1975),* U.S. Department of Justice, Law Enforcement Assistance Administration, National Crime Panel Survey Report, May 1975, Vol. 1.

4. *Myth and Reality of Aging in America,* a study prepared by Louis Harris and Associates, Inc., for The National Council on the Aging, Inc., Washington, D.C. © 1975, p. 133.

5. Lee P. Brown and Marlene A. Y. Rifai, "Crime Prevention for Older Americans: Multnomah County's Victimization Study," *The Police Chief,* February 1976, p. 20.

6. M. Ernst, L. F. Jodry, and H. J. Friedsam, *Reporting and Nonreporting of Crime by Older Americans,* Center for Studies in Aging, North Texas State University, Denton, Texas, 1976, pp. 1–3.

7. Philip J. Gross, "Law Enforcement and the Senior Citizen," *The Police Chief,* February 1976, p. 10.

8. *30 Ways You Can Prevent Crime.* Greenfield, Massachusetts: Channing L. Bete Co., Inc., 1972, p. 3.

9. J. Edgar Hoover, "The War Against Crime is Your War," *The Reader's Digest,* Vol. 93, November 1968, pp. 17–18.

10. Dale T. Beerbower and L. William Sheppard, "Fourth Dimension of the Criminal Justice System," *F.B.I. Law Enforcement Bulletin,* Vol. 45, No. 3, March 1976, p. 24.

11. Ibid.

12. Robert A. Carlston, et al, "Crime Prevention through Environmental Design Program: May 1974–June 1976," National Institute of Law Enforcement and Criminal Justice, LEAA, U.S. Department of Justice, in cooperation with, Westinghouse National Issues Center, Westinghouse Electric Corporation, Arlington, Virginia, 1977, pp. 7–8.

13. Carlson et al, op cit, p. 3.

14. Ibid, p. 8.

15. Ibid.

16. D. Dingemans, S. Garfield and T. Olsen, *Defensible Space in Suburban Townhouse Design: A Case Study of Six California Developments,* Research Report No. 33, Institute of Government Affairs, Davis, California, 1976.

17. C. Ray Jeffery, *Crime Prevention Through Environmental Design* (Beverly Hills/London: Sage Publications, © 1971), p. 224.

18. Daryl F. Gates, "Honeycomb Projects: An Architectural Crime Problem," *The Police Chief,* November 1977, p. 42.

19. "Sources of Information About and Descriptions of Crime Prevention Programs for the Elderly," Administration on Aging and Department of Health, Education and Welfare, No. (OHDS) 77-20223, pp. 1–2.

20. Ron L. Willis and Myra Miller, "Senior Citizen Crime Prevention Programs," *The Police Chief,* February 1976, p. 1.

21. Younger, op cit., p. 14.

22. Ibid.

23. Evelle J. Younger, *Consumer Information Protection Program for Seniors: Overview,* State of California, Attorney General's Office, August 1976, p. 3.

24. Evelle J. Younger, *Consumer Information Protection Program for Seniors,* Vol. 5, No. 1, January 1977, p. 6.

25. Office of Attorney General, State of California, "On Guard—A Guide for the Consumer," Information Pamphlet No. 3.

26. Catherine V. Nelson, participant, "Seminar in Crime Prevention for the Elderly," sponsors, Center for Gerontology, Florida State University and Senior Society Planning Council, Tallahassee, Florida, June 21–July 5, 1977.

27. Evelle J. Younger, *Consumer Information Protection Program for Seniors,* Vol. 4, No. 4, October 1976, pp. 9–10.

28. Wayne M. Bradley, "Cass Corridor Safety for Seniors Project," *The Police Chief,* February 1976, p. 24.

29. Ibid.

30. Ottie Adkins, "Crime Prevention: Huntington's Answer," *The Police Chief,* December 1977, p. 55.

31. *Crime Prevention and Senior Citizens,* Criminal Justice Planning Report, Office of the Mayor, Jacksonville, Florida, 1977, p. 2.

32. Willis and Miller, op cit., p. 2.

33. James H. Crawford, "Number that Thieves Avoid," *The Police Chief,* June 1974, p. 26.

34. "Security For the Elderly: Synopsis, "Office of Crime Prevention, St. Petersburg, Florida, 1977, p. 1.

35. Younger, op cit., p. 13.

36. Younger, op cit., p. 14.

37. C. Neil Benson, Chief Investigator, U.S. Post Office, Washington, D.C., personal communication, January 16, 1977.

38. Ibid.

39. "Confidence Games Against the Elderly," Hearing before the Subcommittee on Federal, State and Community Services of the Select Committee on Aging, House of Representatives, Ninety-fourth Congress, Second Session, held in New York, New York, January 13, 1976, U.S. Government Printing Office, Washington, D.C., 1976, pp. 15–16.

40. Ibid, p. 27.

41. Gerald Cress, "A Sheriff Tries Crime Prevention," *The Journal of Criminal Law, Criminology and Police Science,* Vol. 22, 1931–32, p. 425.

42. Clarence M. Kelley, *Crime Resistance,* FBI, 1975, p. v. and 32.

43. *Crime Against the Elderly: LEAA's Elderly Crime Victimization Programs,* National Institute of Law Enforcement and Criminal Justice, LEAA, U.S. Department of Justice, U.S. Government Printing Office, Washington, D.C., No. 1977-241-090/64, p. 3

44. Jack Goldsmith, "Police and the Older Victims: Keys to a Changing Perspective," *The Police Chief,* February 1976, p. 21.

45. Rochelle Jones, *The Other Generation: The New Power of Older People,* (Englewood Cliffs, New Jersey: Prentice-Hall, Inc., © 1977), p. 234.

46. Goldsmith, op cit., p. 23.

Chapter **4**

The Aged as Volunteers

Female members of the Sun City Posse preparing to load weapons at pistol range.

Courtesy of Maricopa County Sheriff's Office

For quite some time, the criminal justice system has needed something to strengthen it besides dollars. The nation's elderly are available and waiting to be counted. They possess the three keys to American democracy de Tocqueville once wrote of: "involvement, civic pride, and volunteerism."[1] It is up to the criminal justice system to use these keys to unlock a productivity which may reshape the criminal justice system's sad state of affairs. The police have always called for more local support and citizen participation. Now that law enforcement has the ability to cash in on its long time request, will they pass up the opportunity to accept elderly volunteers simply because the volunteers are old and so, they assume, would be "in the way"?

Retirement is often a "touchy" issue among the nation's elderly. They face retirement with mixed feelings of relief and loneliness. Although they no longer must deal with the pressures of the workaday world, and by all means deserve a rest from the hectic surroundings of an urbanized industrial pace, the elderly are quick to recognize the boredom which dominates the "golden years." The distaste which surrounds retirement is a crime. There is absolutely no justifiable reason why people who reach the age of sixty-five to seventy must be put out to pasture. True, "it is an empiric and universal truth that after a certain number of years the human organism undergoes a decline...the process is inescapable."[2] However, it is not mandatory that at the age of sixty-five to seventy people begin to die. It is simply ridiculous to think so. Although businesses, corporations, and even government may equate sixty-five to seventy with the loss of efficiency or productivity, this should not be a generalization.

This chapter deals with the elderly's future productivity. Volunteerism has long been a component of the American heritage. All too often the volunteers have been young, strong, motivated, and ambitious individuals. In the past the aged volunteer has been overlooked as an asset to many organizations, including the criminal justice system. The time is ripe. The elderly are ready to become volunteers in all facets of the criminal justice system, especially law enforcement. The elderly are motivated, ambitious, and desirous. They feel a strong need to get involved in something more than a hobby or leisure activity. Hopefully, after completing this chapter, the reader will understand just how useful the elderly can be.

THE ELDERLY AS A WORKING POPULATION

In years past, age was never really considered a hindrance to man's efficiency or productivity. People worked until they died. Life was simple, yet filled with hardships—the toughest hardship being survival. The growth of industrialism and modern technology has reduced the hardships of life. Society has eliminated man's need to work. Society has devoured life's stimulus (survival) and the resulting response (work) has virtually disappeared. This is the situation which society has bred for the aged.

As Table 4-1 reflects, the male labor force of all the countries cited is mostly comprised of men between the ages of 25 to 55 (over 90 percent of the labor force). However, between the ages of fifty-five and sixty-five, the decline of males in the labor force is nearly cut in half, except for Japan. For American men over the age of sixty-five, participation in the labor force has been drastically cut from 39 percent in 1950 to 24.5 percent in 1970. One bright note is that American women over sixty-five have increased their participation in the labor force from 7.3 percent in 1950 to 10.3 percent in 1970. Though the increase in American female participation has increased and American male participation has decreased in the labor force in the twenty-year period from 1950 to 1970, what should be immediately questioned is whether or not the aged population (males and females over sixty-five years of age) has increased in this same time period.

In general, it can be assumed that the aged labor force has decreased and the aged population has increased. With no change in existing labor condi-

Table 4-1 Percentage of Adults Actively Involved in the Labor Force Over a 20-Year Period in Six Countries[3]

Age	USA 1950	USA 1970	Japan 1950	Japan 1970	France 1946	France 1968	West Germany 1950	West Germany 1970	Sweden 1950	Sweden 1970	UK 1951	UK 1971
Men												
20–24	81.9	79.2	90.5	83.5	91.2	71.3	93.4	86.1	90.0	62.0	95.3	90.5
25–39	92.9	94.3	96.3	98.6	96.7	96.3	96.0	94.6	97.5	90.5	98.1	98.0
40–54	92.7	93.1	97.0	97.9	95.5	94.4	95.7		96.8		98.3	97.9
55–59	86.7	87.0	92.4	94.2	85.4	82.4	87.4	87.8	92.5	88.4	95.4	95.2
60–64	79.4	73.3	65.2	85.8	76.3	65.7	73.0	35.6	79.7	75.7	87.8	86.7
65 +	39.0	24.5		54.5	51.6	19.1	26.8		40.1	15.2	34.8	21.1
TOTAL	78.9	74.7	83.4	84.3	85.5	73.2	63.2	58.9	65.2	54.7	87.9	81.6
Women												
20–24	43.2	55.4	64.0	70.9	59.9	62.4	70.4	68.8	57.3	53.3	65.5	60.1
25–39	32.5	46.0	49.1	49.6	48.9	44.8	42.2		30.2		37.1	47.8
40–54	33.9	52.2	53.2	63.1	51.0	44.6	35.1	47.7	30.0	51.0	34.2	60.5
55–59	25.9	47.6	48.2	53.8	46.1	42.3	29.4	35.5	26.3	41.4	27.7	51.0
60–64	20.5	36.2		43.3	40.2	32.3	21.2		18.9	25.7	14.4	27.9
65 +	7.3	10.3	27.2	19.7	22.0	8.0	9.7	10.1	8.6	3.2	6.1	8.0
TOTAL	29.0	40.5	48.6	50.9	46.2	36.1	31.4	29.9	23.2	29.9	34.5	42.8

Sources: *U.N Demographic Yearbook,* 1956 (New York: United Nations, 1956), pp. 319–38; *Yearbook of Labour Statistics,* 1974 (Geneva: International Labour Office, 1974), pp. 28–40. Jon Hendricks and C. Davis Hendricks, *Aging in Mass Society:* Myths and Realities, © 1977 by Winthrop Publishers, Inc. Reprinted by permission.

tions, society will soon be faced with an enormous aged population—a population which the labor force will have to support. Just what has caused this situation? Unfortunately, mandatory retirement is the chief culprit in the reduction of the labor force and will continue to reduce its elderly ranks. If mandatory retirement remains, a viable solution to using the elderly's talents can be found in volunteerism, especially in the criminal justice system.

Retirement

Retirement should not be a dirty word, although to many elderly the idea of retirement is repulsive. Withdrawal from the labor force can be a relatively easy adjustment or a difficult readjustment. There are many elderly who view retirement as a time when they will be able to relax and enjoy life in such activities as tennis, racquetball, swimming, traveling, and recreation in general. Unfortunately, few elderly people will fall into this category, either because of poor retirement planning in young adulthood or the inescapable fact that they belong to a group comprised of a vast number of Americans —the working class. The working class, which does not plan for the future, faces retirement with nothing to do and no money to do it with. When faced with this predicament, the leisure time associated with retirement becomes boring, frustrating, and worthless. Soon, these elderly will grow tired of themselves, their surroundings, and life. In other words, they begin to die.

Retirement should not be the body's cue to start dying. There are too many resources within the body which can be put to use. All the years of experience that a carpenter, computer specialist, radio technician, school teacher, social worker, girl scout leader, policeman, judge, correctional officer, and statistician (to name a few) has is waiting to be tapped. Care must be used not to take advantage of the elderly volunteer. Volunteerism can provide a mutual understanding between the volunteer and the person or agency enjoying the volunteered services. Volunteerism is a two-way street, with the volunteer often receiving more satisfaction than the person or agency helped. Why has the volunteer market increased? Because mandatory retirement has become a practical response from public and private sectors of the economical world—a practical response which says old workers are no longer an asset, but a debit. How wrong they are!

Mandatory Retirement

Mandatory retirement is easily defined: when a person reaches a certain age, regardless of circumstances or personal situations, he is forced to retire. This certain age has become "seventy." It is interesting to note that although sixty-five is the eligible age for social security and pension programs, "Wilbur Cohen, a member of the policy-making team who participated in the Social Security program, has written that the age of sixty-five was not based on any specific gerontological, scientific or social reasoned argument."[4] Though sixty-five or seventy is not a magical number, a number which denotes uselessness, it has become a number which denotes mandatory retirement; and although some states and organizations have disavowed the meaning of age sixty-five, there are many that lag behind. Dr. Douglas G. Montgomery of the Institute of Aging, Portland State University, Portland, Oregon, offers the following as justifications to end mandatory retirement, which is "dehumanizing to all older Americans."[5]

(1)   Age is a poor indicator of ability to perform. The American Medical Association opposes mandatory retirement because of age.

(2)   Older workers perform as well as younger workers in most areas. The elderly use experience and judgment, resulting in fewer accidents.

(3)   Eliminating mandatory retirement will eliminate financial hardships for older persons. The elderly will not be forced to "survive" on a fixed income.

(4)   Eliminating mandatory retirement will stop adverse physical and psychological effects on individuals. The elderly will not be labeled as unproductive.

(5)   The costs of income maintenance programs, e.g., social security and pension plans, would be reduced.

(6)   Elimination of mandatory retirement will create incomes for the elderly as well as stimulate the economy. This will enable the elderly to achieve a higher quality of life.

(7)   Current public opinion will be supported. A 1974 Harris poll supports eliminating mandatory retirement.

(8)   Challenge the current trend of early retirement.

(9)   Restoring dignity to older citizens will be possible.

(10) Elimination of mandatory retirement will stimulate new thinking, e.g., how to use older persons as a resource.[6]

Due to the Pepper Bill, mandatory retirement has shifted from sixty-five to seventy years of age. This increase of five working years has helped, yet what is so magical about the year seventy? Why does there have to be a limit of employment based on age? Shouldn't mandatory retirement be enforced when a worker becomes less efficient? Competence, not age, is becoming the determining factor for hiring, retaining or promoting."[7]

MYTHS ABOUT THE ELDERLY

Just as mandatory retirement should be eliminated because of its inappropriateness for today's society, so should the myths which surround the aged. Because these myths have been around for a long time, some have come to believe them. Myths are a fallacy, and the sooner the myths which encompass old age are dispelled, the sooner the criminal justice system and society will reap the benefits.

Myths are just that—myths. Myths are not real. Their reality is achieved only by attaching meaning to them. For example, "Blondes have more fun," "Short people speak loudly to overcompensate for their height," "Policemen are superhumans," and "All college professors smoke pipes" are simply myths which have developed because society has allowed them to develop. Can it be said that brunettes are shy, tall people meek, policewomen inferior, or college professors nonsmokers? Of course not! The point is that myths are merely figments of imagination. Many have allowed myths to replace the truth. They have put so much faith in the existence of myths that ignorance has replaced their eyes. People only need look around to realize the elderly are not senile, mentally incompetent, physically disabled, absentminded, stubborn, nor lost in their memories. Though a small portion of the elderly population has acquired a few of these qualities, it is unfair to generalize these characteristics to the entire elderly population. After all, it has already been noted that fewer than 5 percent of the elderly are living in institutional settings; the majority are living in the real world. It's about time this fact is realized.

Those individuals, such as criminal justice personnel responsible for employing volunteers, in a position of power to do something about eliminating these myths, should answer this question:

> Have you considered locating and tapping these hidden assets within your own community? The results of such efforts could produce substantial positive returns for the police, older persons, and the overall community itself.[8]

Realizing that myths are difficult to erase or replace, and fearful that elderly volunteers may be a mistake for a particular criminal justice agency, isn't an effort at erasing these myths about the elderly the least that can be done? In case a true skeptic is reading this particular section, please refer to Table 4-2.

Table 4-2 Mean Trials to Learn a Paired-Associate List[9]

Anticipation (Response) Interval, Sec.	Inspection (Study) Interval, Sec.					
	2.2 Age (Years))		**4.4** Age (Years)		**6.6** Age (Years)	
	20–39	40–66	20–39	40–66	20–39	40–66
2.2	10.0	24.9	9.0	24.5	6.0	19.8
4.4	11.0	12.6	7.0	10.4	7.9	7.2
6.6	6.8	11.4	5.0	6.2	5.0	5.4

Data in this table from Monge and Hultsch (1971, p. 159, Table 2).

...the total time available per item (i.e., the sum of the anticipation and inspection intervals) is not differentially important to people of different ages. Only that portion of the total time allotted to the anticipation interval (response time) makes for age differences.[10]

From Monge and Hultsch's data (Table 4-2), it can be argued that the elderly's learning ability is quite near that of younger age groups. Although it would be premature to generalize this data to learning studies overall,[11] it should be noted that "there is a little disagreement regarding performance in later life, however, there is disagreement whether there is a decline with age in learning ability."[12] In other words, most researchers in the area of learning feel that with the onset of age, a person's performance dwindles; he can no longer run as fast as he did in high school, or outdance everyone on the floor. With age, the body slows down; however, this must not be taken as gospel or as the cause for other human functions to break down. There is disagreement among researchers over the decline of learning ability among the aged. Yet, must it be assumed that slower performance is equated with deadening of the brain? Of course not. An elderly person can undertake any position or task that a younger person can. It may take a little longer to accomplish the results, but that should not detract from the accomplishment.

The general finding is that elderly people need more time for responding than typically is provided; they are disadvantaged when this time is not available. When sufficient time for response is available, the performance of elderly people is only slightly inferior, or not inferior at all, to that of young people.[13]

If the evidence discussed above is not enough to convince the skeptic that myths about the edlerly are only myths, the following emotional questions should be posed: "What are you going to do when you reach sixty-five or seventy and become senile and more of a burden than you're worth to family, friends, and business associates?" You say you won't be like that? In all probability you won't, but how do you propose to convince others?

In order to completely dismantle such myths, the elderly must be given a chance to prove themselves. In addition, young people should begin planning for later life so they will be able to graduate into retirement (if such a thing still exists) knowing they are not being cast aside. The most rational and positive approach to eliminating myths about the elderly and preparing for later years is through volunteerism. Volunteering provides people, both young and old, with an opportunity to remain active and feel worthwhile every moment of every day.

VOLUNTEERING

If an elderly person has a specific or special interest, such as crime prevention, then he is likely to be highly motivated in the quest of such an interest.

> There is only one solution if old age is not to be an absurd parody of our former life, and that is to go on pursuing ends that give our existence a meaning —devotion to individuals, to groups or to causes, social, political, intellectual or creative work....One's life has value so long as one attributes value to the life of others, by means of love, friendship, indignation and compassion.[14]

Volunteering their services is the elderly's answer to retirement. Neither senile nor "ready for pasture," they have a need for their lives to remain fulfilling. Yet, why should they be volunteers? Why not instead sit back and reap the benefits of others' efforts in the areas of crime prevention? A well-known midwest organization, Aid to Victims of Crime, Inc., has responded by stating:

(1) Crime and victimization occur in areas where people are not organized and where there is little sense of community and community participation. The elderly must organize to make their neighborhoods safe and secure by working together on common problems and taking care of each other.[15]

Alice Van Landingham, AARP President, Washington, D.C., lectures to a group of children at Safety Town, which is a safety preventive program for children, sponsored by the Huntington Police Department, Huntington, W. Virginia, 1976.

(2) The need for volunteers comes from a need for citizens to take control of their lives and face some of the major problems of an urban area.

(3) Crime cannot be reduced and victims cannot be served unless there is a genuine positive response on behalf of the citizen. Neighborhood volunteers enable us to contact and serve many more victims of crime than we could if we used just staff.[16]

With expanding medical knowledge concerning disease and nutrition, longevity is offering more years of life than ever before. All too often the euphemisms applied to the aged have envisioned a positive attitude, as, for example, the "golden years." Just what is so "golden" about being discarded by society, playing checkers in the park, or living on a fixed income? It is time to put aside the seeming significance of these labels (golden, leisure, etc.) and accept the reality of the situation. A lack of diversified activity for the aged develops the impression that older people cannot do anything productive. How far from the truth this is! Retired people and all elderly would be willing to participate in volunteer activities "if their abilities were so utilized and visible to the rest of the community. This positive image of the aged might help break some negative stereotypes."[17]

One thing to caution against is adding misery to an already poorly managed criminal justice system. Elderly participation in the criminal justice system must be planned and organized. Nothing worthwhile is ever easy. The various components of the criminal justice system, whether they be law enforcement, courts, or corrections, cannot be expected to suddenly accept elderly volunteers. If this happened, the elderly volunteers would be totally useless to the agency and would reinforce the myth that the elderly are unproductive. Before the elderly volunteers join a criminal justice agency, the administration should carefully evaluate needs, finances, and potential problems. For example, if a police department jumped on the current bandwagon by employing elderly volunteers, and upon their arrival the elderly were not given any useful purpose or role within the agency, it would not take long before the policemen considered the elderly volunteers a nuisance. If the elderly are to be effective in their role as volunteers and the criminal justice agency is to benefit from such an arrangement, the administration should ask and truthfully answer the following questions:

(1) Do we need volunteers in our agency?
(2) Do we have a particular need for elderly volunteers?
(3) Would elderly volunteers be a hindrance to everyday functions?
(4) Would present employees consider elderly volunteers a nuisance?
(5) What job assignments would the elderly volunteers fill?
(6) Would we be assigning elderly volunteers to menial tasks?
(7) Would present employees consider elderly volunteers a threat to their security?

(8)   How many elderly volunteers could we accept?

(9)   What would be the initial cost of training elderly volunteers?

(10) What would be the in-service cost of training elderly volunteers?

(11) Are federal funds or grants available to local or state agencies which employ elderly volunteers?

(12) Is federal money the only reason to employ elderly volunteers?

(13) Is there a possibility of reimbursing elderly volunteers for transportation costs to and from the agency?

(14) What assurance do we have that the elderly will remain after training? What happens if, after initial training, they decide working with our agency is not for them?

(15) Would we need additional insurance coverage for elderly volunteers?

(16) How much authority do we grant elderly volunteers?

(17) Under whose direction should the elderly volunteers come?

(18) Are we responsible for the elderly volunteers' actions during the performance of their role?

(19) How will the general public feel about our use of elderly volunteers?

(20) Are we helping ourselves as well as the elderly by employing them as volunteers?

The above questions only skim the surface. A well-planned and organized criminal justice agency will ensure the proper utilization of elderly volunteers through advance discussion of the situation. Elderly volunteers in the criminal justice system cannot appear out of the clear blue sky; there must be much thought over the need, finances, and potential problems which may occur. Not only are the elderly willing to participate if their abilities are properly matched with agency needs, but the elderly need this active involvement to aid them in their fight against the retirement process and the myths which ensue.

> There is near unanimity among gerontologists that voluntary organizations form an important mechanism for maintaining communal and social integration of older people.... Rosow (1974) points out that expressive memberships may help cushion the loss of instrumental roles.... Erikson's developmental model ...implies that older people might find deep satisfaction by participating in meaningful voluntary pursuits.... There is ample opportunity for older people to be active if such is their desire.[18]

Although there may be ample opportunity for the elderly to volunteer in private and federal organizations, such as Retired Senior Volunteers Program (RSVP), Service Corps of Retired Executives (SCORE), Foster Grandparents, and other VISTA Services, the reality of volunteering their services in a criminal justice agency, especially law enforcement, is poor. In Table 4-3 note that the number of current volunteer programs in operation is extremely low and the number of volunteer programs planned or proposed is even lower. Most volunteers are nonelderly, yet the potential is there for law enforcement agencies to benefit from elderly volunteers.

In Table 4-3 there may be some discrepancy of column totals due to inconsistency in form completion. Recall that for an IACP survey (Table 3-1, p. 68) 500 requests were mailed to various law enforcement agencies and only 180 or 36 percent were returned.

Table 4-3   Current Volunteer Programs in Law Enforcement Agencies[19]

Job Classification	Planned or Proposed	In Operation	Nonsenior Volunteer	Senior Volunteer	Potential for Senior Citizen Involvement
Internal administration:					
Personnel matters	0 (0%)	1 (1%)	4 (2%)	1 (1%)	18 (10%)
Budget preparation	0 (0%)	1 (1%)	3 (2%)	0 (0%)	21 (12%)
Budget control/accounting	0 (0%)	0 (0%)	2 (1%)	0 (0%)	13 (7%)
Data processing	0 (0%)	1 (1%)	3 (2%)	0 (0%)	22 (12%)
Planning and research	1 (1%)	2 (1%)	4 (2%)	1 (1%)	28 (16%)
Legal	2 (1%)	2 (1%)	7 (4%)	0 (0%)	26 (14%)
Training	1 (1%)	1 (1%)	4 (2%)	1 (1%)	36 (20%)
Clerical	3 (2%)	5 (3%)	11 (6%)	2 (1%)	68 (38%)
Other	0 (0%)	2 (1%)	5 (3%)	1 (1%)	6 (3%)
Internal operations:					
Dispatching	1 (1%)	5 (3%)	7 (4%)	0 (0%)	23 (13%)
Emergency operations	0 (0%)	16 (9%)	15 (8%)	4 (2%)	17 (9%)
Booking	1 (1%)	3 (2%)	8 (4%)	2 (1%)	10 (6%)
Arrestee counseling	0 (0%)	4 (2%)	6 (3%)	3 (2%)	22 (12%)
Crime victim counseling	4 (2%)	9 (5%)	10 (6%)	7 (4%)	55 (31%)
Equipment maintenance	1 (0%)	4 (2%)	6 (3%)	0 (0%)	38 (21%)
Criminalistics	0 (0%)	1 (1%)	2 (1%)	1 (1%)	13 (7%)
Property control	0 (0%)	1 (1%)	3 (2%)	2 (1%)	42 (23%)
Other	0 (0%)	12 (7%)	10 (6%)	2 (1%)	2 (1%)
External operations:					
Traffic control	1 (1%)	32 (18%)	30 (17%)	6 (3%)	22 (12%)
Bicycle registration	6 (3%)	13 (7%)	13 (7%)	5 (3%)	91 (51%)
Operation identification	9 (5%)	28 (16%)	24 (13%)	14 (8%)	107 (59%)
Anti-burglary programs	10 (6%)	29 (16%)	23 (13%)	15 (8%)	94 (52%)
Anti-fraud programs	6 (3%)	9 (5%)	9 (5%)	6 (3%)	87 (49%)
Self-defense programs	2 (1%)	10 (6%)	11 (6%)	5 (3%)	35 (19%)
Check-cashing programs	3 (2%)	7 (4%)	7 (4%)	3 (2%)	74 (41%)
Other	4 (2%)	25 (14%)	26 (14%)	14 (8%)	12 (7%)
Patrol					8 (4%)

Tournier has written that the elderly need a second career, not a hobby.[20] The criminal justice system is in such a state of malfunctioning that it could use the service of elderly volunteers who choose a criminal justice agency as their second career. A career which keeps the elderly motivated and feeling useful will also benefit the criminal justice system, if not in satisfaction, at least in additional employees to combat the never-ending flow of defendants into the system.

Before examining the various segments of the criminal justice system for which the elderly could volunteer, realize that, "for those who choose to retain active memberships in voluntary associations,"[21] there are certain rewards to be gained:

(1) Elderly are brought into close contact with others their age.

(2) Through interaction, friendships occur and a mutual exchange of information and opinion takes place.

(3) The elderly realize they are not alone in their problems.[22]

Voluntary association with a criminal justice agency may prove difficult. That is, it may be difficult to find an agency wishing to utilize elderly persons' services; but, once found, the contact will be educational for the elderly as well as the agency.

Aid to Victims of Crime, Inc., has categorized three types of volunteers (in the case of their organization, but the types can be generalized to other organizations in need of volunteers):

(1) The *broker* helps the victim define the problem and works with the victim to find the appropriate resource or alternative.

(2) The *advocate* pleads the cause of the victim to acquire services even though the volunteer may have to confront people, agencies, or institutions.

(3) The *counselor* aids the victim by helping him adjust to a new situation or problem.[23]

This private organization, which actively recruits volunteers, only requests commitment to the program and training. The purpose of training is to ensure quality services to people who have been devastated by violent crime. During the training sessions, special emphasis is placed on communication skills, feelings and the emotional impact of being victimized, information-gathering, information-handling, community resources, and agency guidelines.[24] There is a pressing need for volunteers, especially older volunteers, within all facets of the criminal justice system. Considering the aforementioned discussion of volunteerism, the following volunteer programs can be viewed as typical illustrations of successful volunteer projects for the elderly within the criminal justice system and as potential ideas for successful others.

What Elderly Volunteers Can Do

Law enforcement, courts, and corrections (both traditional and community-based), are in constant need of manpower. Not only are older volunteers a solution to this problem of efficiency that continually faces criminal justice

Mrs. Alta Mae Artrip acts as volunteer for the Huntington Police Department's Operation Lifeline Program.

administrators, but elderly people possess an enormous amount of untapped energy. This energy can be focused on aiding all agencies within the criminal justice responsibility, particularly those directed at crime prevention—"a highly desirable goal because, to the extent criminals are deterred, the tasks and problems not only of the police, but also of the courts and corrections are eased."[25]

Elderly volunteers can strengthen, not weaken, the criminal justice system. Personal safety has become an issue with which each person should be concerned. Safety has become increasingly important to the elderly; so much so that "since this [safety] is a direct responsibility of local government, older voters may in time be able to exert a good deal of effective pressure to secure their own safety."[26] The criminal justice system is in a position to do something about the situation of the elderly before pressure is applied. Criminal justice administrators and employees should accept the elderly volunteer as an equal of all volunteers.

> Never underestimate the power of a volunteer who is well placed and trained for the job. We should look at what volunteers are being asked to do, make it manageable, attractive and enjoyable. Educational training is a stimulus... and gives greater satisfaction for the individual volunteer.[27]

How can the elderly volunteer aid the dysfunctioning, overworked, and overburdened criminal justice system? The elderly volunteers can supply the additional labor needed to operate any organization within the system effectively. The following areas can use the elderly volunteer in their operation. Current examples or suggestions on how to utilize the elderly volunteer within each area will be discussed.

AREAS FOR ELDERLY VOLUNTEERS

(1) Criminal Justice Education or Training
(2) Law Enforcement
(3) Courts
(4) Corrections
(5) Community-Based Corrections
(6) Statistical Research
(7) Community Projects

Criminal Justice Education or Training

Many colleges and universities throughout the United States have begun programs in criminal justice or criminology. The topic of crime has come to mean so much to so many people that the crime problem or the increasing crime rate can no longer be ignored. Just as lawyers say, "Ignorance of the law is not a defense," so society has realized that ignoring crime will not make it disappear. University criminal justice programs are employing Ph.D.'s by the score, and community colleges are constantly searching for instructors with the appropriate academic credentials and "experience" in the criminal justice system. Just as criminal justice has become popular within the academic community, its popularity has spread to the entire community. Not all community residents have the opportunity to attend a university or community college due to prior responsibilities or commitments; thus, universities and community colleges have responded with continuing education programs, mostly available in the evenings or in seminar fashion.

Since most universities and community colleges are now turning to continuing education programs, and since criminal justice is a strong and popular component within these programs, it seems only logical to evaluate local elderly for positions within these programs. For example, most community college continuing education programs are self-supporting; that is, the collegiate institution will make rooms and audio-visual materials available, but the course itself must generate enough revenue to be self-sufficient. Since the majority of continuing education courses are noncredit and are basically offered because of a community response or interest, the instructor need not have the normal academic qualifications such as Masters degree or Ph.D. In other words, a retired policeman, judge, court clerk, correctional officer, counselor, or high-school teacher could be a valuable asset to the program and a tremendous instructor. These elderly could bring not only their willingness to become involved but also their knowledge of the criminal justice field itself. It could provide these individuals with a remarkable opportunity to pass on information or help people understand the functioning of the criminal justice system. In short, they have the experience and knowledge; why not let them share it? Elderly volunteers could even be brought in as guest speakers or lecturers in criminal justice seminars. Their availability and willingness is something which should not be overlooked by criminal justice education or training institutions.

Law Enforcement

Although the number of roles or functions the elderly volunteer can assume are limitless, a review will be made of two programs which have utilized the elderly volunteer: Maricopa County Sheriff's Department and the Cottage Grove Police Department.

Maricopa County

Sheriff Blubaum of the Maricopa County Sheriff's Department, Phoenix, Arizona, regrettably noted that the criminal justice system and law enforcement agencies in particular have not effectively used the elderly volunteer.

Addressing the issue in his 1971 bid for county sheriff, he made a campaign promise to actively involve interested and qualified citizens in a cooperative volunteer program within the Sheriff's Department, especially focusing on the older volunteers.

Sheriff Blubaum pointed out several reasons why older volunteers, a vital resource usually available but more often overlooked or ignored by many law enforcement officials, are essential to effective law enforcement—

Crime Prevention Posse member assisting Reserve officer during search exercise

Courtesy of Maricopa County Sheriff's Office

Sun City Posse members operating radio equipment during normal course of duty.

especially where crime is on the rise and justice seems to be on the wane. He feels citizens should be continually encouraged to participate in a job which literally belongs to each person anyway. It is unfortunate that many law enforcement agencies, plagued with tighter or reduced budgets, fail to acknowledge the elderly volunteer. This type of limited thinking is not only unrealistic, but could become a very serious mistake, considering the unquestionable need for additonal equipment, services, and personnel just to keep pace with the rising crime rate. Blubaum strongly urges utilizing the elderly volunteer as a combatant, rather than stagnating in archaic traditions of professional law enforcement.[28]

To become a volunteer with the Maricopa County Sheriff's Department, a citizen must: (1) file an application with the Department, (2) undergo a thorough background investigation, (3) have no felony convictions, and (4) be of good moral character. It seems the elderly would have no problem in applying. Unique to this program is a twenty-hour seminar in crime prevention fundamentals and techniques.[29] For those academic skeptics and law enforcement alarmists concerned over whether the older volunteer would be an asset or a liability, the evidence to date reinforces the interest and sincerity that such individual volunteers follow throughout their commitment.[30]

Not too far from Phoenix, Arizona, and within the law enforcement responsibilities of Maricopa County, exists a town known as Sun City, Arizona. Sun City, an unincorporated community of 30,000 persons, now boasts of the largest volunteer posse in Arizona, some 250 men and women. Members of the posse must volunteer their time and pay five dollars for a whistle, flashlight and white hardhat—their entire uniform. The Sun City posse, just one of thirty-six posses in Maricopa County, maintains almost continual surveillance of the town. Each posse provides such specialties as: mounted horse patrols, jeep patrols, motorcycle patrols, airplane patrols, desert survival courses, scuba divers and communications posses, crime prevention and security training, community relations and rehabilitation posses for the jail inmates.[31] These are just a few of the ways that elderly volunteers have been trained and assigned useful tasks within law enforcement. Sheriff Blubaum has stated:

> I can't afford not to use volunteers. We couldn't do half the things we're doing now without volunteer help. (Yet several sheriffs in middle-western and eastern counties have told Sheriff Blubaum that what he is doing with volunteers cannot be done in their counties. He smiles and replies...) Usually when anyone says it can't be done, it means he doesn't want to try it. If he wants to do it, he'll find a way.[32]

Cottage Grove

Just as Maricopa County found a way, so too did the Cottage Grove Police Department, Cottage Grove, Oregon. The law enforcement officials of Cottage Grove view the role of volunteer as an essential element of local police efficiency.[33] For an aged person to become a volunteer, thereby aiding the community as well as psychologically benefiting himself, two steps must be taken: filing a volunteer application form and signing a Senior Citizen Crime Prevention Contract. The application form and contract are provided for illustration purposes in Diagram 4-1 and 4-2.[34] Once accepted as a volunteer with Cottage Grove's program, the elderly volunteer is expected to perform the following specific duties:

(1)   Attend all meetings and training sessions that pertain to the general job function, including all meetings of the crime prevention officers of Lane County and the state of Oregon.

Diagram 4—1 Senior Citizen Crime Prevention Contract

I, _____ volunteer my time and efforts to the City of Cottage Grove and the Crime Prevention Program. I agree to work at least two hours a week in training and crime prevention. I understand that I must not discuss anything of a confidential nature obtained through my work with anyone. I will comply with all rules and regulations of the program and the police department. I understand that I am a citizen volunteer and not a police officer. I do not have powers of arrest. Any violation of the law that I see as a volunteer I will report to the police department.

Signed _____

Witnessed By _____

Diagram 4—2 Volunteer Application Form

Name: _____   Social Security Number: _____

Address: _____   Date of Birth: _____

_____   Telephone Number: _____

Sex: _____ Height: _____ Weight: _____

Operator's License Number: _____   State: _____

Name of Spouse: _____

* * * * * * * * *

1. Why do you want to be a Volunteer? _____
_____
_____
_____

2. Have you been a Volunteer before? _____ If so, where and doing what? _____

3. Have you ever been arrested? _____ If so, where and what for?
_____

4. Do you own a Car? _____ If so, Make _____ Year _____ Model _____

5. Would you be willing to use your automobile for short trips for the program? _____

6. Do you have Automobile Insurance? _____

7. Have you (within the past 5 years) had a Traffic Citation? _____ If so, where and what for? _____
_____

Diagram 4-2 (cont.)

8. Have you ever been a Victim of a Crime? _____ If so, where and when? _____

9. How much time in Hours per week can you spend on the program? _____ hours.

10. Do you have any experience in Law Enforcement? _____ If so, What?_____

11. Please list names of clubs and service groups you belong to currently
_____

12. Please list any friends or relatives currently in Law Enforcement
_____
_____

13. Please list three (3) personal references who have known you for over five (5) years.

(1)
Name: _____ Telephone # _____
Address:_____ Years Known _____
_____

(2)
Name: _____ Telephone # _____
Address:_____ Years Known _____
_____

(3)
Name: _____ Telephone # _____
Address:_____ Years Known _____
_____

CERTIFICATION OF APPLICANT:
I, Certify that all statements contained herein are true and correct.

_____
Signature

Date: _____

(2) Work with senior citizen groups in the area of crime prevention.

(3) Establish a crime prevention program within the community through public presentations such as slide programs, talks, video-tape programs, motion pictures, and news reports on radio and television.

(4) Keep a file of statistical information on current and past criminal trends.

(5) Maintain files on completed home inspections and all other pertinent data in this area.

(6)   Work with elderly within the community on various methods of protecting personal items and homes from crime.

(7)   Establish rapport with members of the business community to enable the volunteers to work with them on criminal activity prevention, including building inspections for burglary prevention, information on bad checks, and other pertinent crime prevention information.

(8)   Maintain an active membership in the Crime Prevention Association.

(9)   Organize security surveys designed to reduce risks in both commercial and residential areas.

(10) Stimulate enthusiasm for a positive crime prevention attitude.[35]

These two law enforcement departments are not the only agencies which employ elderly volunteers in some capacity. There are others, but there are still a great deal of law enforcement officials and officers who must be convinced that the elderly volunteer is not a liability. How difficult it is for some to face reality!

Courts

What can the elderly do as volunteers within the judicial component of the criminal justice system? Mainly, they can speak out, voice their satisfactions and dissatisfactions with the current court administration.

Those who have lived in a metropolitan community, such as Detroit, Chicago, New York, Baltimore, Los Angeles, or San Francisco, and have used public transportation networks, must have noticed that a large percentage of the mid-morning and late-afternoon passengers are elderly. Where are they going and coming from? The courthouse is where a sizable portion of the cities' elderly spend their day. They sit in on various trials and view different defendants, witnesses, and court personnel. In short, they are participant observers of the court system. The elderly see the court's strengths and weaknesses. Day after day they sit and observe. For many of the elderly this courtroom observance has become a daily ritual—a part of their lives.

As long as the elderly are compelled to visit the courthouse and are essentially making it their second home, why not effectively employ their talents? Just as with law enforcement, court administrators are hard pressed for funds and personnel. How often those words, "The docket is full...," "We're two months behind the docket already...," echo through the halls of justice. Due to heavy dockets and normal bureaucratic failings, many defendants (innocent or guilty) are usually denied a speedy trial. If additional court personnel could be acquired for the tasks of typing, filing, messenger service, etc., it would allow more to be accomplished in a shorter period of time.

Those who say the elderly would not want to volunteer for such mundane tasks as typing or filing are sadly mistaken. Given the amount of elderly who frequent the felony, misdemeanant, and divorce courts, the facts present themselves: these elderly are interested in the judicial process. If the elderly are given the opportunity to get involved in the "actual" process, even if the volunteer function is typing or filing, how much more fulfilling their lives would be. Of course, the court administrators who decide to employ elderly volunteers must be prepared, organized, and offer initial training in court procedures. For those court personnel willing to invest the time in elderly volunteers, the reward will be an abundance of extra time to assume more difficult tasks previously abandoned because of "everyday" limitations on their time.

One additional role in which the court could use the elderly volunteer is transportation. Many elderly still have automobile licenses. Having them pick up and deliver witnesses for trials, defendants for civil suits, tenants for landlord disputes, handicapped—to pick up and transport to the court those individuals who would otherwise find it difficult to appear—would prevent further delay within the judicial process.

Corrections

Usually, correctional facilities use 95 percent of their budget on the protection of society, for high walls, barbed wire, cells, guards, administrative personnel, food, and the like. On the average, only 5 percent of the budget is allotted to treatment and rehabilitation—a sad state of affairs, mostly the result of minimal budgets and allotment policies. Floggings, whippings, branking, dunking, and capital punishment have disappeared as society has become more humane in its rationale for punishment, and the concept of helping the criminal has surfaced. Unfortunately, sufficient funds to provide this help are invisible. Just as John Howard was successful in persuading the English Parliament of 1779 to enact the Penitentiary Act, and then funds were not allocated for the project, so too seems the fate of treatment and rehabilitation in correctional institutions.

Though correctional administrators clamor and shout that they just do not have enough personnel to run an effective treatment program, they have kept their eyes closed to a readily available volunteer source of elderly professionals. Haven't the elderly counselor, correctional officer, ex-warden, retired surgeon, psychologist, criminologist, social worker, and psychiatrist the ability to provide their professional skills and expertise in a treatment setting a few hours a week? Is it not probable they would enjoy "keeping their feet wet"? What of the nonprofessional elderly individuals—are they not to be allowed to volunteer within a correctional setting? That would be ridiculous, for nonprofessional elderly volunteers can be trained by the current correctional staff or professional elderly volunteers in certain psychotherapies such as behavior modification, reality therapy, or transcendental meditation, which could be used within the correctional setting. The use of elderly volunteers in the corrections field is as limitless as the imagination.

Do not forget juvenile corrections; using elderly volunteers, professional and nonprofessional, applies to this area as well. Since the number of elderly persons is on the rise and the youth population has experienced a decline, the elderly seem an appropriate support unit to agencies and institutions dealing with youthful offenders. If the present birth and death rate continues, the ratio of aged persons to youth might someday enable each youngster to have at least one foster grandparent. With the elderly volunteer having the ability and time to become involved with youth, the youth might not have the time to get delinquently involved with the system.

Community-Based Corrections

Modern community-based corrections "compliments traditional incarceration, probation, and parole—it's an area where people 'do their own thing' more than in any other part of the criminal justice system."[36] Mostly because of this "do-your-own-thing" philosophy, community-based corrections provides the elderly with a unique opportunity for a second career —a full-time career after retirement. A number of elderly people can get together and develop a program which their particular neighborhood or community needs. With enough community support and motivation, it is even possible for the eldery to acquire a Law Enforcement Assistance Administration grant to finance their program.

Whatever community-based correctional program the elderly volunteer for or begin themselves (neighborhood youth centers, diversion programs, halfway houses, work-release programs, drug abuse and alcohol programs, counseling centers, group homes, or foster homes), the following should be carefully considered:

(1) Do you have the ability to understand and withstand provocative behavior without becoming punitive?

(2) Do you possess knowledge of on-the-job counseling techniques? If not, how do you propose to acquire such knowledge?

(3) Do you have sufficient sensitivity to pathological behavior to permit intelligent referral to professional staff and/or agencies?

(4) Do you possess the tact to avoid creating or aggravating problem situations?

(5) Are you willing to augment and support the staff?

(6) Do you have the ability to assess community and family attitudes toward the offender?

(7) Do you possess the ability to keep a discrete silence on critical issues and "classified" information in order to maintain (a) staff morale, (b) caseload morale, and (c) good public relations?

(8)   Do you have the ability to constructively interpret agency or community attitudes and behavior toward the person on the volunteer's caseload?

(9)   Do you have knowledge of the constitutional and civil rights of persons on the case load, and the ability to incorporate that knowledge into the supervisory process?

(10) Do you possess the ability to interpret the system of justice, including laws of arrest, judicial procedure, and a total correctional process, in order to correctly answer questions put by the offender?[37]

Whether or not any volunteer would have the knowledge or ability to answer any of the above questions positively is not the issue here. If the elderly have the ability to volunteer their services in a community-based correctional program, then they have the ability to learn the necessary rules, regulations, and functions to perform their tasks superiorly!

> It is obvious that the number of personnel employed in community-based corrections program cannot possibly manage the many duties that must be performed for effective handling of cases. . . . There is simply not adequate time for counseling or casework. For example, the average workload for a staff member in a child guidance clinic is twelve to fifteen children with problems. Consequently, the use of volunteers is the only possible solution to a very difficult problem. Volunteers are indeed vital to an effective community-based corrections system.[38]

The key to effective community-based corrections is volunteers. The elderly are the key to volunteer support. Again, proper training is essential, but the elderly volunteer's willingness and motivation are the elements which can make community-based corrections a tremendous success.

Statistical Research

The viability of all criminal justice agencies lies in their statistical research. Proper data collection is essential. If programs are to be started, financed, and completed, it is necessary there be more than a margin of success. Theory and research are not separate and distinct entities; they compliment or disgrace each other. For instance, if a particular correctional theory says increased sentence time will reduce recidivism, yet the collected data refutes the theory, then time, energy, and money can be saved in the future. In other words, the data purported that the theory was not holding its own in the real world. Just as easily as data can refute a particular theory, so research can prove a theory's usefulness.

Just imagine how many business people, accountants, statisticians, computer analysts, computer programmers, mathematicians, etc., are among the ranks of the retired. Many of these "very knowledgeable" elderly would enjoy working (volunteering) on a stimulating and challenging research project —especially a project which would utilize their research talents in the quest of evaluating a law enforcement, judicial, or correctional program currently in operation or a program waiting implementation.

In this area of research statistics, the elderly volunteer personnel would more than likely be thoroughly trained for their role. It is the one area in which little time would need be devoted to planning and organizing. Other elderly volunteers interested in this data collection and analysis would enjoy a variety of tasks, such as keypunch operating or typing. The training or brushing up of skills in these particular jobs might take some time, but the investment payoff could come in the form of a completely self-sufficient network of research statisticians and staff. The only operating cost to the criminal justice system would be the use of the machinery—computers, typewriters, keypunch machines—and facilities to accommodate the volunteers. If we don't use this machinery or put it to use as often as possible, it becomes a wasted resource.

Community Projects

There are many community projects that are worthwhile. However, a truly unique project is one that helps elderly persons in need and, at the same time, employs them to furnish the muscle that supplies their needs. The Senior Home Security Program in St. Louis, Missouri, is one such program. Although this project just began in March of 1976, its concept is catching on. As Steve D'Angelo, project director, has stated, "The whole idea of using seniors to help others [seniors] sounds so easy...I get calls from all over the United States from agencies wanting to copy what we are doing here."[39]

What exactly does the Senior Home Security Program do? With funds administered by the Administration on Aging, HEW, the program employs any low-income person over fifty-five years of age. Paying between $2.30 and $4.50 per hour, the jobs employees acquire are those with which they are familiar. For example, a man who has been a plumber, carpenter, or electrician all his life, will be a plumber, carpenter, or electrician in the program. The program employees improve and secure homes of those elderly who are financially or physically unable to do the work themselves. Like any program which is popular and successful, the Senior Home Security Program's funds are dwindling away by increasing demand. The customers are satisfied, the workers satisfied, and potential burglars disgruntled.

This program is just one idea utilizing elderly people to help others. The workers, recipients, and society are being helped. If only other programs would open their doors to the elderly. The volunteers may be old, but they are determined to remain productive and available.

SUMMARY

It is within the scope of the criminal justice system to employ elderly volunteers in all the aforementioned areas. Though there may be some overlap in the areas discussed (statistical research and law enforcement, training and community-based corrections), all are areas which could benefit from the time, knowledge, expertise, and devotion elderly volunteers can offer to an overburdened criminal justice system.

Many social scientists feel that a certain amount of crime is normal. If society rationalizes the normalcy of crime and realizes that, at best, it can only neutralize, not nullify, the crime problem, then an attractive alternative for increasing effectiveness and efficiency within the criminal justice system lies in the use of the aged volunteer. Komara stated, "Crime cannot be corrected or controlled by the police alone, regardless of a police department's size...we have witnessed departments that have nearly doubled in their strength without a comparable drop in their crime statistic."[40] Not using the aged volunteer is a waste of a very productive resource.

The concept of volunteerism is as old as civilization itself. As a result of religious beliefs, patriotic ventures, and the taming of the western United States in the 1800s, volunteers have offered a helping hand to those who needed it. The need for volunteers is even greater today. The criminal justice system would be wise to focus on the most available resource of energy available, at present and in the future—the aged volunteer. A volunteer program using the elderly would foster participation and partnership, publicly and privately. The criminal justice system should turn to direct contact of aged volunteers by its professionals. There is nothing to lose and much to gain from the wisdom and insatiable desire which the aged possess. Although retirement is not necessarily equated with boredom and loneliness, there is no excuse for letting the aged sit idly by when they can offer so much in return for an investment in them.

QUESTIONS

1. Why is elderly volunteerism the key to successful crime prevention programs?
2. Is seventy a justifiable age for retirement?
3. Should a person's productivity be measured by age? Why or why not?
4. Discuss the justifications suggested to end mandatory retirement.
5. Are the myths about the elderly realistic?
6. In what ways does the elderly person benefit from being a volunteer?
7. What elements make the elderly volunteer useful in crime prevention?

8. What is the chief responsibility of criminal justice agencies before employing elderly volunteers?

9. Discuss some of the questions criminal justice administrators should ask themselves about elderly volunteers.

10. Are elderly volunteers as good as other age-group volunteers?

11. Discuss the use of elderly volunteers in various criminal justice areas, such as in education, law enforcement, courts, corrections, community-based corrections, statistical research, and community projects.

12. Discuss the questions community-based correctional volunteers should ask themselves.

13. Why are elderly law enforcement volunteers so successful in Maricopa County, Phoenix, Arizona?

14. Why have elderly volunteers been overlooked by the criminal justice system?

15. Discuss the benefits to be gained by the criminal justice system's use of elderly volunteers.

SUGGESTED READINGS

J. E. Birren, *The Psychology of Aging* (Englewood Cliffs, N.J.: Prentice-Hall, Inc., 1965).

J. Botwinick, *Cognitive Processes in Maturity and Old Age* (New York, N.Y.: Springer Publishing Co., Inc., 1967).

Wilbur Cohen, *Retirement Policies Under Social Security* (Berkeley, California: University of California Press, 1975).

R. W. Tyler, "The Role of the Volunteer," *California Youth Authority* (California Department of Youth Authority in conjunction with Stanford University, 1965), Vol. 18, No. 4, pp. 15–23.

NOTES

1. *Democracy in America,* trans. George Lawrence (London, England: Harper and Row Publishers, 1966).

2. Simone de Beauvoir, *The Coming of Age* p. 800.

3. Jon Hendricks and C. Davis Hendricks, *Aging in Mass Society: Myths and Realities,* © 1977 Winthrop Publishers, Inc., p. 211.

4. Douglas G. Montgomery, "Testimony On the Issues of Mandatory Retirement to a Joint Interim Task Force on Mandatory Retirement, State of Oregon Legislature," (Portland, Oregon: Institute on Aging, Portland State University, September 22, 1977), p. 3.

5. Montgomery, op cit., p. 21.

6. Ibid, pp. 22–3.

7. Tom William, "The New Mandatory Retirement Law and You," *NRTA Journal,* March/April, 1978, p. 23.

8. George Sunderland, "The Older American: Police Problem or Police Asset?," *F.B.I. Law Enforcement Bulletin,* Vol. 45, No. 8, August 1976, p. 8.

9. Rolf Monge and David F. Hultsch, "Paired-Associate Learning as a Function of Adult Age and the Length of the Anticipation and Inspection Intervals," *Journal of Gerontology,* Vol. 26, 1971, pp. 157–62.

10. Ibid, p. 161.

11. Jack Botwinick, Ph.D., *Aging and Behavior: A Comprehensive Integration of Research Findings* (New York, N.Y.: Springer Publ. Co., Inc., 1973), p. 221.

12. Ibid., p. 229.

13. Ibid., p. 229.

14. de Beauvoir, op cit., pp. 802–03.

15. Aid to Victims of Crime, Inc., *Victimization* (pamphlet), University Club Bldg., Suite 705, 601 N. Grand, St. Louis, Missouri, 63101.

16. Aid to Victims of Crime, Inc., *Lend a Hand to Aid a Friend* (pamphlet), loc cit.

17. Gladys Worthington, "Older Persons as Community Service Volunteers," *Social Work,* Vol. 8, No. 4, October 1963, p. 71.

18. Hendricks and Hendricks, op cit., pp. 299–300.

19. Philip J. Gross, "Law Enforcement and the Senior Citizen," *The Police Chief,* February 1976, p. 9.

20. Paul Tournier, *Learn to Grow,* trans. Edwin Husdon (New York, N.Y.: Harper and Row Publishers, 1972), p. 124.

21. Hendricks and Hendricks, op cit., p. 301.

22. Ibid.

23. Aid to Victims of Crime, Inc., *Volunteer Training Manual* (pamphlet), loc cit.

24. Ibid.

25. Chamber of Commerce of the United States, *Marshalling Citizen Power Against Crime,* 1615 H. Street, N.W., Washington, D.C., p. 101.

26. W. Fred Cottrell, *Aging and the Aged* (Dubuque, Iowa: Wm. C. Brown Co., 1974), p. 34.

27. Harriet Naylor, *Volunteers Today—Finding, Training and Working With Them* (New York, N.Y.: Associated Press, 1967).

28. Paul E. Blubaum, "Maricopa County Sheriff's Department Volunteer Program," *The Police Chief,* February 1976, p. 17.

29. Blubaum, op cit., p. 19.

30. Ibid.

31. Glenn White, "Where Citizens Help Control Crime," *Dynamic Maturity,* July 1975, p. 12.

32. White, op cit., p. 13.

33. Ron L. Willis and Myra Miller, "Senior Citizen Crime Prevention Programs," *The Police Chief,* February 1976.

34. Cottage Grove Police Department, Senior Citizens' Volunteer Crime Prevention Unit, 400 Main Street, Cottage Grove, Oregon, 97424.

35. Willis and Miller, op cit.

36. Vernon B. Fox, Community-Based Corrections (Englewood Cliffs, New Jersey: Prentice-Hall, Inc., 1977), pp. xiii–xiv.

37. Adapted from Vernon B. Fox, *Guidelines For Corrections Programs in Community and Junior Colleges* (Washington, D.C.: American Association of Junior Colleges, 1969), pp. 18–19.

38. Fox, op cit., pp. xiii–xiv.

39. Kim Plummer, "They Rebuild Homes and Hopes," *Globe-Democrat,* St. Louis, Missouri, July 2–3, 1977, p. 1E.

40. Donald F. Komara, "Concerned Citizen's Action Hotline," *The Police Chief,* June 1974, p. 19.

Chapter **5**

The Elderly
as Criminals?

Throughout this book we have discussed the plight of the elderly regarding criminal victimization—how the elderly are victimized, how the elderly can prevent victimization, and how they can be a useful asset in reducing crime through volunteer efforts. The image of the elderly thus far has been positive and reinforcing. We will now turn to another plight of the elderly, a plight caused by contemporary society—the elderly as criminals.

This topic is not at all an attempt to negate the elderly, but rather the result of a desire to introduce a new area of research to criminologists, gerontologists, and generalists. There have always been crimes for which the elderly are more suspect than other age groups (child molestation and indecent exposure, for example). However, it is time social scientists took a long, hard look at why some elderly are turning to economic crime. As indicated in Chapter 1, Diagram 1-1 (page 12), the elderly as criminals is an offshoot in the study of crime and gerontology. Although not directly related to the other components discussed thus far, the study of elderly crime is an important issue—an issue where attention should be focused.

> Chancellor Mel Carden says he thought he was about to die when a man claiming he'd been cheated on a land deal held him more than ninety minutes at gunpoint. "He kept the gun jammed in my side or back most of the time. ...He said he was going to blow my guts out...."
>
> The man, identified by police as Harry Lang, age seventy-nine, was handcuffed and taken to the state hosptial....Witnesses said the man claimed Carden had ruled against him in a property dispute in 1975, and that the ruling was based on forged documents. He said he was ordered to sell twenty acres of land that belonged to him because someone had forged his name on a sales option.[1]

News stories such as the above and others dealing with less serious crimes are appearing in newspapers all over the country. What is causing elderly people to turn to crime? Is it a means of expression? Has crime become a way for the elderly to vent their frustrations? Are the elderly becoming indignant and fed up with the uncaring attitude of the bureaucratic system which controls their lives? There is a strong tendency to believe so.

This chapter will stimulate both the beginning student and advanced scholar and open the door to a new field of inquiry by focusing on (1) notable gerontological and criminological theories, (2) crime statistics on the elderly, and (3) a speculative discussion on why the elderly are turning to crime. At the conclusion of this chapter, the reader will have sufficient understanding of the concepts involved to determine whether contemporary elderly crime is a viable research area. There has been very little systematic attention or research given to the elderly as criminals. The minimal amount of information and data concerning elderly criminals is not supportive enough to provide answers to the questions posed above; however, the information which has been gathered is quite interesting and enables much "food for future thought." Although the data is not conclusive at this time and generalizations would be inappropriate, speculation can be offered. Through this speculative discussion of why elderly people turn to crime, it is hoped that researchers will rise to the occasion and that the accumulation of supportive data will enable more conclusive remarks in the future.

Since this is an introductory textbook, the purpose is not to confuse the new student with theoretical concepts, definitions, and jargon of the theories involved, but rather to explain the theories in sufficient terminology so that a reasonable understanding of the theory and the speculative discussion will follow. For those new students, advanced students, and interdisciplinary scholars who wish to investigate the theories further, the bibliography will provide additional information necessary for research.

CRIMINOLOGICAL THEORIES

The Theory of Cultural Deviance

According to the theory of cultural deviance, crime is the inevitable result of diverse cultures. In society, all members of all cultures—as, for example, Black, Spanish, Anglo, Polish, French—are exposed to conventional morality. Conventional morality is the label attached to "what is right" for the majority of people. The majority of people are expected to be socialized (to the dominant culture), rational, and status and goal seekers. However, there are many different cultures which exist in society. Can each different culture be judged on the basis of the dominant culture? Cultural deviance theorists believe so. They pose the question, "How do different cultural norms lead a person to deviate from conventional morality (in such ways as committing crimes)?" Before attempting to answer this question, we must first ask, "What is cultural deviance?"

Cultural deviance is simply any deviance from the majority culture's norms. In this country there are a variety of diverse cultures continually competing and conflicting with other cultures, especially the dominant one. For example, the black culture which exists in the ghetto or lower-class neighborhoods is one which the majority of middle-class whites do not understand or do not want to understand. The middle-class white who sees the rundown housing area of low-class blacks may try to superimpose the middle-class ethos on the black people, for example, replacing single family housing units with multifamily housing complexes. What the middle-class "do-gooder" has failed to realize is that the black culture is based in part on the interaction of black families, where the front porch is the center of social activities. When the center of social activities is replaced with apartments, social interaction may dwindle or become nonexistent, resulting in the breakdown of black culture and the imposition of another culture. When this breakdown in culture occurs, the possibility of crime increases. Criminal behavior is the natural byproduct of the interaction between people and their environment. Using the above example, when blacks lived in crowded neighborhoods, single-family housing and the process of socialization was centered on the front porch. The eyes of the community were watching. When apartment complexes were substituted for single-family units, the eyes disappeared and the crime appeared. This is not to say crime was not present before, for it was; however, crime was kept in check under the community's eyes. Without those eyes, the opportunity for committing crime and "getting away with it" became more realistic.

Just as there are many diverse cultures, there are many different cultural deviance theorists who propose to explain how cultural norms lead the actor to deviate from conventional morality. Though there are many different explanations, all cultural deviance theorists try to explain the concepts of diversity and socialization. The previous example showed how deviance is caused by imposing one culture upon another. Now examine how one theorist in particular, Miller, views deviance. Miller[2] sees the lower class as a generating mileau of lower-class delinquency. In his vision are three concepts: (1) focal concerns, (2) status and belonging, and (3) lower-class features. The focal concerns are issues around which people give widespread attention and have emotional involvement, for example, trouble, toughness, smartness, fate, autonomy, and excitement. There are issues around which adults and adolescents used to organize their behavior. Status and belonging follow from the focal concerns. Being tough, getting into trouble, and being street smart will build one's status and enable him to *belong*. Miller suggests that all lower-class adolescents seek to belong because they do not receive an adequate sense of belonging from their families. (Keep in mind the family that cannot find any time for the elderly relative or the elderly person longing for a sense of belonging.) The lower-class adolescent seeks this belonging on the streets in the form of gangs, and deviance appears. Finally, Miller suggests that the features of lower-class life, such as cultural terms, economic disadvantages, and female monogamy, all aid in the development of deviance.

How does delinquency develop? It develops from a conflict with middle-class values and as a byproduct of focal concerns. Imagine living in a world where middle-class ethos are superimposed on your lower-class existence, in which focal concerns, status, belonging, and lower-class features are your everyday concern—a way to prove to others that you are just as good as they are. That is how deviance develops. Can focal concerns be controlled?

Yes. Through places such as Boys' Clubs and Police Athletic Associations, youth can exercise their focal concerns in a recreational and guided way.

Now picture the elderly person living alone, on a fixed income, with few people showing him respect and many people offering him sympathy because he is old. What are his focal concerns, his status and belonging, and the features which invade his life space? These questions soon will be answered; just mull them over in your mind for now.

Strain Theory

In strain theory, crime is quite naturally caused by strain—the strain of not being able to attain certain goals. In other words, people violate societal norms when the promise of the culture cannot be attained. Man deviates from the norm when his goals are too high (Durkheim)[3] or when the means to attain those goals are not available (Merton).[4] The object is to coordinate goals and means; when this becomes unlikely, deviance surfaces.

In strain theory, people are subjected to stress or pressure. This stress causes people to deviate from the norm. Examples of this are suicide (Durkheim) or delinquent subcultures (Cloward and Ohlin).[5] Of course this theory assumes that there is a common set of values among the members of society and that socialization has been successful. The valid criticisms of this theory are (1) it assumes everyone is seeking the same goal, which is not so, (2) middle-class bias is focused on the lower class, (3) the internalization of norms, and (4) no empirical evidence for the concepts. Davis even suggests that despite the American dream of making it, the lower class is excluded from the competitive game of attaining monetary success through legitimate means.[6] Assuming that Davis is correct, what means does the lower class have available to attain their goals? When lower-class individuals observe the "good life" on television, in stores, or out on the town, and the majority of this lower class are prevented from higher education, better paying jobs, or a chance at the good life, where do they turn? Illegitimate means become a way of attaining the goals superimposed on them by the middle-class culture.

Merton gives an example of how strain theory operates. In considering why the poor become deviants, the following concepts are employed: (1) culture, (2) social structure, and (3) anomie. Culture defines man's goals and the means for achieving them. This assumes the culture is consistent and uniform and that monetary success is the prime goal. The social structure is the stabilized roles people play—for example: if you work hard, you will be successful (employment is the key). Anomie is the malintegration of culture. In other words, the goals and rules have unequal emphasis within a particular society; for example, the goal is to be successful, yet the rules to gain success are very strict. Often the rules make the goals impossible to attain. What causes this malintegration is the strain or "blocked opportunity" when people are told or influenced to pursue that which they cannot attain. Because of this blocked opportunity, they have no legitimate payoff, or reward. Yet the pressure remains, the pressure to achieve monetary success. Thus the source becomes deviance, such as crime.

Diagram 5—1

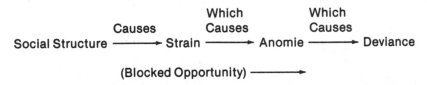

The illegitimate means of attaining goals remove the pressure and strain of one's social structure position. Would full employment end this pressure? Possibly. We know that desires, needs, wants, and goals still remain without employment. It becomes difficult to live with the knowledge that "you want, but cannot have." Imagine the elderly person who works hard all his life to finally be faced with living on social security and, if he's lucky, pension checks. Shouldn't retirement be somewhat easy, especially after all those years of hard work? What will happen to this elderly person who, because of his newly acquired social position as a golden age leisure recipient, finds pressures of inflation, impossibility to work (income) and fewer who care? Will he turn to crime? There is that possibility.

Conflict Theory

According to conflict theory, crime is behavior which conflicts with the interests of those in power. Given conflict, how is social order possible? Must power be redistributed in order to prevent conflict? Is conflict among societal members something which can be alleviated?

Conflict theorists attempt to explain criminal behavior and legal institutions through the use of two concepts—capitalism and conflict. Capitalism is the system in which we live. It is an economic system characterized by private or corporate ownership of goods. These goods are investments which are determined by private decision, not state or local government control. The price, production, and distribution of goods are mainly determined in a free market. Bonger[7] suggests that criminal behavior is a result of tendencies in man which are elicited by capitalism. Since excessive egoism develops under capitalism, capitalism stimulates egoism and competition which, in turn, causes crime. Gordon[8] remarks that crime is a rational response to conditions generated by capitalism. These conditions are competition and inequality of rewards. What is conflict? It is the rational adaptation to the material conditions of society with which people must live. In other words, if a person is hungry because he is poor and unemployed, he rationalizes the theft of food as a condition which society has forced upon him.

Although some conflict theorists do not make a conscious effort to apply Karl Marx[9] in their theories (Turk, Quinney), others do call attention to Marx and two of his concepts: superstructure and surplus population. Superstructure is the concept used to address the questions of social control and the law. The law, its content and operation, is part of the superstructure and reflects the will or interests of the ruling class. The ruling class dominates or exercises social control over all people because it controls the means of material existence. When powerless people feel threatened, or not in control, they rebel. This rebellion, short of revolution, comes in the form of criminal behavior.

Surplus population is a concept also used to address social control and criminal behavior. The surplus population results from industrialization. It is a contradiction of capitalism, a consequence of productivity. As the surplus population increases, it becomes a problem population (example: idle people who are hungry). Marx suggested that crime is what the surplus population does. It leans toward criminal behavior because crime is indeed a rational adaptation to the circumstance of surplus population. Now, what is the likelihood that the surplus population will become deviant? That all depends on a number of elements:

(1) The organization of the superstructure
(2) The efficiency of the superstructure in dealing with the surplus population
(3) The size of the surplus population
(4) The threat of the surplus population
(5) The surplus population's level of organization

Just how does the superstructure keep the surplus population (elderly) in check? How do those in power attempt to prevent it from turning to crime? The main way the dominant order prevents deviance among the surplus population is by providing for its needs, such as food, clothing, medical care, housing—in short, welfare! But is welfare enough today? Has contemporary America caused an excessive surplus population? If the aged population increases and other age groups remain stable, it is possible that, by the year 2000, 40 percent of the population will be gainfully employed and producing the necessities of life for 100 percent of the population. Will the 1980s and beyond continue to dismember the aged from society, adding to the already huge surplus population? If the elderly are to face old age without the comforts of their earlier productivity (income) and be forced to live on fixed incomes, is not crime a viable alternative?

Labelling Theory

Labelling theorists believe that crime is behavior which is offensive to some social audience. To illustrate the concept of social audience, examine Diagram 5-2.

Diagram 5—2 The Criminal Behavior of Indecent Exposure (Streaking)

Social Audience	Meaning Applied
Your Mother	The behavior is unnecessary, but as long as no one gets hurt, it is OK
Your Peers	Terrific!
The Law	It is a Crime

As shown in Diagram 5-2, the crime of streaking can assume different meanings, depending on the social audience viewing the situation. In determining why people deviate, labelling theorists follow the concepts of (1) social audience, (2) designation of deviant acor, and (3) escalation to deviant identity.

As previously explained, social audience is any person or group of persons who assigns meaning to a particular behavior. This meaning is largely a function of the character or level of the social audience. The significance of social audience cannot be diminished, yet to define deviance using the concept of social audience implies there is nothing intrinsically deviant, even murder. Murder is usually defined as the unlawful and unnecessary taking of a life, but isn't it dependent upon the social audience (jury) to determine unlawful and unnecessary? Labelling theory may not tell exactly what is criminal, but the theory does provide for interesting material. For example, why does the FBI consider motor vehicle theft important? Possibly the question to determine is "Is there something more intrinsically wrong with rape than with streaking?" If so, then we should pursue it.

The designation of deviant actor is simply applying the label "deviant" and its subsequent meaning to an individual. For example, if there are 100 arrests for streaking and only five convictions, only five persons are labelled deviant. Isn't this quite a process of assigning meaning? What of those other ninety-five streakers? Usually, what is crucial for the label to be attached (the actor to be designated deviant), is dependent upon (1) the character of the actor, (2) the character of the social audience, and (3) the character of the situation. If the streaking is the actor's first offense, the social audience viewing the streak is not particularly upset, and the streak did not interfere with traffic (such as causing automobile accidents), chances are the actor will not be labelled. However, if any of those factors become crucial, labelling will result. What is necessary and influential in the process of assigning meaning? Lofland[10] addresses:

(1) Knowledge
(2) Reasonableness of category
(3) Prevalent sensitivity
(4) Individual vulnerability
(5) Simple indicators

The social audience must have the knowledge that a deviant category exists. This knowledge may vary historically and geographically. For example, in the 1800s, when boys were deviant, the phrase, "Boys will be boys," was often heard; whereas in the 1950s and 1960s, when boys broke street lamps, the phrase, "You're a juvenile delinquent," was often heard. Geographically, smoking marijuana in Dallas, Texas, carries a stiff penalty if caught; yet every year on the campus of the University of Michigan the Annual Hash Bash is held. Why? In Ann Arbor, Michigan, the social audience does not equate smoking marijuana/hash as a deviant act.

With regard to the "label," the category of deviance must be reasonable. If the label is not with the times, it is not applied. For example, there are few witch hunts today in Salem, Massachusetts. The label could be out of place in the eyes of the criminal as well—some individuals actually convicted of a crime never do fully accept the label "criminal." Prevalent sensitivity refers to how turned on or off society is to coding the behavior as deviant. As long as there is sensitivity to the behavior, there will be a way to label it.

Individual vulnerability means that some people are more vulnerable than others to having labels attached to them. This individual vulnerability is usually a matter of (1) class, power, or race, (2) demeanor, and (3) shared symbolic universe. Imagine a white, middle-class, twenty-eight-year-old criminology professor and a black, lower-class, blue-collar steelworker both driving under the influence of alcohol. Who is more likely to be taken home? Who more likely to be arrested? The same two individuals are stopped for speeding by a policeman. The professor is polite and responds with "yes sir," while the steelworker is angry and responds with abusive language. Which demeanor is more likely to receive a verbal warning, a ticket, and/or arrest? What if both are stopped for speeding and they can see that it is useless, for the cop is determined to issue a ticket. The professor mentions that he teaches criminology at the college and begins to identify with the cop's problems, eventually leading into the topic of discretion, while the steelworker can offer no "shared symbolic universe." Which individual is more likely to escape the ticket because of what he has in common with the

patrolman? The simple indicators are identities which are easy to define—
Blacks, Mexicans, hippies, etc. If a group is numerous and easy to identify,
the more likely it is that the label will be applied. All these components add
or detract to an individual's vulnerability and the designation of the label
"deviant."

The escalation to deviant identity is seen as a consequence of the individual's reaction to the social audience. It happens when the casual or non-
habitual criminal comes to categorize himself as criminal, so that subsequent
acts become part of the self-definition. Lemert[11] suggests that this escalation
is a response to the problems created by the label. The stigma generates a
sense of injustice within the individual, and the person strikes back by committing more crime so that he will feel comfortable with the label. Because
of the label, the individual becomes a more likely suspect for law enforcement dragnets; possibly the individual will be watched more closely. In
order to protect himself from the social audience which has imputed this
label, chances are the individual will acquire an alternative set of standards
and develop or be influenced by subcultures. Lemert refers to this deviance
caused by the label as secondary deviance—deviance which adapts to new
circumstances.

Two criticisms of labelling theory are that it does not explain the initial
deviance, and individuals often violate laws knowingly in a rational choice.
These criticisms are valid, for they form the basis of the following questions:
Why do elderly people deviate? How do the elderly escalate to a deviant
identity? Who is the elderly's dominant social audience? What has become
of the elderly's shared symbolic universe? These concepts will prove useful
in understanding gerontological crime, but first must be learned the second
theoretical component—gerontological theories.

GERONTOLOGICAL THEORIES

Disengagement Theory

Disengagement theory involves the disengagement of the elderly from
their functional roles within society. This theory not only assumes the process
of withdrawals to be satisfying (for both society and the elderly individual),
but also proclaims the disengagement to be functional in that withdrawal
from productive work roles enables younger, more efficient individuals to
assume these roles without an interruption in society and productivity.
Botwinick suggests that the heart of the theory is the fact that people will
withdraw and/or become dissociated from other people and activity with
the advance of old age. Though there is little controversy with this statement,
the majority of controversy is to be found in the theory's belief that the

disengaged person is happy.[12] Yet, if the disengagement is forced by society, how can such an experience be happy?

Why has disengagement theory flourished, even among the numerous critics? One reason is that in America, this land of productivity and efficiency, there is one inescapable fact—all people die. Since everyone is going to die, why sacrifice productivity? Isn't it more rational to keep the system flowing smoothly? Must efficiency be sacrificed so elderly employees can maintain functional roles? Disengagement theorists think not! They believe a practical and applicable solution to the aging process can be found in disengagement. One of their main faults is their presumption that the aging process begins at age sixty-five or seventy, for example, with mandatory retirement. Although this disengagement may be reflected as a single event (retirement), "in fact the process is a gradual one which involves separation of the individual from a great many of his positions and roles."[13] Another of the theory's faults is its functional hypothesis that society cannot function with elderly people filling responsible and productive roles. Look only as far as the political area in your own state, county, or municipality. How many representatives are beyond mandatory retirement, yet remain active and productive in politics? Atchley suggests that disengagement theory is not functional, for if it were, "wouldn't we expect it to apply to political institutions more than to any other [institution]?"[14]

Disengagement theory can be satisfying if it is something the elderly individual wants and understands. However, if an elderly person is forced to retire in order to make way for the young and energetic, can there be happiness and adjustment in later life? The utopian essays of Robert Owen were among the first to expound on the benefits and happiness of old age,[15] but society is no longer an agrarian community. Life expectancy has increased and with it the elderly population. The disengagement theory is clearly an assault on the elderly of this country. If the elderly are to disengage, who is to support their needs? Has automation become insensitive to the plight of aging Americans?

Activity Theory

The proponents of activity theory did not appear until ten years after disengagement theory first surfaced. Activity theory, which has received very little attention (as compared to disengagement theory), is one which maintains that the elderly must remain active in their later years. Activity or involvement after retirement will not only enhance one's self-concept but will make living more satisfying. This theory accepts retirement, yet doesn't accept needless and wasteful idleness by the elderly. Activity theorists realize the functional roles of work will disappear, but if there are ample substitute roles, such as volunteer programs, the elderly will be able to make the adjustment to retirement quite smoothly. Note that these substitute activities must be of a worthwhile nature; otherwise the elderly will not fully benefit from such roles.

A major difficulty with the activity theory is that "it says nothing about what happens to people who cannot maintain the standards of the middle-aged."[16] In other words, it is felt that the elderly person who retires tries to live by the active and energetic norms of the middle-aged person. Obviously, many elderly people cannot assume such active involvement as they did in middle age. However, retirement need not signify the collapse of all activity. The elderly, though not keeping the same pace as twenty years prior, can remain active, useful, and productive.

An elderly person who refuses to be disengaged and is confronted with no alternative role or identity may be forced to search for such a role—something to replace the activity he has lost. When a role is lost or taken from a person, that person must compensate. He must regain the activity. Isn't this sense of "a need for involvement" part of our rugged American heritage, which has always stressed individualism?[17]

Other Theories

Although there are many other theories of gerontology which attempt to describe the aging process, we are basically concerned with disengagement and activity theory only. For information concerning continuity theory, subcultural theory, minority theory and identity crisis theory, the bibliography will provide references.

ARE THERE ELDERLY CRIMINALS?

Although newspaper accounts of bizarre incidents are not reason enough to suspect an increase in the amount of aged persons turning to a life of crime, the St. Petersburg, Florida, Police Department has issued the following statement:

> The number of perpetrators aged sixty and over increased 108 percent from 1974 to 1975. The largest single category was shoplifting. Their favorite theft objects were food products, followed by clothing and medical-related articles. In 85 percent of the incidents, property losses were less than ten dollars.[18]

While the cash amount of property stolen per individual may seem trivial, the total cost of such theft is quite high. Shoplifting has become a great cost to storeowners—a cost which these storeowners pass on to the customers. Though the number of felonies is relatively small, the number of misdemeanors should call attention to a possible trend formation. Yes, shoplifting and pilferage of under ten dollars may be a misdemeanor, but it is still a crime. Why have the elderly turned to such crime? What are the reasons for the 108 percent increase in elderly crime in one year alone?

Most social science literature informs us that criminal behavior subsides when a person reaches twenty or thirty years of age. The question to be asked is, "What has caused this resurgence of criminal activity among the elderly?" Why has St. Petersburg, Florida, experienced increased criminal activity by the elderly (Table 5-1)?

If the cause lies in a social system inadequately prepared to meet the needs of the aged, then social policy to meet these needs must be developed immediately. Verbal battle over the ramifications of policies which aid an elderly person would lessen the implementation of programs designed for the aged. Discussion is needed, but delay in setting up programs is a horological injustice. The longer the organization of programs is stalled, the sooner the social policy towards the elderly stales, and the greater the possibility of elderly turning to crime.

Table 5-1   Crime and the Elderly[19]
(1974–1975)

Crime	Number of Suspects 60 Years and Over	
	1974	1975
Homicide	2	1
Rape	0	0
Robbery	0	0
Aggravated assault	28	37
Simple assault	38	69
Residential breaking and entry	4	7
Auto breaking and entry	1	2
Pickpocketing	1	0
Purse snatching	2	1
Commercial breaking and entry	0	0
Shoplifting	95	250
Larceny		
Auto parts theft	1	0
Bike theft	0	1
Theft from buildings	4	4
Miscellaneous	13	20
Auto theft	1	4
TOTAL	190	396

Table 5-2 Total Arrests by Age[20]
(Age 60 +)

	1972		1973	
	Agencies 6,195		Agencies 6,004	
	Estimated Population 160,416,000		Estimated Population 154,995,000	
Offense Charged	Total Arrests 18 +	Total Arrests 60 +	Total Arrests 18 +	Total Arrests 60 +
Criminal homicide	16,119	602	15,535	558
Forcible rape	15,532	89	15,426	130
Robbery	74,394	244	67,520	339
Aggravated assault	128,325	3,345	128,621	3,575
Burglary (breaking and entry)	154,017	650	146,044	731
Larceny (theft)	341,690	10,209	333,738	9,905
Auto theft	56,587	196	51,512	211
Other assaults	247,316	5,137	222,061	4,443
Sex offenses (except forcible rape and prostitution	40,147	1,504	38,889	1,577
Gambling	68,336	7,525	53,394	5,503
DWI	596,723	29,278	644,888	31,684
Liquor laws	130,781	3,598	109,123	2,899
Drunkenness	1,344,110	118,314	1,154,767	99,638
Disorderly conduct	454,757	15,328	357,997	8,434
Vagrancy	50,133	2,082	44,294	1,772
Suspicion	29,054	473	27,837	543
Forgery and counterfeiting	40,002	283	37,318	240
Fraud	93,008	1,240	82,308	1,128
Embezzlement	6,365	62	5,183	52

Table 5-2 represents data collected from the FBI's Uniform Crime Reports, 1972 to 1976. Before attempting an analysis of the adapted statistics, the following should be noted:

(1) The FBI data collected for the Uniform Crime Reports is voluntary data; that is, law enforcement agencies throughout the United States are under no legal or moral obligation to send their statistics to the FBI for compilation.

(2) Subsequent to the data being volunteered from various law enforcement agencies, note the total number of agencies that volunteered data for any particular year. For example, in 1972, only 6,195 law enforcement agencies supplied data (thus contributing to an inaccurate reflection of the situation).

(3) The elderly population has increased in the time period from 1972 to 1976.

152

Table 5–2 (Continued)

1974		1975		1976	
Agencies 5,298		Agencies 8,051		Agencies 10,119	
Estimated Population 134,082,000		Estimated Population 179,191,000		Estimated Population 175,499,000	
Total Arrests 18+	Total Arrests 60+	Total Arrests 18+	Total Arrests 60+	Total Arrests 18+	Total Arrests 60+
14,422	475	17,585	602	15,186	548
14,349	81	18,100	118	17,942	148
73,136	259	85,318	266	73,306	205
128,214	3,140	166,705	4,194	160,075	4,003
159,008	576	212,963	795	197,425	744
372,966	9,854	526,919	15,193	528,843	15,033
48,043	201	54,660	232	52,429	231
215,438	3,988	282,683	5,176	284,106	5,316
34,422	1,149	39,961	1,397	41,874	1,603
44,004	4,365	47,706	4,763	62,890	5,416
607,731	28,326	891,660	41,252	820,646	37,586
111,890	2,442	161,244	3,685	194,009	4,442
883,199	74,892	1,134,664	88,804	1,031,381	77,208
434,881	11,469	512,283	13,094	431,741	9,720
28,183	1,590	53,954	2,635	26,883	895
22,691	325	21,380	252	23,085	305
34,473	369	50,483	261	49,110	281
86,412	915	141,588	1,399	156,815	1,693
5,437	56	8,623	54	7,693	73

(4) Like all statistics, the FBI Uniform Crime Reports do not reflect the unreported crime. Probably one of the most unreported crimes is shoplifting—a major crime of the elderly.

Table 5-3 reflects data collected from the Jacksonville, Florida, Police Department. Obviously the number of crimes committed by the elderly has increased.

In 1973, Shimizu stated "[in Japan], the criminal trend of the aged appears to be very low (representing criminal rates less than one-tenth of that of the general population). For women, the criminal rate of the aged was slightly higher, though the trend was similar. Comparison of the present data with that of the western countries revealed a lower criminal ratio for the aged against total adult criminals in Japan than in the western countries."[21] With few studies and even less available data in the United States, it is imperative

Table 5–3 Arrests by Age[a] (Jacksonville, Florida)[22]

	1975		1976	
Crime	60–64	65+	60–64	65+
Homicide	1	1	1	3
Robbery	0	1	0	0
Aggravated assault	15	21	13	14
Breaking and entry	2	3	5	2
Larceny	34	43	49	31
Other assaults	5	0	3	6
Fraud, including worthless checks	3	2	5	3
Weapons processing	19	21	10	21
Sex offenses	9	6	6	10
Gambling	11	7	12	7
Driving under the influence	174	116	180	104
Drunkenness	61	25	121	81
Subtotal	334	246	405	282
TOTAL	580		687	

[a]Estimated population for the City of Jacksonville was 573,186 as of July 1, 1977. Estimated population of Jacksonville residents over 65 years of age was 48,020 as of July 1, 1976, or 8.38%.

to note what Shimizu hints at: though Japan considers the aged criminal a minimal threat, Shimizu reflects on the higher criminal ratio for the aged in western countries (United States included). Japan, an industrialized nation modeled after the United States, reflecting democratic principles and policies, has taken a giant step in this area of concern to criminologists and gerontologists alike. It is time for contemporary social scientists to look around them. Innovative studies are not necessarily restricted to the continental boundaries of the United States.

Though the above statistics are not mystifying or outrageous, they do tend to reflect the increase in elderly crime. (Keep in mind the discrepancies listed prior to Table 5-2.) Obviously, crime has increased in all age brackets during this five-year period; however, why has it increased in the elderly age bracket? Why are there so many elderly murderers? robbers? burglars? thieves? gamblers? Why are the elderly violating laws which they obeyed and lived by for years? Of course, without a longitudinal study, it cannot be determined whether the elderly criminals listed in the FBI data of Table 5-2 have always been criminals. For example, the sixty-five-year-old robber may have been the fifty-five-year-old robber in 1966, the forty-five-year-old robber in 1956, the 35-year-old robber in 1946, and so on. Most of the problems people have regarding statistics result from superficial understanding or an inability to completely understand the numbers. Though the data presented in this chapter are not conclusive, they are interesting. Why the 108 percent increase in elderly crime in St. Petersburg? Although it is not possible to generalize at this point, criminology and gerontology researchers should be sufficiently stimulated to study the problems presented here, so that a clearer picture may unfold in the future.

These statistics may reflect some triviality in the view of some academic skeptics, yet those concerned with practical issues in the real world of policy control and implementation of programs will avoid the question of triviality and turn to the importance of this issue—prevention of elderly persons turning to criminal behavior.

Why Elderly Criminals?

Discussed thus far in this chapter have been some criminological and gerontological theories and statistics on elderly criminals; also the suggestion has been made that there is some reason why elderly persons commit crime. As noted in Chapter 1, these theories can make a contribution to understanding an aged person's involvement in criminal activity. For example, retirement may be an extremely difficult adjustment for some elderly persons. Retirement could mean the elimination or drastic reduction of socially acceptable roles. It can be argued that the elderly, facing retirement and the knowledge that they are being "replaced" by young and efficient persons, escalate to a deviant identity—a reaction against their dominant social audience (the retirement age group). It can also be argued that the elderly no longer possess a shared symbolic universe; employers, family, and friends now treat them differently. In most cases, the elderly have fallen from the graces of those in society who assign societal roles and add meaning to life. This total disengagement from society could cause deviance in the form of criminal behavior.

Considering activity theory, what the elderly face upon retiring can be equated to the concept of blocked opportunity. Activity theorists feel that involvement (remaining active) in worklike roles is necessary for the elderly's adjustment to the golden years. Since most normal pathways become blocked to those who join the ranks of the elderly, activity in legitimate enterprises is essentially nonexistent. This frustrating situation could cause elderly persons to become active in other legitimate pathways in order to fulfill needed worklike roles.

Combined with the theories discussed are two other aspects which need to be mentioned. First, the elderly's lifetime occupational role is taken away at retirement, causing him to lose status in a number of ways. Second, unless he prepared himself for retirement financially (which a great majority do not), the everyday financial worries of survival become a great burden. When faced with the loss of status/roles and the loss of financial independence, he may very well feel rejected and frustrated in the situation in which he finds himself. All these theoretical concepts, combined with the reality of poor living standards in later life, may cause the elderly to strike back and commit crime. According to psychologists, when anyone faces dangerous or threatening situations, he either fights or runs. For the elderly person, fleeing from the harsh existence to which he has been exposed may come through death—an honorable and easy way out? Yet, other than suicide, there is no definite way to know when death will come. To fight is the logical, rational, and aggressive way to survive and beat the threat of a "poor life." Who can blame the elderly woman who shoplifts at the corner grocery store or the elderly gentleman who shoplifts at the drugstore? Who can blame the elderly individual who escapes from these harsh living conditions in a bottle of booze? Everyone is at fault for letting such a condition develop.

One final comment on what causes the elderly to turn to criminal behavior —loneliness. If there was ever an elderly's worst enemy, loneliness would have to top the list. After years of working, establishing relationships, friendships, and independence, the elderly face a life style which is totally new to them. The attention which once was focused upon them is no longer there. Companionships have dwindled or ceased to exist. Loneliness has become part of old age. One way to combat this loneliness is to be active and get involved. If the activity available to elderly persons is limited, then substitute activity will eventually be found. If criminal behavior is the result of such an activity search—an activity where companionship and attention once again become central to their lives—then crime it is! A few hypothetical illustrations of the most common crimes to which elderly people turn will help the student better understand the criminal response of the elderly in contemporary society. Remember, this refers to elderly criminals, people who for the most part have internalized legal societal norms/mores and have released themselves from these moral and legal internalizations in order to adjust and survive in their "golden years."

Larceny/Shoplifting

According to *Black's Law Dictionary*,[23] larceny is the fraudulent taking and carrying away of an object without claim of right, with intention of using it for one's own purposes (not the owner's) and without the owner's consent. The crime of shoplifting falls within this definition.

Larceny can be distinguished as either grand or petty. Grand larceny involves taking items worth more than fifty dollars, while petty larceny involves taking items valued under fifty dollars. Generally, crimes are either felonies or misdemeanors. Normally, grand larceny would be a felony (a more serious crime with a greater punishment, e.g., jail time, attached to it), and petty larceny would be a misdemeanor (a less serious crime which usually involves a fine or probation, but no jail time). The majority of elderly people who shoplift are committing petty larceny (a misdemeanor). Regardless of its nature, petty or grand, larceny is a crime. Shoplifting is against the law and those who violate the law should be punished for their actions, regardless of sex, race, or *AGE!*

Shoplifting has almost become a national pastime in America. It has become the individual's reaction to inflation and the high cost of living. People who shoplift have been referred to as avocational predators, "individuals who engage in property predation as a part-time activity to supplement their primary sources of income, which are legitimate."[24]

The elderly are hurt by inflation and price increases more than any other age group because the majority are living on fixed incomes, like social security. They therefore find it extremely difficult to provide themselves with the necessities for living—food, clothing, and shelter (including utilities). Faced with this type of situation, the elderly are striking back, or getting even. When given the opportunity to shoplift a pair of socks, a package of cookies or lunchmeat, or to eat an apple while pushing their cart through a supermarket, the elderly are doing it and rationalizing to themselves that it is OK because it is necessary for them to survive.

Isn't this a sad state of affairs when grandmothers and grandfathers are forced to revert to crime to provide for themselves? Yet it happens every day, and, unfortunately, the number of incidents increases, as well. Has society come to the aid of the financially stricken elderly population? Have the elderly been provided with a life style that would inhibit such criminal behavior? Are not all in society to blame? When does elderly crime stop and society's help begin? It had better start soon. The elderly shoplifter is not only a criminal, but a victim as well—a victim of society's "do nothing or do as little as possible" attitude toward the plight of the aged.

Fraud

Crimes of fraud come in many forms, for example, check forging, counterfeiting, writing bad checks, and embezzling. Whatever the form, the intent behind a fraudulent crime is to deceive another of money or property for one's own personal gain. Glaser describes individuals who have long conformed to the law, yet when faced with an unusual crisis in their lives, deviate from their conformity as crisis-vacillation predators.[25] Morris referred to these criminals as situational offenders.[26] Regardless of the label, the individual attempts to resolve the crisis through criminal acts.

An elderly person who decides to violate the law through fraudulent acts in order to make ends meet financially can do so relatively easily. In today's world people are constantly being bombarded with checking accounts, credit cards, easy loan payments. Indeed, some people have become so addicted to credit cards that they have become habitual spenders. The elderly who possess such credit are literally in the position to buy out the house.

There is usually an upper limit to each credit card. But even when a person can charge no more than $2,500 on each card, the total amount of purchases could easily exceed $10,000 very quickly. For an elderly person with a fixed income, this may be a very legitimate way to alleviate the burden of his needs. When he is confronted with payment, all he need do is file for bankruptcy. The companies who have been "taken" cannot collect any monies from welfare or social security checks. In short, many elderly have successfully defrauded companies. These companies will undoubtedly pass the costs of their losses on to all the consumers.

Fraud is an interesting way for the elderly to combat a poor economic existence. Can the answer be to take away the elderly's credit cards upon retirement? One should hope not. After all, wouldn't that be age discrimination and subsequently unconstitutional? The impersonal organizations which issue credit cards can become very easy marks for the elderly who perceive their situation as hopeless and strike out at all those around them who "can afford" the loss.

Drunkenness

In medical jurisprudence, drunkenness is the condition a person puts himself in through the consumption of intoxicating beverages, resulting in irrational conduct and mannerisms. More literally known as "the drunk," this person escapes from the real world through liquor, beer, or wine. It is an attempt to relieve the pressures of his existence.

Recently, drunkenness has been referred to as a victimless crime—a crime which affects no one but the person involved in the act. Depending on the locale, drunkenness may or may not be a legal crime. However, it can be assumed to be a moral, emotional, or psychological crime. Drunkenness is a behavior which is readily accessible and usually very inexpensive. An elderly person with a fixed income could easily afford the habit. What is causing the elderly to turn to the bottle? An answer could be the loneliness caused by disengagement or lack of activity; however, it is more likely a response to the total situation. The loss of status, work roles, independence, financial freedom, attention, companionship, and respect for self eventually erode an elderly person and cause him to engage in drunkenness. A legal crime? It depends on the location. A shame? Definitely. Society has caused this problem and it is up to society to alleviate the consequences of the elderly's condition.

PERCEIVING ELDERLY CRIME AS A SOCIAL PROBLEM

Assuming elderly crime to be the gravest of all social problems, we can attempt to resolve such a social ill. Using a guidance approach described by Etzioni,[27] let us plug in the problem of elderly criminality to see if prevention is possible.

The first question we must ask ourselves is, "Are we concerned about elderly crime?" If we are, then we must determine whether our concern stems from subjective or objective considerations. If the problem's existence is due to only subjective concerns, the problem would exist merely in our minds, hearts and emotions. Although our concern would be deep, a solution to the problem of elderly criminality would be difficult to engage. On the other hand, if the problem's existence stemmed from objective concerns, such as rising elderly crime data, inflation, fixed incomes, or mandatory retirement, then we could realistically employ measures to eliminate the cause(s) of the problem.

Once we have objectively determined that elderly crime is a social problem in need of resolution, we must further decide where to aim our measures to eradicate the problem. Should we concentrate on the elderly themselves or should we focus on societal and government policies and programs? If we assume that people, especially the elderly, are inherently law-abiding and they try to remain that way, but that governmental disregard and social conditions force a criminal response from the elderly, then our measures to prevent elderly crime must be focused at governmental and societal institutions—who control, or are at least responsive to and responsible for, inflation, fixed income, mandatory retirement, etc.

So how can we go about preventing elderly crime? How can we zero in on those public institutions responsible for the elderly's state of affairs? What do we need to persuade society and government to initiate programs that will reduce the potential for elderly criminality? Continuing with Etzioni's concepts, we must concentrate on the following areas: knowledge, goal setting, organization and consensus—all of which operate simultaneously.

Prior to convincing society and the government of the elderly crime problem, we must first gather sufficient knowledge to demonstrate that such a problem exists. Obtaining reliable and valid data will further substantiate our objective proclamation of the problem's existence. Once we have accumulated an abundance of facts and figures, it will then be necessary to make sense of the information by synthesizing and interpreting the raw assemblage of facts for summary and presentation; thus, the knowledge gathered will not fall upon deaf ears or be easily refuted as a matter of statistical interpretation. The data must be as conclusive as possible.

The formulation of a theory to present the data, with recommendations to test a hypothesis to resolve the problem, should be incorporated. Though a theory to eradicate the problem of elderly crime may be weak due to normative underpinnings and the complexity of social problems, it may nonetheless provide the basis for research and stimulate a resolution for the problem. Knowledge and theories which utilize knowledge are useless, unless we can convince policy makers that our measures will be successful. Before attempting to initiate a nationwide program to eliminate elderly crime, it is necessary to test the theory (based on our data) and possibly reformulate the program before committing millions of dollars to a questionable venture. An evaluation of our program on a small-scale operation will aid in its overall adoption into social policy. The feedback from our program may point to a solution which lies elsewhere or is effective only in a particular area, for example, suburban vs. urban crime. Yet, once we have tested our program and found it appropriate for the reduction of elderly criminality, we are ready for the next developmental stage in the solution—goal setting.

Can we expect societal and governmental institutions, once shown the problem, to immediately initiate programs designed to alleviate it? Assuming bureaucratic tendencies toward nonhaste, how can we push along those responsible for deciding which measures to implement? How can we prevent these institutions from merely paying lip service to a program designed to reduce elderly crime? One way to ensure success is to pressure such institutions to translate "yes, we'll do something," into specific commitments of action. Changing general acknowledgements of a problem into working solutions often takes time. In setting the goals, we must ensure a logical, step-by-step introduction to resolving the issue. We can't initiate programs overnight and expect all of society to understand the rationale for implementing such programs. A specific commitment to a goal, such as the elimination of mandatory retirement, must be nurtured if we are to experience success of the goal and acceptance by the citizenry. If it hadn't been for long hard preparation and determination on the part of those connected with the Pepper Bill, mandatory retirement would not have changed from sixty-five to seventy years of age.

We've gathered the knowledge about our problem and set realistic goals, but the attainment of our goals is dependent upon our ability to organize. Even the best-laid plans will fall by the wayside if not properly organized and implemented. Implementation occurs with the aid of compliance, which comes in many forms, most notably coercion, utilitarian, and normative means. While coercion relies on force and utilitarian on financial incentives, normative means employ existing beliefs as the foundation for compliance. Without doubt, the greatest advantage of gaining compliance through normative means is its ability to heighten commitment. There is no more deeply embedded compliance than that achieved by normative measures. Though we've chosen normative compliance to aid in the organization of our goals, we must still determine which of the following will facilitate a strong commitment to our program to reduce elderly crime: (1) private organizations, (2) government, or (3) voluntary, nonprofit organizations.

Noting that profit plays a key role in any activity that private organizations enter, what would they have to gain from a program which helped reduce elderly crime? What would they have to lose by not getting involved in such a program? Additional monetary loss through crimes such as shoplifing? Obviously, these questions deserve much thought. And what of the government, the supposed guardians of those who are without the power to gain support for their programs? Are they efficient and internally organized to operate a "successful" program (one which does not have the usual bureaucratic trappings)?

We will find that both the public and private sector have obvious failings if we are to utilize a compliance strategy based on normative means. Thus, the voluntary, nonprofit organizations are our most likely candidates for organizing and implementing our goals, for it is here that norms play an important role. For instance, the American Association of Retired Persons (AARP), Gray Panthers, and thousands of senior citizen groups have one thing in common—the advancement of the aged person within society. These organizations possess the naturally normative compliance to a program aimed at reducing a problem which a greater number of them will need to face as they grow older (and as current societal and governmental failings continue, e.g., fixed incomes).

Do they have the power to organize and implement goals to reduce elderly criminality? By far, their mobilization outsurpasses any efforts made by the government or private organizations' utilization of power. The aged's voluntary, nonprofit affiliation to organizations is normatively based and they know their priority—themselves. With the government, we never know what priority will be given to eliminating a particular social problem. If the problem's existence is such that the government feels obligated, they will assume responsibility. But the question remains—for how long? And the private sector—what is the cost-benefit? The ability of these voluntary, nonprofit groups to elicit government action depends on their size, cohesiveness, mobility, and allies to the cause. Obviously, the size of such organizations is tremendous. As noted earlier in this book, the aged will number approximately 20,000,000 by the twenty-first century. Although it might seem unlikely for such a large group to mobilize their numbers behind an issue or program, the fact remains they can (especially when there is a normative commitment to the program). It would be curious to note how many letters and postcards flooded the politicians' offices by elderly and nonelderly constituents, proving their cohesiveness to the end of mandatory retirement at age sixty-five.

The nonelderly are the elderly's best allies. They have a stake in programs which affect the elderly. The nonelderly have shown consensus regarding elderly concerns. They have both a reallocative and symbolic stake in eliminating the causes which force the elderly to a life of crime. Reallocatively, they have an interest in maintaining their same level of existence in later years—not wanting to face inflation with fixed incomes. Symbolically, the nonelderly share the same beliefs and values (again, a normative coalition) regarding problems to which the elderly are exposed.

Etzioni has described and enabled us to discuss how the prevention of elderly crime may be approached—by gathering the data, organizing ourselves, setting goals, utilizing our power and gaining consensus to introduce programs to reduce or eliminate the opportunity or reasons for elderly crime. We are left with the choice of accomplishing the above to defeat one of the gravest social ills the elderly may be forced to face—criminality.

PREVENTING ELDERLY CRIME

We are not at a total loss. Elderly crime is and will continue to be most of all a response to the elderly's present economic condition. Closely following the poor economic conditions are personal, emotional and psychological pressures which persuade the elderly to engage in criminal behavior. Society has let this condition develop. As a whole, we no longer care or concern ourselves with the elderly as we did in the past. Historically, the elderly were treated with more respect than is now afforded to them. This societal disregard for the elderly has been influenced by (1) a weakening of kinship ties, (2) a rapidly changing industrial and technological society, (3) a growing elderly population, and (4) American culture's dominant emphasis on productivity.[28]

The stress and lack of opportunity to reintegrate themselves into the modern culture is posing new and increasing difficulties for the elderly. Our culture would never allow treatment of the elderly as the Hopi, Creek, and Crow Indians and the Bushmen of South Africa once did (lead the aged person to a hut specifically built away from the village for the purpose of abandoning him, leaving only a little food and water).[29] Nor, like the Eskimo, would we "persuade the old to go and lie in the snow and wait for death... or shut them into an igloo...or forget them on an ice-floe when the tribe is out fishing."[30] Yet, does our culture treat the elderly as the Yaghan tribe? The Yaghans, now extinct, used to treat their aged with respect and reverence —always providing the elderly with the best of what meager means were available.[31]

Yes, different cultures have treated the aged in numerous ways. Some cultures have killed, some have respected. Which is ours? As Simon de Beauvoir points out, "What are called civilized nations apply the same methods: killing alone is forbidden, unless it is disguised."[32] Are we killing our elderly? Are we forcing the elderly to engage in crime to supplement their meager existence? The most logical way to prevent elderly crime is by providing for the needs of the elderly. This must include all the needs— food, clothing, shelter, love, compassion, and attention. Just as the elderly must get involved in the criminal justice system, we must get involved with the elderly. We can no longer turn our backs on the problem of elderly crime. There is no need for it. Of all crime, elderly crime can be resolved so easily. The elderly, for the most part, have lived law-abiding lives. All that is necessary to prevent them from committing crime is to ensure that their later years will be void of frustration, extreme poverty, and aggravation. For the younger criminals experiencing these same feelings, it will take more than providing life's necessities; but for the elderly, it may make the difference between a life of crime or a life!

SUMMARY

Have we proposed a theory for elderly crime? No. But we have engaged in a speculative discussion of why the elderly turn to crime when faced with few alternatives. Disengagement theory has shown why the elderly become frustrated with life; activity theory has shown how to eliminate that frustration. The criminological theories of cultural deviance, strain, conflict, and labeling have enabled us to comprehend some of the bases behind criminal behavior. In short, we have provided information and hopefully stimulated thought. Though studies indicate the elderly are not engaging in much serious crime,[33] the level of misdemeanant offenses, such as shoplifting, is on the increase. Generally, the elderly are being driven to crime. Who is to blame? Should the elderly criminal be punished in the traditional sense of the word? Or should society embark on an effort to eliminate elderly crime by eliminating the social and economic conditions which encompass the "golden years"?

Due to the nature of the speculative discussion of elderly crime, criticism is expected. However, we hope for constructive criticism, which will enable the growth and development of projects to eliminate elderly criminalization. Criticism from those who do not understand, or refuse to understand, the forces which lead the elderly to choose crime, will only add to that element known in social science circles as "scientific ignorance."

QUESTIONS

1. Do you feel elderly criminalization is an important issue?
2. Why has there been little research involving elderly criminals?
3. What is cultural deviance?
4. Is Miller's lower class milieu a sufficient explanation of cultural deviance?
5. Explain strain theory.
6. Discuss capitalism, surplus population, and superstructure as they pertain to conflict theory.
7. What issues do labelling theorists consider relevant?
8. Will disengagement from society cause the elderly to turn to crime?

9. Will remaining active after retirement prevent the elderly from criminal behavior?

10. Is there evidence to show an upswing in elderly criminalization?

11. Is elderly crime a consequence of the elderly's victimization (within society)?

12. Why do elderly people engage in shoplifting? fraud? drunkenness?

13. Can financial solvency prevent elderly crime?

14. What emotional and psychological problems can influence an elderly person to commit criminal acts?

15. How can we prevent elderly crime?

SUGGESTED READINGS

William Chamblis, "Functional and Conflict Theories of Crime" (New York, N.Y.: MSS Modular Publications, Module 17, 1974), pp. 1-23.

Albert K. Cohen, *Delinquent Boys* (Glencoe, Ill.: The Free Press, 1955).

Fred Cottrell and Robert C. Atchley, *Retired Women: A Preliminary Report* (Oxford, Ohio: Scripps Foundation, 1969).

Elaine Cumming, L. R. Dean, D. S. Newell and I. McCaffrey, "Disengagement—A Tentative Theory of Aging," *Sociometry,* Vol. 23, 1960, pp. 23-5.

Robert J. Havighurst, "Successful Aging," Richard H. Williams, Clark Tibbitts and Wilma Donahue (eds), *Processes of Aging* (New York, N.Y.: Atherton Press, 1963), Vol. 1, pp. 299-320.

George L. Maddox, Jr., "Themes and Issues in Sociological Theories of Human Aging," *Human Development,* Vol. 13, 1970, pp. 17-27.

George L. Maddox, Jr., "Disengagement Theory: A Critical Evaluation," *Gerontologist,* Vol. 4, 1964, pp. 80-2.

David Matza, *Becoming Deviant* (Englewood Cliffs, N.J.: Prentice-Hall, Inc., 1969).

Richard Quinney, *The Social Reality of Crime* (Boston, Mass.: Little Brown and Co., 1970).

Edwin Schur, *Labelling Deviant Behavior* (New York, N.Y.: Harper and Row Publishers, 1971).

Steven Spitzer, "Toward a Marian Theory of Deviance," *Social Problems,* June 1975, pp. 638-51.

E. H. Sutherland, and Donald Cressey, *Criminology,* 8th ed. (Philadelphia, Pa.: J. B. Lippincott Co., 1970).

Ian Taylor, Paul Walton, and Jock Young, *The New Criminology* (New York, N.Y.: Harper and Row Publishers, 1973).

Austin Turk, "Conflict and Criminality," *American Sociological Review,* Vol. 31, June, 1966.

NOTES

1. "Another Victim Freed," *The Tallahasee Democrat,* Tallahassee, Florida, February 17, 1977.

2. Walter Miller, "Lower Class Culture as a Generating Milieu of Gang Delinquency," *Journal of Social Issues,* Vol. 14, 1958, pp. 5–19.

3. Emile Durkheim, *Suicide* (Glencoe, Ill.: The Free Press, 1951), and *The Division of Labor in Society* (New York, N.Y.: The Free Press, 1964).

4. Robert Merton, *Social Theory and Social Structure* (New York, N.Y.: The Free Press, 1957).

5. Richard Cloward and Lloyd Ohlin, *Delinquency and Opportunity* (New York, N.Y.: The Free Press, 1960).

6. Nanette J. Davis, *Sociological Constructions of Deviance: Perceptions and Issues in the Field* (Dubuque, Iowa: Wm. C. Brown Co., 1975).

7. William Bonger, *Criminality and Economic Conditions* (Bloomington, Indiana: University Press, 1969).

8. David Gordon, "Capitalism, Class and Crime in America," *Crime and Delinquency,* April 1973, pp. 163–186.

9. Karl Marx, *Theories of Surplus Value,* trans. G. A. Bonner and Emile Burns (New York, N.Y.: A. M. Kelley, 1969).

10. John Lofland, *Deviance and Identity* (Englewood Cliffs, N.J.: Prentice-Hall, Inc. 1969).

11. Edwin M. Lemart, *Human Deviance, Social Problems and Social Control* (Englewood Cliffs, N.J.: Prentice-Hall, Inc., 1967).

12. Jack Botwinick, Ph.D., *Aging and Behavior: A Comprehensive Integration of Research Findings* (New York, N.Y.: Springer Publ. Co., Inc., 1973), p. 52.

13. Robert C. Atchley, *The Social Forces in Later Life: An Introduction to Social Gerontology* (Belmont, Calif.: Wadsworth Publishing Co., Inc., 1972), p. 32.

14. Ibid., p. 32.

15. Margaret Clark and Barbara G. Anderson, *Culture and Aging: An Anthropological Study of Older Americans* (Springfield, Ill.: Charles C. Thomas Publisher, 1967), p. 349.

16. Atchley, op cit., p. 35.

17. J. A. Kuypers and V. L. Bengston, "Competence and Social Breakdown: A Social-Psychology View of Aging," *Human Development,* Vol. 16, No. 2, 1973, pp. 37–49.

18. *Crime and the Elderly,* St. Petersburg Police Department, St. Petersburg, Florida, 1974–1975.

19. Ibid.

20. Adapted from *Uniform Crime Reports,* Washington, D.C.: Federal Bureau of Investigation, 1972–1976.

21. *Arrest Analysis,* Jacksonville Police Department, Jacksonville, Florida, 1975–1976.

22. Makoto Shimizu, "A Study on the Crimes of the Aged in Japan," *Acta Criminologiae et Medicinae Legalis Japonica,* Vol. 39, No. 5/6, December 1973, p. 212.

23. Henry Campbell Black, *Black's Law Dictionary,* revised fourth edition, (St. Paul, Minnesota: West Publishing Co., 1968).

24. Daniel Glaser, *Adult Crime and Social Policy* (Englewood Cliffs, N.J.: Prentice-Hall, Inc., 1972), p. 56.

25. D. Glaser, op cit., p. 58.

26. Albert Morris, "The Comprehensive Classification of Adult Offenders," *Journal of Criminal Law, Criminology and Police Science,* Vol. 56, June 1965, pp. 197–202.

27. Amitai Etzioni, *Social Problems* (Englewood Cliffs, New Jersey: Prentice-Hall, Inc., 1976).

28. M. Clark and B. G. Anderson, op cit., pp. 13–17.

29. Simone de Beauvoir, *The Coming of Age* (New York, N.Y.: Putnam/London, England: Andre Deutsch, Ltd./Paris, France: Editions Gallimard, 1972), p. 77.

30. Ibid.

31. Ibid.

32. Ibid., p. 131.

33. George Sunderland, "The Older American: Police Problem or Police Asset," *F.B.I. Law Enforcement Bulletin,* Vol. 45, No. 8, August 1976, p. 5.

Chapter 6

Summary and Recommendations

Here at the completion of our reading, what have we learned? What can we recommend? Is the elderly American vulnerable to crime? Is it realistic to assume crime prevention is the key to reducing elderly victimization? Are volunteer projects within the criminal justice system a viable approach for keeping the elderly active beyond retirement? Can elderly crime be reduced? All the answers are YES!

Public opinion polls and surveys have continually earmarked crime as a major concern. Although all people are potential victims of crime, the elderly are more so than many other age groups. With the population of aged persons increasing each year (and the crime rate as well), the study of the venerable (vulnerable) Americans has become a necessity. In what way can the issue of crime and gerontology be effectively approached? The following recommendations seem a most logical response: (1) continuing education programs specifically for the elderly, and (2) developing techniques for improving elderly victimization reporting. Although other recommendations will be discussed, these provide the stability necessary for research into this area.

CONTINUING EDUCATION FOR THE ELDERLY

Education does not stop when a person acquires an A.A., B.A., M.A. or Ph.D. degree. If anything, acquiring these degrees should be a springboard for continual learning through life. Education is not terminal. As old age is approached, people should educate themselves to the problems which surround this particular phase of life. As has been explained throughout, the aged are more prone to criminal victimization than any other age group. Yet, something can be done about it. Elderly persons should not sit at home waiting to be burglarized, nor remain prisoners within their homes for fear of being victimized on the streets. Criminal justice education, specifically designed for crime prevention techniques, is a key to eliminating the social, psychological, physical, and economic impact of victimization. Once the elderly are properly educated, the chances of their being victimized will be substantially reduced, and their fear of crime may disappear altogether.

Continuing education can aid the elderly as well as the community. Community service is a basic function of universities and colleges. Community service provides cultural, recreational, and educational programs for the benefit (advancement) or pleasure of community residents. Through the use of seminars, workshops, conferences, films, and courses, local residents are able to gain a sense of community and an understanding of problems germane to their locality.

168

A particular program which bears the responsibility of community service is one involved in continuing adult education. Unfortunately, there is one adult group which rarely benefits from such a program—the elderly. This is a group that continuing adult education programs have rarely acknowledged. Along with all who have jumped on the "crime and the elderly" bandwagon, the continuing adult education programs are now in a position to jump also. It is not too often that there appears a workable solution to two contemporary issues of interest to colleges, community residents, and particularly the aged. Yet, by offering a course involving the issues of crime and gerontology, a dual goal can be accomplished: (1) universities, colleges, and community colleges can perform a much-needed community service, and (2) the course can actively involve the elderly in the much-publicized problem of crime. A continuing adult education course involving crime and gerontology can expand an educational institution's urban involvement by offering a new curriculum and foster a close working relationship with community groups (as well as criminal justice agencies).[1] To be effective, a course on crime and gerontology needs to deal with all the issues raised in this book, particularly (1) the elderly victims, (2) crime prevention programs for the elderly, and (3) the importance of the aged as volunteers within the various criminal justice agencies.

Properly developed and administered, a continuing adult education course on crime and gerontology can enable the aged to battle their fear of victimization and learn what to do to prevent victimization, thus enabling a fulfilling life in their later years. It must also be noted here that continuing education for the elderly is not the responsibility of colleges and universities alone. There are many local, state, federal, civic, and religious groups/organizations which have expressed a concern and a willingness to become involved in the elderly's struggle with crime.

IMPROVING ELDERLY CRIME REPORTING

For the young or old, reporting crimes to the police has not been successful. Approximately 50 percent of all crimes go unreported. Some of the reasons for not reporting crimes are (1) the victim not wanting the offender to get in trouble with the law (the offender may be a friend or relative), (2) the fear of reprisal by the offender, (3) the feeling that police are ineffective, (4) the confusion or lack of knowledge of exactly how to report a crime, and (5) the development of hostile feelings toward the criminal justice system (victim might feel the penalty would not be harsh enough).[2] These reasons for not reporting crime can be overcome through education and/or training.

Within an educational setting as the one just described, reasons for reporting crimes can be discussed and internalized, and techniques to make reporting more effective can be demonstrated and practiced. Some reasons for reporting crime are (1) a moral responsibility, (2) the possibility of keeping an offender from victimizing someone else (often criminals keep committing crime because they keep getting away with it), and (3) the fact that the more involved an elderly person is in the criminal justice system, the more communication between the elderly and law enforcement, courts, and corrections will develop.

Regarding techniques for improving reporting of crimes, the elderly can be taught to (1) properly identify all valuable personal property, such as engraving belongings with social security number, (2) learn how to describe a suspicious person, remembering common but important details, such as sex, race, age, height, weight, clothing, distinguishing scars, type of automobile, and direction of escape, (3) realize that, when victimized, reporting to the police is only a first step, they should also report to organizations (for example, victims of mail order fraud should notify the post office, victims of swindles should notify the bank), and (4) seek support from religious and civic organizations; they will provide help when called upon.

The point which must be reinforced throughout education/training programs is that the elderly victim need not face the victimization alone. There are individuals and organizations to help; all the elderly must do is make contact. Whatever information an elderly person has regarding a crime might be the key in solving the crime and apprehending the offender. As mentioned earlier in this text, police awareness of the problems the elderly face and their subsequent treatment of elderly victims will foster or hinder future reporting, regardless of all the reasons why elderly victims should report crimes or all the techniques learned in reporting crimes.

GENERAL RECOMMENDATIONS

Realistically, all individuals are potential victims of crime and of the process of aging. Concerns involving crime and the elderly should be aimed in the following directions.

(1) *Continuing education programs.* As discussed, continuing education programs for the elderly specifically dealing with crime prevention is undoubtedly the most feasible way to get the elderly involved and to get crime prevention material to the elderly. This can be accomplished through the community service aspect of colleges and universities as well as neighborhood senior citizen groups and civic and religious organizations genuinely concerned with elderly criminal victimization. Particular attention should be focused on (a) when criminals are more likely to commit crimes and which type of crimes, (b) how to make the home less penetrable and more secure, (c) tips on preventing purse snatching, pickpocketing, and swindling tech-

niques, (d) what to observe about a suspicious person or activity, and (e) distributing educational pamphlets on all areas of crime prevention.[3]

(2) *Improvement of techniques/rationales for elderly victimization reporting.* A basis for cooperation should evolve within the community. Educational institutions, media, local organizations, and criminal justice agencies should hold meetings, seminars, lectures, courses, and community relation programs focusing on improving the reporting of crimes by elderly victims. For example: (a) brief radio and television announcements which urge the reporting of crimes can be presented as public service announcements, (b) a special telephone number can be designated specifically for reporting crimes, or a secret witness hotline created for the elderly who desire to report a crime but wish to remain uninvolved (it's a step in the right direction), and (c) agencies such as the Better Business Bureau and Chamber of Commerce or newspapers can be informed about recurring swindles occurring in the elderly community.[4] In addition, the development of self-report studies and victimization surveys would enable a more thorough picture of the reality of crime and its relationship to the elderly.

(3) *Special research.* The public should not be in favor of just pouring dollars on a social problem, as Johnson's War on Poverty, for example. Therefore a closer analysis of successful crime prevention programs is needed to enable fiscal managers to spend funds more effectively. There is overall agreement that a problem does exist regarding crime and the aged, e.g., the amount of LEAA money recently poured into several state programs specifically for the elderly. An important question left to answer is, "How can this money be spent effectively and efficiently?"

(4) *Involvement.* Keep in mind that the mere spending of money is not, in and of itself, a guarantee of success in programs involving crime and the elderly. Dedication on the part of criminal justice professionals and volunteers involved in the programs is the key to a workable solution—reduction, possibly eradication, of crimes against the aged. There is enough knowledge to adequately deal with crimes against the aged now. If future research provides a more fruitful approach in dealing with the problem, then it can be implemented. However, we cannot sit idly by. Neither can we wait for criminal justice agencies to get off their "high horses." There is not enough initiative on the part of criminal justice agencies to disseminate and implement currently successful programs, especially those which employ the elderly as volunteers. Valuable resources can no longer be wasted; the elderly must be enjoined in the criminal justice ranks.

(5) *Interdisciplinary study.* Criminal justice professionals are not the only ones who can provide input to this problem of elderly victimization (and criminalization). For example, the economist can provide valuable information on the cost/benefit analysis of crime prevention and volunteer programs; the historian can develop perspectives on the local needs and

community habits of the elderly; the political scientist can provide for an in-depth study of the aged's political power and proper use of that power; and many other disciplines can be actively involved in research, theory, and implementing ideas. The psychologist, sociologist, social worker, and, of course, the criminologist, and gerontologist all have something positive to offer in the study of crime and the elderly. It is time to begin to foster the interchange of ideas and concepts in the hope of accumulating scientifically-based knowledge regarding this issue.

(6) *Harsher penalties/swifter punishment.* Criminals often victimize the elderly because it is easy to do and the chances of apprehension are slim. For criminals who victimize the elderly (who are not able to protect themselves as well as other age groups), the trial should be swift (not giving the elderly a chance to back out of pressing charges or grow tired of the long delay) and the sentence should be the maximum (even for first offenders). If the criminals who prey upon the elderly know that society is serious about this type of crime, the possibility exists of reducing the extent of elderly victimization.

(7) *Victim compensation.* Criminal justice authorities have concentrated on the offender and paid little attention to the victim. This condition has lasted much too long. With all the millions of dollars that has been poured into rehabilitation of the criminals, yet failed (the recidivism rate has not been drastically reduced), there must be funds available for the innocent bystander, the victim. Crime victim programs are relatively new, California being the first of the states to introduce its program in 1965, followed by New York in 1966, and Hawaii in 1967.[5] At present, less than half of the states have some form of victim compensation program. Victims are tax-payers, and, as such, should voice their feelings and rights concerning compensation to their legislatures and representatives at once. Although elderly victims suffer worse losses than victims in other age groups, all victims can unite. The time is ripe—victims are being heard.

(8) *Home security.* Home security is of the utmost importance to the elderly. The following recommendations were made to the U.S. Congress.

(a) Title XX of the Social Security Act should be amended to include among the services eligible for federal assistance the installation of devices that will prevent unauthorized entry and promote the security of the elderly in their homes.

(b) Title II, Part B, Section 222 (A) (12) of the Economic Opportunity Act of 1964, should be amended to include the installation of security devices and other minor modifications to improve the security in homes of elderly residents.

(c) Title III, Section 305 (b) (4) of the Older Americans Act of 1965 should be amended to provide for broader assistance under the residential repair and renovation programs to include construction modifications and the installation of security devices. Also, Section 308 (a) (1) (A) should be amended to include construction modifications and the installation of devices that will promote the security of the elderly in their homes.[6]

The above are just a few legislative recommendations made *In Search of Security*. Other recommendations involving Home Security are made to the (a) Department of Housing and Urban Development, (b) Law Enforcement Assistance Administration, (c) Administration on Aging, and (d) local government agencies. For a more complete picture of what recommendations are currently pending in Congress and government agencies, you are urged to contact your congressional representative and provide support for such legislative recommendations.

(9) *Films*. The most explosive media today are television and films. Films offer the uniqueness of visual and audible stimuli; thus, the viewer can grasp the material quicker and the issues become more salient. The following film topics are suggested:

(a) Elderly Victimization. A film depicting why the elderly are more prone to victimization. It should be filled with personal stories, examples, and illustrations showing how and why violent crimes, property crimes, and confidence games are committed against the elderly. An integral part of this film should be devoted to the subject of fear of crime among the elderly and how such fear can be eliminated.

(b) Elderly Crime Prevention. A film which illustrates step-by-step directions of how to prevent being a victim, e.g., methods to prevent residential burglary, operation identification, methods to prevent the purse snatcher, bunco prevention, and how to discourage the fast-talking con artist. This film would show a crime and then proceed to explain how the crime could have been prevented—which is often nothing more than common sense.

(c) Elderly Volunteers. A film which addresses the positive aspects of elderly volunteers within the criminal justice system, focusing on (1) where to volunteer, (2) setting up local volunteer projects, (3) how to deal with inhibited and unresponsive criminal justice agencies, and (4) training the elderly for volunteer duty. This film should illustrate the frustration the elderly may encounter in trying to volunteer, followed by the acceptance of the volunteer and all the responsibilities and problems both the criminal justice agency and the volunteer will have to face.

(d) Police and the Aged Victim. A film which includes (1) identification of the aged population within a community, (2) development of special law enforcement concerning the elderly, and (3) designing a program for police-older victim relations. The film would actually spell out what the cop should do at the scene of the crime, so as not to alienate the elderly victim. The police are the criminal justice component the elderly first encounter when victimized; therefore, it is mandatory that the police be responsive and aware of the special problems and needs the elderly victim experiences.

(e) Developing Law Enforcement Prevention for the Elderly. A film which (1) develops a crime prevention program for the elderly, more specifically, lay out plans on how a police department can initiate a special elderly crime prevention unit within the police department, (2) teaches law enforcement administrators how to appreciate and productively use the aged volunteer, and (3) increases each patrolman's knowledge of the aged, thereby ridding the law enforcement officer of the stereotype image of the elderly.

Films are an expressive way to make a point. The above are ideas, merely focal points, for a unique presentation of the problems involved in elderly victimization.

(10) *Recommendation for recommenders.* It is all very well to recommend a project or program for the elderly in their dealings with crime, but before jumping onto the bandwagon, a careful analysis should be sought to determine whether such a problem exists in a community.

(a) First, collect the data. Determine where the elderly population lives within the community and accumulate information regarding sex, age, income level, etc. This data will be useful when deciding which program to implement from a cost/benefit analysis.

(b) Second, acquire help from community organizations. Make sure there will be sufficient support for the program once it is operationalized. If possible, use volunteers from these organizations in the collection of data.

(c) Third, estimate the cost of the program. Are there local, state, or federal funds available through grants or stipends? Will funds be donated from the organizations providing help? Will other organizations donate funds instead of services? A good program will fail if there is not enough money to keep it going.

(d) Fourth, evaluate the program. This will ensure that the program is accomplishing its objectives. If evaluative experts have not donated their services, it might be necessary to employ them.[7]

These general recommendations should provide the necessary stimulus for research and development in the crime and gerontology area. If the author has succeeded in doing nothing more than broadening the reader's interest throughout this text, it has been enough. With time, all will realize the significance of Crime and Gerontology.

STUDENT PROJECTS

(1) Organize a crime prevention/crime assistance seminar for local elderly groups. Invite local experts in crime prevention and victim assistance to sit on a panel to provide information and respond to audience questions and concerns.

(2)   Prepare and send out an elderly victimization survey. Determine if there is a need for elderly victimization programs in your area or within specific areas of your town, e.g., central business district. Inform local law enforcement officials and politicians of your results and offer possible recommendations.

(3)   Elicit responses from various criminal justice agencies on the possibility of using elderly volunteers in their organizations. If the agencies seem positive to such a suggestion, inform your local office for the aging, volunteering your services to put a program together. If the response seems negative, attempt to determine the cause of the negativity.

(4)   Contact your local politicians and inform them of your concern over elderly victimization. Ask for information regarding currently existing programs to reduce elderly victimization. If necessary, and within reason, organize a legal demonstration to focus attention on the problem.

(5)   Does your state have a victim compensation program? How long has t been in operation? How much funding is available? Are they educating he elderly public of their existence? How does an elderly victim apply for compensation? How is the program administered?

(6)   Organize a few students and volunteer a weekend to home improvement for an elderly resident in need of home crime prevention. If necessary, contact federal and state agencies for possible funding or aid.

(7)   Produce a documentary film on the problems of crime and the elderly. Utilize the information you have gathered from the above projects or personal research as the basis for your film.

(8)   Interview elderly persons convicted of noncapital felonies and misdemeanors. Write a paper presenting the elderly rationalizations for turning to crime.

(9)   Develop an interdisciplinary workshop on the problems the aged face, e.g., politically, sociologically, biologically, criminologically, gerontologically, etc. Begin an annual conference for concerns of the elderly on your campus.

(10)   Become involved in a senior citizen's group in whatever capacity you can.

OVERVIEW

Chapter 1 briefly synopsized the issues concerning crime and gerontology, giving an introduction to the ensuing chapters which dealt with each concern in more detail. Why the elderly are more vulnerable to crime than other age groups was reasoned in Chapter 2. Chapter 3 illustrated crime prevention for the elderly, and Chapter 4 discussed the issue of elderly volunteers. The importance of research in the area of the aged as criminals was instigated in Chapter 5.

It is time for the Criminal Justice System to consider appropriate policy to deal with crime and the aged. There is no question that research is needed. It is time for talk to subside and the various criminal justice components to focus their attention on the removal of the word "vulnerable" in reference to our most venerable citizens.

QUESTIONS

1. Which two recommendations are the strongest for effectively dealing with all the issues of crime and the elderly? Why?

2. Are continuing education programs for the elderly realistic?

3. Who is responsible for implementing continuing education programs? and what purposes would such programs achieve?

4. How can elderly victimization reporting be improved?

5. Continue the list of recommendations suggested in this chapter. Be innovative.

SUGGESTED READINGS

James Brooks, "Compensating Victims of Crime: The Recommendations of Program Administrators," *Law and Society Review,* Spring, 1973.

John E. Conklin, "Dimensions of Community Response to the Crime Problem," *Social Problems,* XVII, Winter, 1971, pp. 373–84.

Criminal Victimization in the U.S. (1975), Vol. 1, National Crime Panel Survey Report, U.S. Department of Justice, LEAA, May 1975.

NOTES

1. Martin D. Jenkins and Bernard H. Ross, "The Urban Involvement of Higher Education," *Journal of Higher Education,* Vol. XLVI, No. 4, July/August, 1975.

2. Sharon Baggett and Marvin Ernst, "From Research to Application—Development of Police and Older Adult Training Modules," *The Police Chief,* February, 1977, p. 35.

3. Raymon Forston and James Kitchens, *Criminal Victimization of the Aged: The Houston Model Neighborhood Area, Community Report #1,* Center for Community Services, School of Community Service, North Texas State University, Denton, Texas, 1974, pp. 41–2.

4. Forston and Kitchens, op cit., pp. 43–6.

5. Cindy Rose, "Crime," *The Tallahassee Democrat,* May 8, 1977.

6. "In Search of Security: A National Perspective on Elderly Crime Victimization," Report by the Subcommittee on Housing and Consumer Interests of the Select Committe on Aging, 95th Congress, 1st Session, Washington, D.C.: U.S. Government Printing Office, April, 1977, pp. 81-5.

7. Ibid., pp. 48-9.

Appendix **A**

State and Regional Agencies on Aging

STATE OFFICES

Alabama

Commission on Aging
740 Madison Avenue
Montgomery, Alabama 36104

Alaska

Office on Aging
Department of Health and Social Services
Pouch H
Juneau, Alaska 99811

Arizona

Bureau on Aging
Department of Economic Security
543 East McDowell
Room 217
Phoenix, Arizona 85004

Arkansas

Office on Aging and Adult Services
Department of Social and Rehabilitation
    Services
Seventh and Gaines
Post Office Box 2179
Little Rock, Arkansas 72202

California

Department of Aging
Health and Welfare Agency
918 J Street
Sacramento, California 95814

Colorado

Division of Services for the Aging
Department of Social Services
1575 Sherman Street
Denver, Colorado 80203

Connecticut

Department on Aging
90 Washington Street
Room 312
Hartford, Connecticut 06115

Delaware

Division of Aging
Department of Health and Social Services
2413 Lancaster Avenue
Wilmington, Delaware 19805

District of Columbia

Office of Aging
Office of the Mayor
1329 E Street, N.W.
Washington, D.C. 20004

Florida

Program Office of Aging and Adult Services
Department of Health and Rehabilitation
    Services
1323 Winewood Boulevard
Tallahassee, Florida 32301

Source: State Agencies on Aging and Regional Offices (Directory), Administration on Aging, Office of Human Development (Washington, D.C.: U.S. Department of Health, Education and Welfare, April, 1977), DHEW Publication No. (OHD) 77-20283.

Georgia

Office of Aging
Department of Human Resources
47 Trinity Avenue, S.W.
Atlanta, Georgia 30334

Guam

Office of Aging
Social Service Administration
Government of Guam
Post Office Box 2816
Agana, Guam 96910

Hawaii

Commission on Aging
1149 Bethel Street
Room 311
Honolulu, Hawaii 96813

Idaho

Idaho Office on Aging
Statehouse
Boise, Idaho 83720

Illinois

Department on Aging
2401 West Jefferson Street
Springfield, Illinois 62706

Indiana

Commission on Aging and Aged
Graphic Arts Building
215 North Senate Avenue
Indianapolis, Indiana 46202

Iowa

Commission on Aging
415 West Tenth Street
Jewett Building
Des Moines, Iowa 50319

Kansas

Division of Social Services
Services for the Aging Section
Department of Social and Rehabilitation
    Services
State Office Building
Topeka, Kansas

Kentucky

Center for Aging and Community
    Development
Department for Human Resources
403 Wapping Street
Frankfort, Kentucky 40601

Louisiana

Bureau of Aging Services
Division of Human Resources
Health and Human Resources Administration
Post Office Box 44282, Capitol Station
Baton Rouge, Louisiana 70804

Maine

Bureau of Maine's Elderly
Community Services Unit
Department of Human Services
State House
Augusta, Maine 04333

Maryland

Office on Aging
State Office Building
301 West Preston Street
Baltimore, Maryland 21201

Massachusetts

Department of Elder Affairs
110 Tremont Street
Boston, Massachusetts 02108

Michigan

Office of Services to the Aging
300 East Michigan Street
Post Office Box 30026
Lansing, Michigan 48913

Minnesota

Governor's Citizens Council on Aging
Suite 204
Metro Square Building
Seventh and Robert Streets
Saint Paul, Minnesota 55101

Mississippi

Council on Aging
Post Office Box 5136
Fondren Station
510 George Street
Jackson, Mississippi 39216

Missouri

Office of Aging
Division of Special Services
Department of Social Services
Broadway State Office Building
Post Office Box 570
Jefferson City, Missouri 65101

Montana

Aging Services Bureau
Department of Social and Rehabilitation
    Services
Post Office Box 1723
Helena, Montana 59601

Nebraska

Commission on Aging
State House Station 94784
Post Office Box 94784
Lincoln, Nebraska 68509

Nevada

Division for Aging Services
Department of Human Resources
505 East King Street
Kinkead Building, Room 101
Carson City, Nevada 89710

New Hampshire

Council on Aging
Post Office Box 786
14 Depot Street
Concord, New Hampshire 03301

New Jersey

Division on Aging
Department of Community Affairs
Post Office Box 2768
363 West State Street
Trenton, New Jersey 08625

New Mexico

Commission on Aging
408 Galisteo-Villagra Building
Santa Fe, New Mexico 87503

New York

Office for the Aging
Agency Building Number 2
Empire State Plaza
Albany, New York 12223

New York City Field Office

2 World Trade Center
Room 5036
New York City, New York 10047

North Carolina

North Carolina Division for Aging
Department of Human Resources
213 Hillsborough Street
Raleigh, North Carolina 27603

North Dakota

Aging Services
Social Services Board of North Dakota
State Capitol Building
Bismarck, North Dakota 58505

Ohio

Commission on Aging
50 West Broad Street
Columbus, Ohio 43216

Oklahoma

Special Unit on Aging
Department of Institutions, Social
    and Rehabilitation Service
Post Office Box 25352
Oklahoma City, Oklahoma 73125

Oregon

Program on Aging
Human Resources Department
772 Commercial Street, S.E.
Salem, Oregon 97310

Pennsylvania

Office for the Aging
Department of Public Welfare
Health and Welfare Building
Room 540, Post Office Box 2675
Seventh and Forster Streets
Harrisburg, Pennsylvania 17120

Puerto Rico

Gericulture Commission
Department of Social Services
Post Office Box 11697
Santurce, Puerto Rico 00908

Vermont

Office on Aging
Agency of Human Services
81 River Street, Heritage 1
Montpelier, Vermont 05602

Virginia

Office on Aging
830 East Main Street
Suite 950
Richmond, Virginia 23219

Virgin Islands

Commission on Aging
Post Office Box 539
Charlotte Amalie
Saint Thomas, Virgin Islands 00801

Washington

Office on Aging
Department of Social and Health Services
Post Office Box 1788 M.S. 45-2
Olympia, Washington 98504

West Virginia

Commission on Aging
State Capitol
Charleston, West Virginia 25305

Wisconsin

Division on Aging
Department of Health and Social Services
1 West Wilson Street
Room 686
Madison, Wisconsin 53703

Wyoming

Aging Services
Department of Health and Social Services
Division of Public Assistance and Social
    Services
New State Office Building West
Room 288
Cheyenne, Wyoming 82002

REGIONAL OFFICES

Region I

Connecticut, Maine, Massachusetts, New
    Hampshire, Rhode Island, Vermont
J.F. Kennedy Federal Building
Government Center
Room 2007
Boston, Massachusetts

Region II

New Jersey, New York, Puerto Rico, Virgin
    Islands
26 Federal Plaza
Room 4106
Broadway and Lafayette Streets
New York City, New York 10007

Region III

Delaware, District of Columbia, Maryland,
    Pennsylvania, Virginia, West Virginia
Post Office Box 13716
3535 Market Street
Fifth Floor
Philadelphia, Pennsylvania 19101

Region IV

Alabama, Florida, Georgia, Kentucky,
    Mississippi, North Carolina, South
    Carolina, Tennessee
50 Seventh Street, N.E.
Room 326
Atlanta, Georgia 30323

Region V

Illinois, Indiana, Michigan, Minnesota,
    Ohio, Wisconsin
Fifteenth Floor
300 South Wacker Drive
Chicago, Illinois 60606

Region VI

Arkansas, Louisiana, New Mexico,
    Oklahoma, Texas
Fidelity Union Tower Building
Room 500
1507 Pacific Avenue
Dallas, Texas 752001

Region VII

Iowa, Kansas, Missouri, Nebraska
601 East Twelfth Street
Kansas City, Missouri 64106

Region VIII

Colorado, Montana, North Dakota, South
    Dakota, Utah, Wyoming
Nineteenth and Stout Streets
Seventh Floor
Federal Office Building
Denver, Colorado 80202

Region IX

Arizona, California, Hawaii, Nevada,
    Samoa, Guam, Trust Territory
50 U.N. Plaza
Room 206
San Francisco, California 94102

Region X

Alaska, Idaho, Oregon, Washington
Mail Stop 622
Arcade Plaza Building
1321 Second Avenue
Seattle, Washington 98101

Appendix **B**

Organizations to Contact for Information Regarding Elderly Concerns

A.C.T.I.O.N.

Older Americans Volunteer Program
806 Connecticut Avenue, N.W.
Washington, D.C. 20525

Administration on Aging

Department of Health Education and Welfare
330 Independence Avenue, S.W.
Washington, D.C. 20201

Adult Education Association

810 Eighteenth Street, N.W.
Washington, D.C. 20006

American Geriatrics Society

10 Columbus Circle
New York, New York 10019

**American Association of Retired Persons
and National Retired Teachers Association**

1909 K Street, N.W.
Washington, D.C. 20049

American Health Care Association

1200 Fifteenth Street, N.W.
Washington, D.C. 20005

American Public Welfare

1155 Sixteenth Street, N.W.
Suite 201
Washington, D.C. 20036

Concerned Citizens for Better Government

1346 Connecticut Avenue, N.W.
Room 1213
Washington, D.C. 20036

Gerontological Society

1 Dupont Circle
Suite 520
Washington, D.C. 20036

Gray Panthers

3700 Chestnut Street
Philadelphia, Pennsylvania 19104

**National Association of Retired Federal
Employees**

1533 New Hampshire Avenue, N.W.
Washington, D.C. 20036

National Center for Voluntary Action

1785 Massachusetts Avenue, N.W.
Washington, D.C. 20036

National Council of Citizens

1511 K Street, N.W.
Washington, D.C. 20005

National Council on Aging

1828 L Street, N.W.
Washington, D.C. 20036

National Geriatrics Society

212 West Wisconsin Avenue
Third Floor
Milwaukee, Wisconsin 53203

National Senior Citizens Law Center

1709 West Eight Street
Los Angeles, California 90017

National Urban Coalition

1201 Connecticut Avenue, N.W.
Washington, D.C. 20036

U.S. Senate Special Committee on Aging

G-233 Senate Office Building
Washington, D.C. 20510

For education programs consult:

National Directory of Educational Programs in Gerontology, First Edition, Washington, D.C.: Department of Health Education and Welfare, Office of Human Development, Administration on Aging, 1976.

For information in your local area, contact your state's Agency or Commission on Aging.

Appendix C

Publications Emphasizing Elderly Concerns

AAHA Action Bulletin

American Association of Homes for the
Aging
374 National Press Building
Washington, D.C. 20004

AARP News Bulletin

American Association of Retired Persons
1225 Connecticut Avenue, N.W.
Washington, D.C. 20036

Advances in Gerontological Research

Academic Press
111 Fifth Avenue
New York, New York 10003

Aging

Superintendent of Documents
Government Printing Office
Washington, D.C. 20402

Aging and Human Development

Greenwood Periodicals
51 Riverside Avenue
Westport, Connecticut 06880

Aging International

International Federation on Aging
1909 K Street, N.W.
Suite 690
Washington, D.C. 20049

Current Literature on Aging

National Council on Aging
1828 L Street, N.W.
Washington, D.C. 20036

Dynamic Maturity

American Association of Retired Persons
1909 K Street, N.W.
Washington, D.C. 20049

Facts on Aging

Welfare Administration
Office of Aging
Department of Health, Education and Welfare
Washington, D.C. 20201

Gerontologist

Gerontological Society
1 Dupont Circle
Suite 250
Washington, D.C. 20036

Highlights of Legislation on Aging

Welfare Administration
Office of Aging
Department of Health, Education and Welfare
Washington, D.C. 20201

Journal of the American Geriatrics Society

American Geriatrics Society, Inc.
Columbus Circle
New York, New York 10019

Journal of Geriatric Psychiatry

International University Press
239 Park Avenue, South
New York, New York 10003

Journal of Gerontology

Gerontological Society
660 South Euclid Avenue
Saint Louis, Missouri 63110

Mature Years

Methodist Publishing House
201 Eighth Avenue, South
Nashville, Tennessee

Modern Maturity

American Association of Retired Persons
215 Long Beach Boulevard
Long Beach, California 90802

National Directory on Housing for Older People

National Council on Aging
1828 L Street, N.W.
Washington, D.C. 20036

National Geriatrics Society Newsletters

National Geriatrics Society
6750 Old York Road
Philadelphia, Pennsylvania 19126

On Growing Old

Canadian Council on Social Development
55 Parkdale Avenue
Ottawa, Ontario, Canada
K1Y, 1E5

Patterns for Progress in Aging

Superintendent of Documents
Government Printing Office
Washington, D.C. 20402

President's Council on Aging, Newsletter

President's Council on Aging
Washington, D.C. 20201

Senior Citizens Reporter

Council of Golden Ring Clubs
25 East Seventy-Eighth Street
New York, New York 10021

Southern Conference on Gerontology, Proceedings of

University of Florida Press
15 N.W. Fifteenth Street
Gainesville, Florida 32601

Voluntary Organizations in the Field of Aging, Director of

United States Congress
Senate Committee on Labor and Welfare
Government Printing Office
Washington, D.C.

Bibliography

Action on Aging Legislation in Ninety-Fourth Congress, Special Committee on Aging, U.S. Senate, November, 1976.

Adkins, Ottie, "Crimes Against the Elderly," *The Police Chief,* January, 1975.

Adkins, Ottie, "Crime Prevention: Huntington's Answer," *The Police Chief,* December, 1977.

Aid to Elderly Victims of Crime. Kansas City, Kansas: Mid-America Regional Council Commission on Aging, 1976.

"Another Victim Freed," *The Tallahassee Democrat,* February 17, 1977.

Arrest Analysis. Jacksonville Police Department, 1975–76.

Atchley, Robert C., *The Social Forces in Later Life: An Introduction to Social Gerontology.* Belmont, California: Wadsworth Publishing Co., Inc., 1972.

Atchley, Robert C., *The Sociology of Retirement.* Cambridge, Massachusetts: Schenkman, 1976.

Baggett, Sharon and Marvin Ernst, "From Research to Application—Development of Police and Older Adult Training Modules," *The Police Chief,* February, 1977.

Bailey, Marilynn, "Civilians Join Police on Patrols," Rochester, New York: *Rochester Democrat Chronicle,* June 18, 1973.

Barfield, Richard E. and James N. Morgan, "Trends in Planned Early Retirement," *The Gerontologist,* Vol. 18, No. 1, February 1978.

Beattie, W. M., Jr., "Plight of Older People in Urban Areas," *Aging,* Vol. 59, January 1968.

Beerbower, Dale T. and L. William Sheppard, "Fourth Dimension of the Criminal Justice System," *F.B.I. Law Enforcement Bulletin,* Vol. 45, No. 3, March, 1976.

Bell, William G., "Community Care for the Elderly: An Alternative to Institutionalization," *Gerontologist,* Vol. 13, No. 3, Part I, Autumn, 1973.

Benson, C. Neil, Chief Investigator, personal communication. Washington, D.C.: U.S. Post Office, January 26, 1977.

Birren, J. E., *The Psychology of Aging.* Englewood Cliffs, New Jersey: Prentice-Hall, Inc., 1965.

Black, Henry Campbell, *Black's Law Dictionary,* revised fourth edition. St. Paul, Minnesota: West Publishing Company, 1968.

Blubaum, Paul E., "Maricopa County Sheriff's Department Volunteer Program," *The Police Chief,* February, 1976.

Bonger, William, *Criminality and Economic Conditions.* Bloomington, Indiana: University Press, 1969.

Bordua, David J., "Comments on Police-Community Relations," *Connecticut Law Review,* 1, December, 1968, pp. 306–31.

Botwinick, Jack, *Aging and Behavior: A Comprehensive Integration of Research Findings.* New York, New York: Springer Publishing Co., Inc., 1973.

Botwinick, Jack, *Cognitive Processes in Maturity and Old Age.* New York, New York: Springer Publishing Co., Inc., 1967.

Boyd, Rosamonde R., "Preliterate Prologues to Modern Aging Roles," in *Foundations of Practical Gerontology,* eds., Rosamonde Ramsay Boyd and Charles G. Oakes, Columbia, South Carolina: University of South Carolina Press, 1973.

Eds., Boyd, Rosamonde Ramsay and Charles G. Oakes, *Foundations of Practical Gerontology.* Columbia, South Carolina: University of South Carolina Press, 1973.

Bradley, Wayne M., "Cass Corridor Safety for Seniors Project," *The Police Chief,* February, 1976.

Brickfield, Cyril F., "How We're Fighting Crime," *NRTA Journal,* July/August, 1978.

Brickler, Alice, participant, "Seminar in Crime Prevention for the Elderly," sponsors, Center for Gerontology, Florida State University and Senior Society Planning Council, Tallahassee, Florida, June 21 to July 5, 1977.

Bridges, Curtis, "Crime Prevention: A New Emphasis in Policing," *The Police Chief,* October, 1977.

Brooks, James, "Compensating Victims of Crime: The Recommendations of Program Administrators," *Law and Society Review,* Vol. 7, Spring, 1973.

Brostoff, Phyllis M., *Metropolitan Police Contacts with the Elderly.* Washington, D.C.: The Washington School of Psychiatry, November 1971.

Brown, Lee P. and Marlene A. Young Rifai, "Crime Prevention for Older Americans: Multnomah County's Victimization Study," *The Police Chief,* February, 1976.

Bull, C. N., and J. B. Aucoin, "Voluntary Association Participation and Life Satisfaction: A Replication Note," *Journal of Gerontology,* Vol. 30, No. 1, 1975, pp. 73–6.

Burdick, Hannah, participant, "Seminar in Crime Prevention for the Elderly," sponsors, Center for Gerontology, Florida State University and Senior Society Planning Council, Tallahassee, Florida, June 21 to July 5, 1977.

Butler, Robert N. and Myrna I. Lewis, *Aging and Mental Health: Positive Psychosocial Approaches.* St. Louis, Missouri: The C. V. Mosby Company, 1973.

Butler, Robert N., *Why Survive? Being Old in America.* New York, New York: Harper and Row Publishers, 1975.

Cairns, Wayne L., "Senior Citizens Turn Cop Spotters," *The Police Chief,* February, 1977.

Califano, Joseph A., Jr., "The Aging of America," *Vital Speeches of the Day,* Vol. XLIV, No. 15, May 15, 1978.

Carlston, Robert A., Philip D. DeWitt, Lewis F. Hanes and Edward J. Pesce, "Crime Prevention through Environmental Design Program: May 1974 to June 1976," National Institute of Law Enforcement and Criminal Justice, U.S. Department of Justice, L.E.A.A., in cooperation with Westinghouse National Issues Center, Westinghouse Electric Corporation, Arlington, Virginia, 1977.

Chamblis, William J., "Functional and Conflict Theories of Crime," New York, New York: MSS Modular Publications, Module 17, 1974, pp. 1-23.

"Citizen Patrol Formed," Fargo, North Dakota: *Fargo Forum,* January 11, 1975.

Clark, Margaret and Barbara G. Anderson, *Culture and Aging: An Antropological Study of Older Americans.* Springfield, Illinois: Charles C. Thomas Publisher, 1967.

Clemente, Frank and Michael B. Kleiman, "Fear of Crime Among the Aged," *Gerontologist,* Vol. 16, No. 3, June, 1976, pp. 207-10.

Clemente, Frank, Patricia A. Rexroad, and Carl Hirsch, "The Participation of the Black Aged in Voluntary Association," *Journal of Gerontology,* Vol. 30, No. 4, 1975.

Cloward, Richard and Lloyd Ohlin, *Delinquency and Opportunity.* New York, New York: The Free Press, 1960.

Cohen, Albert K., *Delinquent Boys.* Glencoe, Illinois: The Free Press, 1955.

Cohen, Wilbur, *Retirement Policies Under Social Security.* Berkley, California: University of California Press, 1957.

Condit, T. W., S. Greenbaum and G. Nicholson, *Forgotten Victims—An Advocate's Anthology.* Sacramento, California Office of Criminal Justice Planning, Alameda Regional Criminal Justice Planning Board, 1977.

"Confidence Games Against the Elderly," Hearing before the Subcommittee on Federal, State and Community Services of the Select Committee on Aging, House of Representatives, 94th Congress, 2nd Session, held in New York, New York, January 13, 1976. Washington, D.C.: U.S. Government Printing Office, 1976.

Conklin, John E., "Dimensions of Community Response to the Crime Problem," *Social Problems,* XVII, Winter, 1971, pp. 373-84.

Cook, Fay Lomax and Thomas D. Cook, "Evaluating the Rhetoric of Crisis: A Case Study of Criminal Victimization of the Elderly," *Social Service Review,* Vol. 50, December, 1976, pp. 641-2.

Cottage Grove Police Department, Senior Citizens Volunteer Crime Prevention Unit, 400 Main Street, Cottage Grove, Oregon, 97424.

Cottrell, W. Fred, *Aging and the Aged.* Dubuque, Iowa: Wm. C. Brown Co., 1974.

Cottrell, Fred and Robert C. Atchley, *Retired Women: A Preliminary Report.* Oxford, Ohio: Scripps Foundation, 1969.

Cowgill, Donald O., "Aging and Modernization: A Revision of the Theory," in *Late Life: Communities and Environmental Policy,* ed. Jaber F. Gubrium, Springfield, Illinois: Charles C. Thomas Publisher, 1974.

Cowgill, Donald O. and Lowell D. Holmes, *Aging and Modernization.* New York, New York: Appleton-Century-Crofts, 1972.

Crawford, James H., "Number that Thieves Avoid," *The Police Chief,* June, 1974.

Cress, Gerald, "A Sheriff Tries Crime Prevention," *The Journal of Criminal Law, Criminology and Police Science,* Vol. 22, 1931–32.

Crime Against Aging Americans—The Kansas City Study. Kansas City, Missouri: Midwest Research Institute, 1975.

Crime and the Elderly. St. Petersburg, Florida: St. Petersburg Police Department, 1974–75.

Crime Against the Elderly: L.E.A.A.'s Elderly Crime Victimization Programs, No. 1977-241-090/64, National Institute of Law Enforcement and Criminal Justice, U.S. Department of Justice, L.E.A.A., Washington, D.C.: U.S. Government Printing Office, 1977.

Crime Prevention and Senior Citizens, Report. Jacksonville, Florida: Office of the Mayor, Criminal Justice Planning, 1977.

Crime Prevention Handbook for Senior Citizens. Kansas City, Missouri: Midwest Research Institute, 1977.

Crime Prevention Handbook for Senior Citizens. Washington, D.C.: Law Enforcement Assistance Administration, June 1977.

Criminal Victimization in the U.S. (1975), Vol. 1, National Crime Panel Survey Report, U.S. Department of Justice, L.E.A.A., May, 1975.

Criminal Victimization in the United States, 1974: A National Crime Survey Report, U.S. Department of Justice, Law Enforcement Assistance Administration, National Criminal Justice Information and Statistics Service, December 1977, p.13.

Criminal Victimization in the United States, 1975: A National Crime Survey Report, U.S. Department of Justice, Law Enforcement Assistance Administration, National Criminal Justice Information and Statistics Service, December 1977, p. 13.

Cull, John G. and Richard E. Hardy, *The Neglected Older American: Social and Rehabilitation Services.* Springfield, Illinois: Charles C. Thomas Publisher, 1973.

Cumming, E., L. R. Dean, D. S. Newell and I. McCaffrey, "Disengagement—A Tentative Theory of Aging," *Sociometry,* Vol. 23, No. 1, 1960.

Cunningham, Carl L., "Crime Against the Aging Victim," *Midwest Research Institute Quarterly,* Spring, 1973.

Curtis, Gayhe E., participant, "Seminar in Crime Prevention for the Elderly," Center for Gerontology, Florida State University and Senior Society Planning Council, Tallahassee, Florida, sponsors, June 21 to July 5, 1977.

Curtis, J., "Voluntary Association Joining: A Cross-National Comparative Note," *American Sociological Review,* Vol. XXXVI, No. 5, 1971, pp. 872–80.

Dadich, Gerald J., "Crime, the Elderly and Community Relations," *The Police Chief,* February, 1977.

Davis, Edward M., "Crime and the Elderly," *The Police Chief,* February, 1977.

Davis, Nanette J., *Sociological Constructions of Deviance: Perceptions and Issues in the Field.* Dubuque, Iowa: Wm. C. Brown Co., 1975.

D'Angelo, Stephen, "Senior Home Security Program, St. Louis, Missouri," *The Police Chief,* February, 1977.

de Beauvoir, Simone, *The Coming of Age.* New York, New York: Putnam/London, England: Andre Deutsch, Ltd./Paris, France: Editions Gallimard, 1972.

DeLoache, Frank, "For the Aged, A Free Way To Lock Out Crime," St. Petersburg, Florida: *St. Petersburg Times,* September 12, 1977, p. 18.

Democracy in America, trans. George Lawrence. London, England: Harper and Row Publishers, 1966.

Dingemans, Dennis J. and Robert H. Schinzel, "Defensible Space Design of Housing for Crime Prevention," *The Police Chief,* November, 1977.

Dingemans, Dennis, Susan Garfield and Tonya Olsen, *Defensible Space in Suburban Townhouse Design: A Case Study of Six California Developments.* Davis, California: Institute of Government Affairs, Research Report No. 33, 1976.

Dorsey, R. A., participant, "Seminar in Crime Prevention for the Elderly," sponsors, Center for Gerontology, Florida State University and Senior Society Planning Council, Tallahassee, Florida, June 21 to July 5, 1977.

Ducovny, Amram M., *The Billion Dollar Swindle: Frauds Against the Elderly.* New York, New York: Fleet Press, 1969.

Durkheim, Emile, *Suicide.* Glencoe, Illinois: The Free Press, 1951.

Durkheim, Emile, *The Division of Labor in Society.* New York: The Free Press, 1964.

Eisdorfer, C. and M. Powell Lawton, *The Psychology of Adult Development and Aging.* Washington, D.C.: American Psychological Association, 1973.

Elderly Crime Victimization (Federal Law Enforcement Agencies—L.E.A.A. and F.B.I.), Hearings before the U.S. Congress, House Select Committee on Aging, Subcommittee on Housing and Consumer Interests, 94th Congress, 2nd Session, held April 12–13, 1976. Washington, D.C.: U.S. Government Printing Office, 1976.

Eliason, Kevin, "Citizen on Patrol," *Law and Order,* November, 1970.

Ernst, Marvin, L. Frederick Jodry and H. J. Friedsam, *Reporting and Non-Reporting of Crime by Older Americans.* Denton, Texas: Center for Studies in Aging, North Texas State University, 1976.

Etzioni, Amitai, *Social Problems,* Englewood Cliffs, New Jersey: Prentice-Hall, Inc., 1976.

Farace, Theodore and Andrew Camera, "Confidence Games," *The Police Chief,* January, 1975.

Federal Bureau of Investigation, White Collar Crime Section, Criminal Investigative Division, "Anatomy of an Advanced-Fee Swindle," *The Police Chief,* September, 1977.

Forston, Raymon and James Kitchens, *Criminal Victimization of the Aged: The Houston Model Neighborhood Area,* Community Service Report No. 1, Center for

Community Services, School of Community Service. Denton, Texas: North Texas State University, 1974.

Fox, Harry G., "Grannies with Badges," *Law and Order,* August, 1970.

Fox, Vernon B., *Community-Based Corrections.* Englewood Cliffs, New Jersey: Prentice-Hall, Inc., 1977.

Fox, Vernon B., *Guidelines For Corrections Programs in Community and Junior Colleges.* Washington, D.C.: American Association of Junior Colleges, 1969.

Fox, Vernon B., *Introduction to Criminology.* Englewood Cliffs, New Jersey: Prentice-Hall, Inc., 1977.

Fraenkel, J., *Crime and Criminals: What Should We Do About Them.* Englewood Cliffs, New Jersey: Prentice-Hall, Inc., 1977.

Furstenburg, Frank, "Public Reactions to Crime in the Streets," *American Scholar,* Autumn, 1970, pp. 601–10.

Gallo, John M., statement, "Crimes Against the Elderly," Hearing before the Subcommittee on Federal, State and Community Services of the Select Committee on Aging, House of Representatives, 94th Congress, 2nd Session, held in New York, New York, December 13, 1976. Washington, D.C.: U.S. Government Printing Office, 1977.

Gates, Daryl F., "Honeycomb Projects: An Architectural Crime Problem," *The Police Chief,* November, 1977.

Gentry, Curt, *The Vulnerable Americans.* Garden City, New York, New York. Doubleday and Company, Inc., 1966.

Gertz, Marc G. and Susette Talarico, "Problems of Reliability and Validity in Criminal Justice Research," *Journal of Criminal Justice,* Vol. 5, No. 3, Fall, 1977, pp. 217–24.

Gibbons, Don C., *Society, Crime and Criminal Careers.* Englewood Cliffs, New Jersey: Prentice-Hall, Inc., 1968.

Glaser, Daniel, *Adult Crime and Social Policy.* Englewood Cliffs, New Jersey: Prentice-Hall, Inc., 1972.

Goldsmith, Jack, "Community Crime Prevention and the Elderly: A Segmental Approach," *Crime Prevention Review,* State of California: Attorney General's Office, July, 1975.

Goldsmith, Jack, "Police and the Older Victim: Keys to a Changing Perspective," *The Police Chief,* February, 1976.

Goldsmith, Jack and Sharon S. Goldsmith, *Crime and the Elderly—Challenge and Response.* Lexington, Massachusetts: Lexington Brooks, 1976.

Goldsmith, Jack and Noel E. Tomas, "Crimes Against the Elderly: A Continuing National Crisis," *Aging,* June/July, 1974.

Goldsmith, S. S. and Jack Goldsmith, "Crime, The Aging and Public Policy," *Perspective on Aging,* Vol. 4, No. 3, May/June, 1975.

Good, Edward, *Community Crime Prevention: An Exemplary Project, Seattle, Washington.* Seattle, Washington: Community Crime Prevention Program, City of Seattle, Law and Justice Planning Office, 607 Alaska Blvd., 98104, June, 1977.

Gordon, David, "Capitalism, Class and Crime in America," *Crime and Delinquency,* April, 1973, pp. 163–86.

Goudy, Willis J., Edward A. Powers and Patricia Keith, "Work and Retirement: A Test of Attitudinal Relationships," *Journal of Gerontology,* Vol. 30, No. 2, 1975.

Griffith, Liddon, *Mugging: You Can Protect Yourself,* Englewood Cliffs, N.J.: Prentice-Hall, Inc., 1978.

Gross, Philip J., "Law Enforcement and the Senior Citizen," *The Police Chief,* February, 1976.

Gross, Selma and Daniel J. Lipstein, "Crime Prevention Education for the Elderly in Baltimore City," *The Police Chief,* October, 1977.

Gubrium, Jaber F., *The Myths of the Golden Years: A Socio-Environmental Theory of Aging.* Springfield, Illinois: Charles C. Thomas Publisher, 1973.

Gubrium, Jaber F., *Time, Roles and Self in Old Age.* New York, New York: Human Sciences Press, Behavioral Publications, Inc., 1976.

Gubrium, Jaber F., "Victimization in Old Age: Available Evidence and Three Hypotheses," *Crime and Delinquency,* July, 1974.

Hahn, P. H., *Crimes Against the Elderly—A Study in Victimology.* Santa Cruz, California: Davis Publications, 1976.

Havighurst, Robert J., "Successful Aging," in *Processes of Aging,* Vol. 1, pp. 299–320, eds. Richard H. Williams, Clark Tibbitts and Wilma Donahue, New York, New York: Atherton Press, 1963.

Hendricks, Jon and C. Davis Hendricks, *Aging in Mass Society: Myths and Realities.* Cambridge, Massachusetts: Winthrop Publishers, Inc., 1977.

Hindeland, Michael J., *Criminal Victimization in Eight American Cities, Final Report.* Washington, D.C.: Law Enforcement Assistance Administration, 1975.

Hoover, J. Edgar, "The War Against Crime is Your War," *The Reader's Digest,* Vol. 93, November, 1968.

Houck, Russell, "Operation Lifeline," *The Police Chief,* March, 1975.

Hypes, Diane, "New Approaches to Crime Prevention," *The Police Chief,* May 1975.

"IACP Executive Director Talks About Crime and the Elderly," *Aging,* Nos. 281–282, March/April, 1978, pp. 18–22.

"In Search of Security: A National Perspective on Elderly Crime Victimization," Report by the Subcommittee on Housing and Consumer Interests of the Select Committee on Aging, 95th Congress, 1st Session, Washington, D.C.: U.S. Government Printing Office, April, 1977.

Irvin, John, *The Felon.* Englewood Cliffs, New Jersey: Prentice-Hall, Inc., 1970.

Jeffery, C. Ray, *Crime Prevention Through Environmental Design.* Beverly Hills, California: Sage Publication, 1971.

Jenkins, Martin D. and Bernard H. Ross, "The Urban Involvement of Higher Education," *Journal of Higher Education,* Vol. XLVI, No. 4, July/August, 1975.

Jones, Rochelle, *The Other Generation: The New Power in Older People.* Englewood Cliffs, New Jersey: Prentice-Hall, Inc., 1977.

Kahana, E., *Perspectives of Aged on Victimization, Ageism, and Their Problems in Urban Society.* Detroit, Michigan: Wayne State University, 1974.

Keller, O. and C. Badder, "The Crimes That Old Persons Commit," *Gerontologist,* No. 8, 1968, pp. 43–50.

Kelley, Clarence M., *Crime Resistance.* Wasshington, D.C.: Federal Bureau of Investigation, 1975.

Kelley, Clarence M., "Message From the Director...," *F.B.I. Law Enforcement Bulletin,* Vol. 45, No. 1, January, 1976.

Kelley, Clarence M., "Message From the Director...," *F.B.I. Law Enforcement Bulletin,* Vol. 46, No. 1, January, 1977.

Kimmel, Douglas C., *Adulthood and Aging: An Interdisciplinary Developmental View.* New York, New York: John Wiley and Sons, 1974.

Koller, Marvin R., *Social Gerontology.* New York, New York: Random House, 1968.

Komara, Donald F., "Concerned Citizen's Action Hotline," *The Police Chief,* June, 1974.

Kubler-Ross, Elisabeth, *On Death and Dying.* New York, New York: Macmillan, 1969.

Kuypers, J. A. and V. L. Bengston, "Competence and Social Breakdown: A Social-Psychology View of Aging," *Human Development,* Vol. 16, No. 2, 1973, pp. 37–49.

Langer, E., "Growing Old in America: Frauds, Quackery, Swindle the Aged and Compound Their Troubles," *Science,* Vol. 140, May 3, 1963, pp. 470–2.

Larson, Reed, "Thirty Years of Research on the Subjective Well-Being of Older Americans," *Journal of Gerontology,* Vol. 33, No. 1, 1978.

Lemert, Edwin M., *Human Deviance, Social Problems and Social Control.* Englewood Cliffs, New Jersey: Prentice-Hall, Inc., 1967.

Lemon, B. W., V. L. Bengston and J. A. Petersen, "An Exploration of the Activity Theory of Aging: Activity Types and Life Expectation Among In-Movers to a Retirement Community," *Journal of Gerontology,* Vol. 27, No. 4, 1972, pp. 511–23.

Lend A Hand To Aid A Friend. St. Louis, Missouri: Aid to Victims of Crime, Inc., University Club Bldg., Suite 705, 601 N. Grand, 63101.

Lofland, John, *Deviance and Identity.* Englewood Cliffs, New Jersey: Prentice-Hall, Inc., 1969.

Lozier, John and Ronald Althouse, "Retirement to the Porch in Rural Appalachia," *International Journal of Aging and Human Development,* Vol. 6, No. 1, 1975.

Lozier, John and Ronald Althouse, "Social Enforcement of Behavior Toward Elders in an Appalachian Mountain Settlement," *Gerontologist,* Vol. 14, No. 1, February, 1974.

Maddox, George L., Jr., "Disengagement Theory: A Critical Evaluation," *Gerontologist,* Vol. 4, 1964, pp. 80–2.

Maddox, George L., "Growing Old: Getting Beyond the Stereotypes," in *Foundations of Practical Gerontology,* eds. Rosamonde Ramsay Boyd and Charles G. Oakes, University of South Carolina Press, 1973.

Maddox, George L., Jr., "Themes and Issues in Sociological Theories of Human Aging," *Human Development,* Vol. 13, 1970, pp. 17–27.

Malinchak, Alan A., "The Embarrassing Problem of Elderly Criminals," *Proceedings of the 23rd Annual Conference on Corrections,* Tallahassee, Florida: Florida State University, March 5–7, 1978.

Malinchak, Alan A. and Douglas Wright, "Older Americans and Crime: The Scope of Elderly Victimization," *Aging,* Nos. 281–282, March/April, 1978, pp. 10–17.

Marshalling Citizen Power Against Crime. Washington, D.C.: Chamber of Commerce of the United States, 1615 H. Street N.W., 20006, 1970.

Marx, Karl, *Theories of Surplus Value,* translated from the German by G. A. Bonner and Emile Burns. New York, New York: A. M. Kelley, 1969.

Matza, David, *Becoming Deviant.* Englewood Cliffs, New Jersey: Prentice-Hall, Inc., 1969.

McClure, Barbara Puls, "Crimes Against the Elderly," Library of Congress Congressional Research Service: Education and Public Welfare Division, HV 7251-A, 75-23OED, October 21, 1975.

McCreary, Charles P. and Ivan N. Mensh, "Personality Differences Associated with Age in Law Assistance," *Journal of Gerontology,* Vol. 32, No. 2, 1977, pp. 164–7.

McKenna, Kenneth, "For the Eldery the Street is a Jungle," New York, New York: *New York Daily News,* November 14, 1974.

Mechanic, David, *Mental Health and Social Policy.* Englewood Cliffs, New Jersey: Prentice-Hall, Inc., 1970.

Mendelson, M. A., *Tender Loving Greed—How the Incredibly Lucrative Nursing Home "Industry" Is Exploiting America's Old People and Defrauding Us All.* New York, New York: Alfred A. Knopf, 1974.

Merton, Robert, *Social Theory and Social Structure.* New York, New York: The Free Press, 1957.

Miller, Stephen J., "The Social Dilemma of the Aging Leisure Participant," in *Older People and Their Social World,* eds. A. Rose and W. Petersen, Philadelphia, Pennsylvania: F. A. Davis, 1965, pp. 77–92.

Miller, Walter, "Lower Class Culture as a Generating Milieu of Gang Delinquency," *Journal of Social Issues,* Vol. 14, 1958, pp. 5–19.

Monge, Rolf and David F. Hultsch, "Paired-Associate Learning as a Function of Adult Age and the Length of the Anticipation and Inspection Intervals," *Journal of Gerontology,* Vol. 26, 1971, pp. 157–162.

Montgomery, Douglas G., "Testimony On the Issues of Mandatory Retirement to a Joint Interim Task Force on Mandatory Retirement, State of Oregon Legislature," Portland, Oregon: Institute on Aging, Portland State University, September 22, 1977.

Morris, Albert, "The Comprehensive Classification of Adult Offenders," *Journal of Criminal Law, Criminology and Police Science,* Vol. 56, June, 1965, pp. 197–202.

Myth and Reality of Aging in America, a study prepared by Louis Harris and Associates, Inc. for The National Council on the Aging, Inc., Washington, D.C. © 1975.

Naylor, Harriet H., "Volunteerism With and by the Elderly," in *Foundations of*

Practical Gerontology, eds. Rosamonde Ramsay Boyd and Charles G. Oakes, Columbia, South Carolina: University of South Carolina Press, 1973.

Naylor, Harriet, *Volunteers Today—Finding, Training and Working with Them.* New York, New York: Associated Press, 1967.

Nelson, Catherine V., participant, "Seminar in Crime Prevention for the Elderly," sponsors, Center for Gerontology, Florida State University and Senior Society Planning Council, Tallahassee, Florida, June 21 to July 5, 1977.

Neugarten, Bernice L., *Middle Age and Aging: A Reader in Social Psychology.* Chicago, Illinois: University of Chicago Press, 1968.

Newman, Oscar, *Defensible Space: Crime Prevention Through Urban Design.* New York, New York: MacMillan, 1972.

Nohl, Max W., "Crime Prevention from the Cradle Up," *The Journal of Criminal Law, Criminology and Police Science,* Vol. 28, 1937–38.

"On Guard—A Guide for the Consumer," Information Pamphlet No. 3, State of California: Office of Attorney General.

Palmore, Erdman, B., *Normal Aging: Reports From the Duke Study,* 2 Volumes. Durham, North Carolina: Duke University Press, 1970–4.

Plummer, Kim, "They Rebuild Homes and Hopes," St. Louis, Missouri: *Globe-Democrat,* July 2–3, 1977, p. 1E.

Pomrenke, Norman E., C. E. Cherry and H. Burton, "A New Approach to Crime Prevention—Community Services," *The Police Chief,* April, 1967.

Pope, Carl E. and William Feyerherm, "A Review of Recent Trends: The Effects of Crime on the Elderly," *The Police Chief,* February, 1976.

Quinney, Richard, *The Social Reality of Crime.* Boston, Massachusetts: Little Brown and Company, 1970.

Reinhold, Robert, "Youth Gives Way to Graying of America," *The Tallahassee Democrat,* February 13, 1977.

Richards, Daniel E., "Victims Often Encourage a Burglar," Flint, Michigan: *The Flint Journal,* January, 12, 1975, p. B1.

Rifai, Marlene A. Young, "The Response of the Older Adult to Criminal Victimization," *The Police Chief,* February, 1977.

Riley, Matilda, *Aging and Society,* 3 Volumes. New York, New York: Russell Sage Foundation, 1972.

Ritchey, Larry W., "Crime: Can the Older Adult do Anything About It," *The Police Chief,* February, 1977, pp. 40–1.

Rose, Arnold, "The Subculture of the Aging: A Framework for Research in Social Gerontology," in *Older People and Their Social World,* eds. A. Rose and W. Peterson. Philadelphia, Pennsylvania: F. A. Davis, 1965, pp. 3–16.

Rose, Cindy, "Crime," *The Tallahassee Democrat,* May 8, 1977.

Sarle, Stephen C., "The Con-Artist: Can He Be Stopped," *The Police Chief,* September, 1977.

Schafer, Stephen, *Victimology: The Victim and His Criminal.* Reston, Virginia: Reston Publishing Company, Inc., 1977.

Schur, Edwin M., *Labelling Deviant Behavior*. New York, New York: Harper and Row Publishers, 1971.

Schur, Edwin M., *Our Criminal Society: The Social and Legal Sources of Crime in America*. Englewood Cliffs, New Jersey: Prentice-Hall, Inc., 1969.

Schweizer, Louis G., "Helping the Elderly," *F.B.I. Law Enforcement Bulletin*, Vol. 42, No. 2, December, 1973.

Scott-Maxwell, Florida "We Are the Sum of Our Days (Abridged)," in *Culture and Aging: An Anthropological Study of Older Americans*, by Margaret Clark and Barbara G. Anderson, Springfield, Illinois: Charles C. Thomas, Publisher, 1967.

Security For the Elderly: Synopsis. St. Petersburg, Florida, Office of Crime Prevention, 1977.

Services and Programs. Boulder, Colorado: Hall of Justice, Boulder County Juvenile Court, 1972.

Shimizu, Makoto, "A Study on the Crimes of the Aged in Japan," *Acta Criminologiae et Medicinae Legalis Japonica*, Vol. 39, No. 5/6, December, 1973.

Shook, Howard C., "Who Pleads for the Victim," *The Police Chief*, January, 1978.

Shuler, Judy, "Civic Duty Prompts Auxiliary Police to Work Free," Anchorage, Alaska: *Anchorage Daily Times*, February 6, 1973.

Slicker, Martin, "A Public Policy Perspective: The Elderly and the Criminal Justice System," *The Police Chief*, February, 1977, pp. 23–5.

"Sources of Information About and Descriptions of Crime Prevention Programs for the Elderly," No. (OHDS) 77-20223, Washington, D.C.: Administration on Aging and Department of Health, Education and Welfare.

Spitzer, Steven, "Toward a Marxian Theory of Deviance," *Social Problems*, June 1975, pp. 638–51.

Springer, John L., *Consumer Swindlers and How to Avoid Them*. New York, New York: Henry R. Regnery Company, 1970.

"Statement of Understanding Between the Law Enforcement Assistance Administration and the Administration on Aging," Information Memorandum AOA-IM-76-66, Washington, D.C.: Department of Health, Education and Welfare, Office of the Secretary, May 10, 1976.

Streib, Gordon F., "Are the Aged a Minority Group?" in *Applied Sociology*, eds. A. W. Gouldner and S. M. Miller. New York, New York: The Free Press of Glencoe, 1965.

Sudnow, D., *Passing On*. Englewood Cliffs, New Jersey: Prentice-Hall, Inc., 1967.

Sundeen, Richard A. and James T. Mathieu, "The Fear of Crime and Its Consequences Among Elderly In Three Urban Communities," *Gerontologist*, Vol. 16, No. 3, June, 1976, pp. 211–19.

Sunderland, George, "Crime Prevention for the Elderly," *Ekistics*, Vol. 39, No. 231, February, 1975, pp. 91–2.

Sunderland, George, "The Older American: Police Problem or Police Asset?," *F.B.I. Law Enforcement Bulletin*, Vol. 45, No. 8, August, 1976.

Sutherland, E. H. and Donald Cressey, *Criminology,* 8th edition. Philadelphia, Pennsylvania: J. B. Lippincott Company, 1970.

Taylor, Ian, Paul Walton and Jock Young, *The New Criminology.* New York, New York: Harper and Row Publishers, 1973.

30 Ways You Can Prevent Crime. Greenfield, Massachusetts: Channing L. Bete Co., Inc., 1972.

Tibbitts, Clark and Wilma Donahue, *Aging in Today's Society.* Englewood Cliffs, New Jersey: Prentice-Hall, Inc., 1960.

Tighe, John H., "A Survey of Crime Against the Elderly," *The Police Chief,* February 1977.

Tournier, Paul, *Learn to Grow Old,* trans. Edwin Hudson. New York, New York: Harper and Row Publishers, 1972.

Turk, Austin, "Conflict and Criminality," *American Sociological Review,* Vol. 31, June, 1966.

Tyler, R. W., "The Role of the Volunteer," *California Youth Authority,* Vol. 18, No. 4, California Department of Youth Authority in conjunction with Stanford University.

Uniform Crime Reports. Washington, D.C.: Federal Bureau of Investigation, 1972–76.

Victimization. St. Louis, Missouri: Aid to Victims of Crime, Inc., University Club Bldg., Suite 705, 601 N. Grand, 63101.

Vogelsang, Fred, "Employment for the Low-Income Elderly," *Journal of Housing,* Vol. 22, 1973, pp. 540–4.

Volunteers in Law Enforcement Program. Washington, D.C.: U.S. Department of Justice, L.E.A.A., 1972.

Volunteer Training Manual. St. Louis, Missouri: Aid to Victims of Crime, Inc., University Club Bldg., Suite 705, 601 N. Grand, 63101.

Whiskin, F., "Delinquency in the Aged," *Journal of Geriatric Psychiatry,* Vol. 1, 1968, pp. 243–52.

White, Glenn, "Where Citizens Help Control Crime," *Dynamic Maturity,* July, 1975.

Willis, Ron L. and Myra Miller, "Senior Citizen Crime Prevention Programs," *The Police Chief,* February, 1976.

Willman, Tom, "The New Mandatory Retirement Law and You," *NRTA Journal,* March/April 1978.

Wolf, Robert, "An Aid to Designing Prevention Programs," *The Police Chief,* February, 1977.

Worthington, Gladys, "Older Persons as Community Service Volunteers," *Social Work,* Vol. 8, No. 4, October, 1963.

Youmans, E. Grant, "Some Views on Human Aging," in *Foundations of Practical Gerontology,* eds. Rosamonde Ramsay Boyd and Charles G. Oakes, Columbia, South Carolina: University of South Carolina Press, 1973.

Younger, Evelle J., *Consumer Information Protection Program for Seniors: Overview.* State of California: Attorney General's Office, August, 1976.

Younger, Evelle J., "Consumer Information Protection Program for Seniors," Vol. 4, No. 4, October, 1976.

Younger, Evelle, J., "Consumer Information Protection Program for Seniors," Vol. 5, No. 1, January, 1977.

Younger, Evelle, J., *On Guard,* Vol. 4, No. 4, State of California: Attorney General's Office, October, 1976.

Younger, Evelle, J., "The California Experience: Prevention of Criminal Victimization of the Elderly," *The Police Chief,* February, 1976.

Younger, Evelle J., "Welfare, Social Security, Pension Check and Food Stamp Frauds," *On Guard,* Vol. 4, No. 4, State of California: Attorney General's Office, October, 1976.

Your Retirement Anti-Crime Guide. Washington, D.C.: American Association of Retired Persons and National Retired Teachers Association, 1973.

Index